Collected Novellas

S.B. Borgersen

COLLECTED NOVELLAS

Passport to Perdita

Eva Matson

Fishermen's Fingers

PASSPORT TO PERDITA

A novella

'If you look for truth, you may find comfort in the end.'

C.S. Lewis

'The other side of life? It is true all life has another side, and we will only find it if we look.'

Perdita Drummond

For Tilly

1.

Gordon Drummond buried his father three days ago. He remembers nothing of the funeral except how cold and empty he felt in the family pew at the front of the church. How stinging freezing the cemetery was and that his nose just wouldn't stop running. He had no handkerchief in the pocket of his borrowed dark grey overcoat, but he'd had the foresight to grab a piece of paper towel from the kitchen before leaving for the church. The rough dollar store paper towel made his nose red and sore.

It is still sore now as he sits on the sofa pondering where his life will go from this point. He pokes the wood stove with the brass poker, using the stabbing action his mother taught him years before, and sits back watching the flames come to life through the glass-fronted door. He swallows hard. "It's going to be okay, Pea," he says to his dog.

The ageing white whippet jumps onto the sofa and curls herself on Gordon's lap, arches her neck until her nose is firmly tucked under her hind leg and closes her eyes. Gordon scratches behind her folded ears, "Goodnight, Pea," he says. "Just us now, old girl."

Gordon watches—without really seeing—the solitary black flea speed through the fine white hairs of the whippet. He is thinking back to the funeral. He can still feel hands gently patting his shoulder afterwards. Faces melded, one with the other. The words, 'Sorry for your loss,' mouthed in lipsticked 'O's wriggle though his mind like the elusive flea running to the dog's groin. One by one the faces begin to come back to him. Some are old friends of his dad's. And some are complete strangers. Not people from around here at all. He watches the black flea as it emerges briefly before burrowing back through the fine white hairs of Pea's coat. What Gordon sees, as he watches the flea, is clear now—a dark figure of a woman stepping carefully through the snowy pathways of the cemetery. Dressed all in black, she has long, dark mahogany hair and no hat. She speaks to no one and is gone before he catches even a glimpse of her face.

He cannot bring himself to go to bed. The fire has a rosy glow, and with Pea now curled behind his legs, he undoes the waistband of his jeans, pulls the plaid wool blanket over his shoulders and lays back, staring at the ceiling.

It is quiet without Dad, he thinks. The old man would normally be making that late night cup of tea about now. Reading through the local weekly newspaper, again, looking through the obituaries for names of old friends; people he went to school with, checking out the deals in the flyers, muttering through his cigarette about the price of steak and toilet paper. All before Pea's final nightly walk around the loop.

Gordon supposes that the dog was always really his father's dog, even though she was not intended to be. She came as an eight-week-old puppy from Ontario. All bones and beseeching seal-like eyes. "My, but you're so perdy," said Andrew Ainslie Drummond, dipping his little finger into his milky tea and letting the puppy suckle. That was the beginning of the bond between the two.

Gordon was an only child. His father travelled with his work as a cable mechanism specialist. His mother, Maryanne, was somewhat of a single parent because of her husband's long absences in South America. Gordon was her constant companion from an early age. He didn't know people talked—speculated about their situation—he was too young then.

"Why don't you divorce the bastard?" said her friend Ivy. More than once.

"You could find yourself another man, a good man, take care of you and the boy," said Ivy's friend Ruby.

But Gordon's mother, Maryanne, shook her head every time, saying nothing. She was a good mother, and Andrew always made sure the finances were in order. Ensuring Gordon always had good clothes for school and a new pair of shoes each September.

As the years passed, even though he was a good student, Gordon relinquished the idea of college, preferring to stay close to home, near his mother. He found that figure work and accounting were his strengths and a job in payroll at the mill suited him just fine.

Gordon and his mother were inseparable.

"Unhealthy," said wise Ivy, "for a grown man to spend so much time with his mother." Ivy didn't have the full picture. No-one did.

When Gordon came home from work, Maryanne had his supper ready on the table. Usually, seafood chowder using scallops and haddock and sometimes lobster from the wharf. Or a lamb stew, sometimes a roast with beef, all the meat from the farm on the hill. With Blueberry Grunt or Upside-Down Pineapple Pudding for dessert, recipes from Maryanne's mother's old recipe book with its falling-out pages and hand-written notes in the margins. When he was a little boy, Gordon leafed through the recipe books, admiring the line drawings, reading the ingredients slowly, "What's 'lb'," he said, "and 'oz'?"

"They are pounds and ounces," she said gently, "that's how people weighed the things for the cakes and bread before cups and spoons." She showed him the old scales and he played for hours with the little brass weights and the larger heavier ones, once dropping one on his big toe which swelled up causing all kinds of panic for a few days.

At eight years old he thought that pounds and ounces were much more complicated than cups and spoons but painstakingly wrote a conversion chart for his mother, showing her how many ounces of flour equalled a cup. Maryanne taped it inside the kitchen cupboard door, the cupboard where she kept her rolling pin and mixing bowls.

The two spent evenings and weekends together. In winter they sat by the fire discussing planting plans for the spring garden; radishes and heirloom tomatoes, maybe. Zucchini and spinach. And sunflowers, Maryanne always planted some sunflower seeds. She liked the seeds for the winter bird feeders. Finches were her special delight. In the summer, mother and son went fishing at the lake, or weeded the vegetable patch, finishing as the sun dipped down by walking a dog. Not Pea, this was before Pea came along. But there was always a dog with Gordon and Maryanne.

Maryanne died twenty years ago, after seven months of battling pancreatic cancer. Andrew returned home from South America when the illness began. He never left her side in all those seven months. This meant Gordon began living with his father in what was, to begin with, an uncomfortable situation. But slowly as the months and then years passed, they fell into a balletic rhythm. Moving around the kitchen preparing individual breakfasts. Reaching for a knife or a plate. Not touching, knowing who would go to the left, or to the right. They sat opposite each other at the kitchen table, Andrew with his weekly newspaper. Gordon staring through the window, down across the bay, to the town on the other side.

His father applied for his old age pension and stayed. Gordon worked to keep them both going, and his father took care of the home and had a hot supper ready when Gordon arrived home each evening at 5.30. Andrew cooked fancy suppers he'd learned to make on his travels through South America. Dishes involving eggplant and fennel. Desserts using mangoes and fruits never heard of before in this part of rural Nova Scotia.

On his way home from the office, Gordon wondered, with a pleasant anticipation, just what concoctions his father might have prepared. It was an arrangement that worked. They got to know each other. In a quiet, non-conversational way. Went fishing together on the lake. Kept up Maryanne's garden. Always planting sunflowers ready for the winter and the bird feeders. Without knowing it, Gordon gave Andrew a taste of Maryanne's life. Many evenings they sat on the deck, watching the sun go down.

"Was she happy?" said Andrew looking into the distance.

"I guess," was Gordon's reply, "but define happy."

"Did she cry for me?"

Gordon was shocked at the question, "If she did, she hid that from me, Dad," he said. "She was strong and very brave, there were times we had nothing. But we made the best of what we had."

Andrew said nothing, stared into the distance. A tear rolled down his cheek.

"What?" said Gordon. "Did you want her to spend the years mourning for you?" He knew the words were harsh the second he spat them out, but still felt some things needed saying. "You left us, you know that," he said in a gentler tone.

"I'm sorry, Son."

"It's a bit late for that," said Gordon, offering his father a cold bottle of beer, "but we can't turn the clock back, can we? We must make the best of things, when you're ready, I'll show you some of the things she did with her life."

Andrew's death was unexpected. He was fit and healthy for someone in their eighties and always joked with his doctor who said, 'You're in good shape for your age.' When Gordon got home from work to find Andrew flat on his back on the kitchen floor, the phone still in his hand, he was in disbelief. But he knew, when he looked down at Andrew, he knew that it was all over, that the body lying on the floor was not his dad anymore, that the spirit had gone, and it was just his cold body. Gordon had heard people talk about this at work, how people's features change once their heart stops beating. How they take on a false waxen look. And that is what Gordon remembers now. More than anything. More than the twenty years of living side by side, of the fishing trips, and the exotic suppers. Even the funeral. He wants to remember that if he can, but it just won't come.

As Gordon sinks back on the sofa with Pea, he looks up at the ceiling and sees the indelible image of his father, lying just as he did on the kitchen floor. Waxen and yellow. Gordon sobs.

2.

"Come with us Gordie, come with us, you'll love it." Joslyn Wentzell from work is on the phone.

"I don't think," says Gordon. "What about Pea-pod?"

"You can bring her," says Joslyn, "it's a picnic. You can bring your dog and your cooler, it's always loads of fun."

"I'll think about it," says Gordon. He puts the phone down but rests his hand on the receiver. He is having trouble with this new-found social life people are foisting upon him. He supposes it is kindness but doesn't react well to charity. He feels torn. Should he go? The Dog Days Picnic sounds like a casual event. Something where you can just sit around on the lawn with your dog and let them all sniff each other. He can't imagine Joslyn has an ulterior motive. Gordon is in his sixties and with no history of a female partnership. Maybe he seems like a dream come true for someone like Joslyn. "No," Gordon shakes his head and mutters, "I have no time for such nonsense."

In true Nova Scotia style, Gordon is late for his appointment at the lawyer's office. Reg Conrad welcomes him with a handshake and, "Coffee?"

"Okay," says Gordon, "I came out in a rush, didn't get chance..."

"Cream and...?"

"Yup, that's good," says Gordon.

Reg Conrad went to The Bay Elementary School with Gordon. They were both 'bookish', the term used in those days for someone who was geeky or nerdish. They spent recesses together, sitting on a flat rock in the corner of the schoolyard sharing each other's discoveries of something scientific, or a hero comic book.

"How's it going, Gordie?"

"Ya know. Okay I guess."

"Bet it's quiet in your neck of the woods."

"Too quiet, can't hear myself think sometimes," says Gordon. "Where did life go, Reg?"

Reg looks across the desk at his old school friend slumped in the worn leather visitors' chair. Stubble on his chin. Balding head that once was so thick in blond curls. A paunch of a belly beginning to project through the green plaid shirt. He suspects Gordon hasn't eaten properly since Andrew died.

"Good question," he says, "I often ask myself too. Especially when I look in the mirror in a morning." He pauses. Closes the files on his desk. "Tell you what, Gordie, why don't we leave this paper work for now and go down the coast for a drive, maybe take in some lunch. I know a great place."

"Don't you have other appointments?" says Gordon.

"I'll get 'em cancelled," says Reg. "There's nothing urgent, all routine stuff."

They walk into the outer office, side by side, same step, just as they did as nine-year-olds. "Louise, can you cancel the rest of today for me?" says Reg. The secretary looks up, surprised.

"Just say something urgent has cropped up—you'll handle it," says Reg with a smile. "We'll take my car shall we?" Still smiling, he says to Gordon. "You might like it; it's a hybrid."

The drive along Highway 103 to Lower West Pubnico takes just over two hours of very little traffic. The plow has been through, and high banks of dirty snow thrown up against the pines and spruce bordering the highway make Gordon think of distant lands, of the postcards his father sent each month from the Andes, from Chile, from Panama, and from Venezuela. He closes his eyes. Willie Nelson is singing, 'On the Road

Again,' from the quadraphonic music system in Reg's Lexus ...Goin'
places that I've never been. Seein' things that I may never see again...
Gordon can't help but wonder about the life his father had, the life he,
Gordon, was not a part of except for the regular postcards and his mother's
monthly cheque arriving in an airmail envelope. He wondered why
Andrew never talked to him about it in the twenty years they'd finally had
together. And sometimes he regrets he never asked.

"What's that?" says Reg.

"What?"

"You asked me something," says Reg.

"Oh. Oh no, I was probably dreaming," says Gordon. "Just
wondering, that's all. Wondering what Dad's life was like all those years
he was away. Wondering why he never talked about it."

"Did you never go visit him?" says Reg.

"Never invited." says Gordon as they turn off the highway at trunk
road 335. The white houses and over-powering churches of the Acadian
communities seem like a foreign land to Gordon.

"Never been down here, Gordie?" says Reg.

"I'm ashamed to say, I haven't."

"Not even to gawk at the wind farm?"

"Nope."

"We'll put that right before we do anything else," says Reg, "it's only
12.30, we've loads of time to eat."

They drive to the end of the point and park the Lexus. The seventeen
turbines tower above them. "They say here they are seventy-eight metres
tall," says Reg looking up from the information board.

"Do you feel weird?" says Gordon, "do you think they give off some
sort of vibe?"

"The locals don't like them," says Reg. "They can hear them all the
time. Apparently, there are some cases of stress."

"Progress, I suppose," says Gordon climbing back into the car.

"Your dad knew about such stuff, didn't he?" says Reg.

"He never said," says Gordon, "I always thought his work was to do with cables under water. At least that's what Ma always said."

The restaurant parking lot has five other cars. "Not busy, still I suppose a Tuesday in the middle of winter is not the most popular time for eating out."

But inside, the place is packed with local lobster fishermen. "Good sign," says Gordon.

Reg nods and steers Gordon to a quiet table in the corner. "They do a real good chowder," says Reg. "The liver dinner is good too."

When the server comes over with menus, Reg tells her, "We've already decided. It's the chowder, the liver dinner and two beers. Keith's. Thanks, Kelly."

"You've been here before then," says Gordon.

"Oh yes," says Reg, "it's good to get away from the bay. For some reason people want to share all their legal questions with you over the dinner or supper table. I don't get a break."

"And you're too mild mannered to tell them?" says Gordon. "You don't change, do you, Reg." It wasn't a question.

"But today I'm going to make an exception, for you, I thought we needed a change of scenery, and we can still talk about, well, what we need to talk about. Plus, you do look hungry, Gord."

Gordon says nothing. He hates to admit he's not taking care of himself. It is ten days since the funeral, and he can't remember if he's cooked or done any laundry. At least he had a shower before the appointment at Reg's office, but he knows now that he forgot to shave and that his shirt is wrinkled from not being ironed. "Sorry," he says, "I don't know where my mind is right now."

"It's natural," says Reg. "I've seen folks like this so many times before, well in my job I would. But Gordie, you've got no-one to share this with. We've got quite a lot of paperwork to get through, and I have some stuff for you that your dad left with me."

Gordon raises his grey eyebrows, says nothing, crumbling the freshly baked tea biscuit on his side plate. He rubs the crumbs back and forth between his thumb and forefinger until there is nothing left on the plate but a sandy pile. He wipes his hands on the table napkin. "Sorry," he says, "this is happening a lot right now."

"Do you think a vacation might help?" says Reg.

"Ha!" Gordon attempts a laugh. "You've got to be kidding. I don't think I've ever been anywhere away from here in my life, unless you count that time we went with the Scouts to PEI."

"Then maybe it's time, Gordie. Maybe it's time to live a little."

The two men, old school friends, eat their meal without saying too much. They sip their cold beer and look out across the road to the busy wharf, the lobster boats and the large trucks rumbling in from the buyers. Gordon begins to realise it was a good idea to get away from familiar surroundings. But he has no idea that Reg wants him with open eyes and mind for what he has in store when they get back to the office.

3.

"I'm going to tell you a story," says Joslyn. She has come round to Gordon's after work with a pie. They sit in the kitchen; the wood stove is doing a good job. Pea is curled up on an old quilt in front of the fire with Louie, Joslyn's retired greyhound. The two dogs look alike. Both white with black dots here and there. "Like a matching pair," Joslyn says.

Gordon doesn't want to make too much of that. He likes Joslyn as a work colleague, but he doesn't want to think of matching pairs. Not right now in any case. He has too many other things on his mind.

"I do appreciate you coming round," he says, "and the pie is excellent—you remembered how much I love pumpkin."

"Not just a pretty face," she replies with a grin, crinkling up her nose, exaggerating the wrinkles around her eyes. "I thought you might be hungry for some home cooking; it was never really your thing, was it?"

Gordon laughs; a dry laugh. But it's a laugh; something he hasn't done in a while. He feels a slight ease in his tension. "No, but you know that. Mom was the cook until she died, then Dad took over. Pathetic isn't it, for someone my age. I don't really know how to look after myself. But I'm learning," he adds, too quickly, wanting to preempt any suggestion on Joslyn's part.

She laughs again, "Don't worry," she says. "Not trying to muscle in, I've seen too many others make that mistake."

Gordon hasn't a clue what she's talking about, but delves into his pie, hoping the cinnamon doesn't cause the heartburn he had the last time. "You said you were going to tell me a story," he says through a mouthful of pie.

"Oh yes, you didn't come with us to the Dog Days picnic, I know. My goodness, you missed a good day."

Gordon gets up to put the coffee pot on the stove and settles back down to listen.

Joslyn continues, "There's a young girl volunteer at the kennels. She is always there when a new load of greyhounds come up from the track in Florida. She helps out with cleaning the kennels, walking the dogs, bathing them, talking to them, soothing them. She just loves them to bits."

"How old?" says Gordon.

"What, the dogs? Oh, you mean the girl. I guess she's about eighteen I suppose."

"Jos?"

"Yup."

"Would you mind if you don't tell me now. I'm guessing this is a lovely sad and happy story. I'd just rather you keep it for another time. Sorry."

"Jeez, Gord, no, I'm sorry, I keep forgetting all you've been through. I was going to tell you how she'd been through a bad patch and working with the dogs has helped her turn her life around. Don't take any notice of my babble. But seriously, is there anything else I can do to help?"

"Well, it's funny you should ask..."

"Yeah?"

"Two things, and I should have told you this before you came over. It's just that I keep forgetting..."

"Yes?"

"Well, I think Pea has a flea or two."

"Oh Lordie Gordie, that ain't nothing," says Joslyn, "I'll take care of that for you. Let me take her home with me for half an hour. Bring her back all right as rain, how about that?"

"That would be great, such a relief. I noticed right after the funeral, but I had so much on my mind."

"It's funny that there're fleas about right now, but I hear a lot of people saying. So what was the other thing?"

"Other?" says Gordon.

"Yes, you said there were two things."

"I don't know how to put this Jos, but I may need to go away for a time. Maybe a couple of months, there's something I have to do for Dad. I just wonder if Pea-pod could come and stay with you and Louie."

4.

Gordon had never before opened the large oak desk in the parlour. It sits, where it always has, on the opposite wall to the bay window. It is a large drop-fronted desk with ornate barley-twist scrolls along each side. First, his mother took care of it. Polishing it each week with lavender polish. Dusting it each Wednesday. Keeping all the bills in one pigeonhole, and the receipts in another. Personal addresses in one section. Stamps and envelopes in another. The big drawer, also locked, was where folders with insurance policies, birth certificates and other such documents were kept. Such things had always been a mystery to Gordon. His mother never taught him that side of life; she took care of those things for him.

When his father eventually returned home, he took care of the desk, keeping the keys on his keychain in his pocket.

Gordon thinks now that was irresponsible of them. He had no idea there was so much to running a home. Things like property tax and stuff like that. He was just thankful there was no mortgage. The property had belonged to his grandparents, who inherited it through the family. The house, always known as The Drummond, stood back from the road, slightly elevated above its neighbours, looking down to its own waterfront, its dock, and across the bay to town. After the legal talks with Reg, Gordon knew the house and land were now all his. And he knew the value. Such properties were changing hands for more than a million dollars right now. It certainly gave him reason to think and think hard. Especially after Reg mentioned maybe Gordie should start to 'live a little'. That was the way Gordon remembered Reg putting it, again, during the second trip down the coast for a discussion over lunch.

"Life's too short, you know," said Reg. "Take a trip down to South America; see what your old man was really up to."

Gordie had laughed then, "I don't even have a passport," he said, "never had one, never needed one."

But the seed of the idea began to take root.

He sits at the desk and turns the key in the top lock and gently lowers the heavy lid to rest on the pulled-out barley scroll arms. The contents are impossibly tidy. He wants to take time going through everything and begins with the top pigeonhole on the right. The bills. There is just one. An invoice for Fedex. It is in the name of Mr. A.A. Drummond. All it states is, for courier services to Chile $59.95.

Gordon scratches the side of his nose. It is twenty years since his father was in Chile. Why would he be sending something by courier only a few days before his death? There is nothing to connect the bill with anything, so Gordon continues to the next pigeonhole. The receipts. They consist of mostly slips for gas and groceries. Gordon isn't sure why such receipts would need keeping. He isn't sure if they could be used for income tax. He fingers the curling corners of the tiny scraps of paper, mostly cash register stubs. Well-thumbed. Checked over more than once. Stapled by each month. Organised. Everything accounted for. One bundle, folded, right at the bottom of the heap, is from Fedex. For courier services to Chile. Ten years' worth. Mostly for around $20 each time. Gordon takes a deep breath and wonders just what business his father was conducting in Chile right until he died.

He calls Reg. "I've no idea," says Reg, "he was pretty vague with me, just wanted you to have the keys to the desk so that you would have everything to go through at your leisure. If you want me to come over and help, any time, Gord, you just have to say."

"It's okay for now," says Gordon, "It just bothers me seeing all these courier documents. He must've been sending something when I was at work because I have no recollection of Fedex calling at the house at all. Ever. I wonder why he never said anything."

"Have you thought anymore about going to find out in person?" says Reg. "Again, if you want company, I might be able to help."

"You're a good friend, Reg. I'll give it more thought. I may well take you up on that offer." Gordon replaces the old telephone receiver. He can't bring himself to go any further through the desk, but knows it will have to be done, so he unlocks the drawer and takes out the file folders, bringing them over to the coffee table. He makes himself a sandwich with his favourite local bacon and sits back with Pea at his side.

"Now then, old girl, let's take a look through these, see if they can shed any light," he says.

Daylight fades into wintery dusk before Gordon has made any headway with the files. He gets up, stretches, closes the curtains, throws another log on the fire. "I suppose you need to go out," he says to the dog, who looks up at him with her melting eyes as if to say, 'thank you for reading my mind.' She uncoils herself from the sofa, two front legs on the rug first and then allows the back ones to drop down after her. Gordon puts on her red fleece coat for her, then his own thick plaid jacket before making their way down the driveway to the ice-covered dock.

The moon is high over the frozen bay, but still, it reflects on the blue-white expanse. The silence is overwhelming, and Gordon reminds himself how lucky he is to live in such a serene part of the world. He sees recent fox tracks, finding some reassurance that wildlife is still wild and kicking. He knows how cold it must be for them, but up in the woods behind the house there is plenty of shelter, cavernous hollows beneath tree roots and granite boulders. He knows the property like he knows his own face. He is pretty sure he is blessed.

But still there is the loneliness. The fear that he has no family left now. If only he'd had brothers or sisters. Even cousins, that would have been something. But there is no-one. Just him and Pea and a couple of colleagues who want to be friends. And his old school friend Reg. His lawyer.

Gordon tries imagining what his life will be like now. An empty house to come home to. Learning how to cook, clean and do his own laundry. Maybe he should go looking for a wife, or at least a companion. All these questions. And no answers popping out of the woodwork. Still, for some reason Reg thinks Gordon's father has left all possible answers in the large oak desk and maybe, just maybe, he should stick at it tonight.

"Come on then, old girl," he says to the whippet, "let's get back inside where it's warm."

She looks up at him as if she understands, and together they walk back up to the house and in through the back door to the kitchen.

Joslyn shows Gordon how to do online research. He uses a computer at work but never had the desire to have one at home. "Google is your friend," she says, getting as close to Gordon as she can, showing him how to search for keywords on the new laptop he's bought in town. "What are you looking for exactly?" She leans across, letting her breast catch his shoulder.

But Gordon is reticent. Either to respond to her advances or to share any concerns he has about his father's activities with anyone other than Reg. "Just stuff," he says. "Things about other countries; I'm thinking of travelling a bit as you know, that's why I asked if you could take care of her for me." He reaches down under the dining table where Pea is curled against his legs.

"But if you tell me more, I can help," she says.

"It's okay, Jos, honestly, I'm just doodling around for something to do, idle curiosity you might call it."

So they leave it at that and open a couple of beers, watching the afternoon sun dip down over the horizon. "You won't find what you're looking for out over there," she says, grinning.

He looks up, he knows her well enough to be honest, "I know, he says, I'm just regretting not doing more with my life, that's all."

"Don't have regrets," she says, "you're a good man, Gordon Drummond. You don't have to be a jet-setting millionaire to be a good man."

Gordon is glad Joslyn doesn't know the whole story, not that he knows all of it himself. But the more he finds out, the more he realises he will never need to worry about money again. Loneliness maybe, but not money. Then he reminds himself of the one thing his mother often said, that money doesn't buy happiness, bringing his thoughts right back to where he started.

After Joslyn leaves in her rattling Toyota pickup, he goes back to the laptop and searches the cost of flights to Valparaiso, Chile, the one place that seems a constant in all the papers of his father. He is pleasantly surprised to find that $1500 will buy a return ticket from Halifax to Santiago, but not to Valparaiso. He would want to stopover there for a week or so to check out some Chilean bonds he'd found in a yellow wax paper envelope in the desk drawer. He looks at the calendar and thinks mid-February to mid-April would be the best time. That would give him the opportunity to get more information together and make arrangements. The biggest one being to apply for early retirement.

Having thought all this through, Gordon feels a quickening in his stomach, an excitement never felt before as he contemplates a real life-changer. He picks up the eight-page passport application Reg dropped off yesterday and begins to fill out the details.

He feels just like he did when he went away with the Scouts to The Island. He was thirteen and his mother bought him new underwear and socks and some play clothes from Bob's Store in town. She washed and ironed and folded them all and packed them in a small cardboard suitcase for him, attaching a luggage label stating that 'this case belongs to Gordon Andrew Drummond, Indian Point, Lunenburg County. If found, please return.' Gordon kept the label in a box of small treasures in his bedroom with his scout badges and some black marbles. He wonders, only fleetingly, if the label would do to attach to his suitcase for his trip to South America. Which brings him to thinking about suitcases.

He doesn't really want to splash out on a new one. His father's travel equipment is all in the bedroom that was first his parents', then his mother's and then, finally, his father's. He climbs the stairs, stepping gently on the sixth tread, which always creaks, and opens the door to the room he has probably only ever been in half a dozen times. It is dark, with the royal blue flowered curtains closed. The large bed is cloaked in a matching royal blue satin bedspread. The head of the bed is high, dark mahogany and finely carved with angels and exotic fruit. Gordon had never studied the detail of the bed head before. He runs his hands across the highly polished top, still wondering at the strange relationship that was his parents' marriage.

On top of the matching armoire is a set of three old suitcases; stacked on top of each other. Gordon stands on a chair and lifts down the top one. It is in a faded green canvas and has leather corners with studs. It is heavier than he thought it would be, but the second is even heavier. When it comes to the third, the biggest, Gordon finds he needs all his strength to lift the case down.

He places each one on the over-sized bed and tries to open them. They are locked. Just like he knew they would be. Every possible key from the desk and also the package Reg handed to him are in his pocket. Gordon has got accustomed to finding things locked and learned quickly that there is no need to be running back and forth trying keys. Old suitcase keys are easy to recognise. "They don't make them like this anymore," he mutters, turning the key in the lock of the smallest case.

Gordon is not ready for the contents. There are two purple velvet drawstring bags about six inches square with hand embroidered monograms—'D'—in yellow gold silk. He takes a deep breath and pulls out small trinkets, lockets mostly, on gold chains. There are five in total. He holds his breath and carefully pulls back the catch on the first. There is a photograph of a young girl. And a lock of dark brown hair.

Gordon lays back on the bed with a pillow propped up against the carved headboard. He angles the shade of the bedside light to give him a better view of the photograph in the locket. He guesses the girl to be about five or six years old, and that the lock of hair would be from her first haircut, maybe to start school. He doesn't recognise the face. He knows his father's sister was fair and died of lung problems when she was only two years old. Gordon has no idea who this might be. Only one locket has a curl of hair, the others have photographs of adults, again no-one he recognises. He carefully replaces them in the velvet pouch and opens the other. This one contains an identity card in a foreign language. Bound in red leather with gold lettering, his father's name, A. Drummond, and the name of a company. Gordon assumes the firm he worked for. He has no idea why his father would keep it in a velvet pouch in a locked suitcase.

He leaves the suitcase open on the bed and goes downstairs, taking the ID card with him. Turning on the laptop, he begins some research into the company name. And variations of the name. Gordon is shocked that results quickly list down the screen for Perdita Drummond Gold. It is a mining company. There is a quote from The Financial Post regarding a court case against the mine and unresolved disputes over its impact on the environment.

Gordon shivers. He knows now that he has cracked open the lid on a world totally unknown to him and he has no idea what to do about it. He looks at the old Gebrueder clock on the mantel. It is twenty minutes to ten. Gordon picks up the phone and dials Reg's number.

6.

"This scares me shitless," Gordon says to Reg.

"Slow down, slow down," says Reg, "start again, what in the be-Jesus have you found?"

"I opened a suitcase," says Gordon, "found an ID card."

"Yes, yes?"

"I looked it up on the computer," says Gordon, feeling a tad braver than ten minutes ago, "and found it's an ID card for a gold mine in Chile."

"Holy suff'rin'," says Reg. "I had no idea. Do you want me to come over?"

"It's late," says Gordon, "I know, but I'll never sleep with all this lot laid out in front of me. And there's more."

"More?"

"Yes, there's a locket and some hair. No-one I recognise."

"I've a bottle of Scotch, not yet opened. Stay right where you are, Gordie, I'll be right over."

Gordon puts down the phone and says, "Do you need to get out, stretch your legs, old girl?" to Pea. "If so, we'd better git 'er done before Reg gets here, we may be at this all night."

They are still out on the dock when Reg's Lexus pulls up and the three walk into the house together. The kitchen has a warmth only a wood stove can give; slightly smoky, comforting. Reg takes off his snow covered boots and pulls a pair of carpet slippers out of his coat pocket. "Thought these would be a good idea," he says, "I suspect we are in for a long night."

Gordon pads around the kitchen in his sock feet. Thick fishermen's socks that keep the cold out. The two men sit at the kitchen table with Pea at their feet on a blanket. Gordon fetches two tumblers and Reg opens the Scotch.

"It's been a long time since I've done anything like this," says Reg.

Gordon raises an eyebrow. "So, it's happened before?"

"No. God no. Nothing like this," says Reg. "But there have been times when clients have gone through a rough patch, and I've helped them sort things out. It usually happens at night."

"Is that how you see me. And this?" says Gordon.

"No Gordie. This is different. Very different. Let's get a drink in us and then we can make a start."

By 3 am. the two have emptied all three suitcases. The contents tell quite the story. There are many photographs of people Gordon doesn't know. Except those of his father, wearing shorts, standing under tropical trees. Smiling a smile Gordon has never seen before. And with other people, sitting outside bars, around tables. Bottles with foreign labels strewn around. Photos taken in nightclubs. On riverbanks. And in mountains.

The other people include a tall woman with long, dark, flowing hair. Two small children in shifts. Gordon assumes they are girls from the hair styles too. He wonders who the lock of hair in the locket belongs to.

"Reg, what do you reckon at the pictures?" says Gordon.

"Hard to say," says Reg, "but at first glance, I'd say your father had another family."

Gordon says nothing. Reg has confirmed what he already feels. A mix of shock and excitement. Excitement at the possibility that he isn't alone in the world after all. That he does have family somewhere.

And that somewhere looks like it's in Chile. South America. But his feeling is mixed with a tinge of sadness. To think that all those years, when his father was away, he was with another family. Coming home from work in the evenings to sit down with them and have supper. To go out at weekends on trips to rivers, and mountains, and stand under exotic trees. And then in the evenings, to sit in nightclubs with another woman. Another wife? Wearing clothes never to be seen in these here parts. While Gordon's mother, Andrew's REAL wife, scrimped and saved to make ends meet. Who never had a social life of her own, never cavorted with another man. Who dedicated her life to Gordon.

"I need another drink," says Gordon. Together the two men sit back at the table, glasses in hand and look at each other.

"You, well we I suppose, have taken the lid off a crock of worms by the looks of things," says Reg. "Sometimes I wish people would sort out their messes before they shuffle off to the graveyard, and not leave this trail of unanswered questions for those left behind."

Gordon nods. "You've seen this before then?"

"Not quite like this. No, nothing quite this deep."

There is a silence that carries their thoughts around the kitchen, over their heads, swirling around the old wooden shelves with their dishes and pots. In and out of the pantry with its stock of canned tomatoes and peaches and beans until it disappears and reappears as words again.

"The thing is Reg..."

"Hmmm."

"The things is... what do I do about it?"

"We." says Reg. "We. If you would like, I'll help you with this. WE can find out as much as we can without alerting anyone. That means not hurting anyone either. So far, you are the only person who knows something of both sides of the story, well I guess so. Or would your father have been open with these other people?" He waves his hands across the piles of photos, "open about the fact that he had a family back here in Canada?"

"Don't know," says Gordon, "but you know there were strangers at the funeral. There was a woman..."

"I remember," says Reg. "I stood near the back you know. I don't know if you realised I was there, but I did come, for you as much as anyone. I did see a strange face or two. Not folks from around here. But your dad did travel a lot years ago. And he did come to see me, first when he came back, to sort out your mother's estate, and then off and on, to ask me to handle his own affairs."

Gordon looks up at Reg. "Thanks," he says.

"What for?"

"Just thanks, I reckon we should sleep on this and look at it with fresh eyes in the morning."

"You're right," says Reg, "I can't drive you know, not after all this whisky. Can I have the sofa?'

"Sure," says Gordon, I'll fetch pillows and blankets, "you know you'll have Pea for company."

"Lovely," says Reg.

Gordon tosses and turns all night. Whether it is because someone else is in the house, or because images of foreign women and palm trees keep floating through his mind, he doesn't know. By 5 a.m., he knows it's no good and goes down to the kitchen to make coffee. What he sees is evidence that Reg couldn't sleep either. The table has neat piles of photographs, all categorised and dated with sticky notes on top. Stacks of papers again with yellow sticky notes—three piles saying Chile, New York, Panama. And on top of everything is a passport. It is an old passport with the corner clipped and 'cancelled' stamped across the name: Mr. Andrew Ainslie Drummond.

Gordon puts down the coffeepot and looks for Reg. No sign of Reg or Pea, so he knows they're out for a walk. There has been a fine falling of snow through the night. Reg's car is covered, as is the front lawn rolling down to the dock. Two sets of prints trail through the snow. Reg's boots and Pea's fine little paw prints. Heading in the direction of the estuary. Gordon knows it will not be long before Pea's feet are too cold to withstand the snow and they'll be back wanting to be warmed. He starts a pot of oatmeal alongside the coffee, picks up the passport and sits in his father's armchair by the stove.

7.

"What do you think?" says Reg, coming through the entryway, shaking off the snow.

"Shocked," says Gordon. "But there had to be something, didn't there? He couldn't have just lived down there all those years, just to work and send money back. I wonder if Mom knew."

"I think she might've," says Reg. "That's the sad part. In addition, it seems he might have more assets than's in his will here. You'd better sit down."

"Let me feed Pea her breakfast first," says Gordon, "then you can show me what you've come up with. Coffee?"

"Can I?" Reg indicates the laptop.

"Sure," says Gordon, ladling out a couple of spoonfuls of oatmeal for Pea, putting it by the window to cool.

"While you were sleeping, I found a law office in Santiago, Chile. I reckon if we speak with them, they may shed some light," says Reg, turning the laptop around for Gordon to see the website. "There may have been a second will, dealing with all of his assets down there."

"Is that allowed?" says Gordon.

"I think so, especially if he had residence there, and all things were kept absolutely separate, as we see they are. And you may or may not like this idea, but I think we should do it face to face. One-on-one, if you like."

Gordon stops between the stove and the table, coffeepot in hand, "You mean go down there?"

"Yes."

"I'd already decided I should," says Gordon, "although, as you know, I haven't a clue how to go about it. I did send off for my passport though."

"That's good," says Reg, "I did wonder. I think it best if we both go, like I suggested earlier."

They book flights with Air Canada online. Reg uses his loyalty card for upgrades and the dates are pretty much what Gordon suggested. February to April. Reg assures Gordon that taking time off is no problem for him; he has new partners hired and has been looking for a way to step back a little, take some time for himself.

"This'll be a trip of a lifetime for me," says Reg.

"Me too," says Gordon, "I've already made arrangements for Pea to stay with Jos. It was a bit difficult; I reckon Jos fancies me, and wanted to tag along." The two men laugh. Good belly laughs. Something Gordon hasn't done for weeks.

"It's Christmas next week," says Reg. "What do you fancy doing?"

"Me?" says Gordon. "Haven't even thought about it, haven't you got family and stuff?'

"No-one," says Reg. "Seems we are in the same boat you and me, Gordie. Same boat. What a pair."

"I always thought you had family, wife and kids; sorry we didn't see much of each other over the years Reg."

"She left me after eight months of marriage," says Reg. "Never heard from her again. So I never bothered, wasn't worth the hassle. Women! Anyway, Christmas? Do you fancy The Lodge?"

Christmas comes. There was something alien about staying in an hotel, getting dressed in a suit and tie for dinner, being waited on. "This is the life," says Gordon to Reg as they sit by the roaring fire after the turkey-with-all-the-trimmings dinner. Sipping brandies. Wearing paper hats. They turn together and look out at the ocean, the Atlantic rolling gently in on the icy white sands. At the couples walking arm in arm along the beach, in red knitted toques and knee-high boots. At the children running back and forth to the icy waves, shrieking then running back to the dunes, hiding behind the ice laden grasses, rushing out screaming in joy and thrill, as only children can do.

"Lucky," says Gordon.

"Yes," says Reg, "but things aren't always what they seem."

In the eight weeks following Christmas, the two men prepare for their trip. Gordon's passport arrives. He keeps it in the oak desk and every day or so; he takes it out and turns the pristine pages, thinking how proud his father would be, and his mother too. Or would they? Would they think he was disturbing things, things that should be left just as they are, hidden within suitcases or desk drawers, or with lawyers in far-off lands? It didn't matter now; the decision was made, and Gordon and Reg were all geared up for the trip.

Reg booked them into the Radisson Plaza on the Avenida Vitacura, quite close to the offices of the lawyers he had made arrangements with. Gordon was glad to have Reg as his friend and ally on this, otherwise he just wouldn't have known where to start. He guesses he would have got on a plane in Halifax and got off in Chile and just taken it from there.

But Reg was more methodical. He knew that they would need all the time they could get to talk with people and sort things out.

In the meantime, they both signed up for Spanish for Beginners through Parks and Recreation. The classes are held in their old High School from seven to nine on Wednesday evenings beginning January 5th.

In some ways, Bagpipes for Beginners being held in the music room down the hall doesn't hurt things at all. It seems to add to the experience, to the uniqueness of it all. Gordon is beginning to find his life has taken on a whole new level. He is doing things and going places he never dreamed of. Evening classes were certainly never part of his life plan.

As he stumbles through hola to adios on night one to a correos and una parada de taxis by week three, he knows that by the time he and Reg leave Halifax, they should at least be able to greet people and ask for a taxi.

When the time comes, the morning before the night flight, Gordon drives Pea over to Joslyn's place. It is an uneasy parting, the two have never been separated before. Gordon finds Joslyn making dog food for Louie and Pea. She is grinding ginger root with spinach and zucchini. She has meat and bones from the farm and the kitchen smells like Gordon's used to smell, when his mother was alive, cooking stews for him.

"They'll be getting it some good," he says.

"This? Oh, this is the norm in this house, take a look at these." She opens the oven door where six dozen cookies are baking. "Banana, sardine and molasses," she says. "Some good all right."

"I'm going to leave yhe ou with this," says Gordon. "It's to cover her costs and in case you have to take her to the vet or something. Anything you need." He places a sealed envelope containing two thousand dollars in one hundred-dollar bills on the side table. Even that doesn't make him feel any better about leaving his one constant and loyal companion and friend, Pea. "Be a good girl," he says, "I'll be home before you know it." He looks up at Joslyn, "I'll email you," he says, "let you know how I'm doing; I can text you too, now you've shown me how, even post some photos on Facebook. And thank you again, you are making this possible you know."

Gordon and Joslyn hug, a tight squeeze, and then he turns on his heels and leaves. Trying not to look back. Trying not to hear the sad cries of his sweet Pea. It sounds just like the seals moaning out on the ice.

8.

The drive to Halifax's Stanfield International Airport is uneventful. Reg has arranged for one of his employees to drive them, in his Lexus, thereby saving the worry of parking and leaving the car for eight weeks. They know they are in for a twenty-hour trip all told, counting check-in times and the change in Toronto, but flight AC 615 takes off on time at 20.25. Gordon, who has never flown before, is surprised that the plane feels just like getting on a bus. They have seats in the front section and as soon as they are settled the cabin crew come around with newspapers and coffee.

The change at Toronto Pearson takes Gordon by surprise, but Reg has passes for the Maple Leaf Lounge where, again, they are treated like VIPs until it's time for AC092 to Santiago.

Reg looks across at Gordon as the cabin crew tuck him up in the first-class pod, offering him pyjamas and hot chocolate. He smiles, wanting only the best for his friend now, and hopes that this is not some wild goose chase. Hoping that good will come from it. That there is no more anguish.

Within half an hour, the two men are asleep and when the lights are turned up with the smell of breakfast, they wake and look across the aisle at each other, "Are we nearly there then?" says Gordon.

Reg laughs, "I guess we are, that didn't hurt one bit, did it."

The procedure on landing in Santiago takes them by surprise. "We are on vacation. Holiday," says Reg, when an immigration officer asks the purpose of the visit. He had already told Gordon to say as little as possible.

The immigration officials look at Gordon's Canadian passport and say, 'Pliss, come this way pliss, Sir."

"I will come too, if I may," says Reg.

"Ah, no, only Mr. Drummond," says the immigration official.

"But I am his lawyer," says Reg. Knowing immediately that it was the wrong thing to say, wishing he could bite his tongue, take the words back.

For ten hours the two men are questioned. Their baggage gone through item by item. Kept separate, neither knew just what the other was saying, or not saying. Gordon heeded Reg's advice and said very little, not letting on he understood a bit of Spanish. Slowly coming to realise that his father's name must be on file. Something to do with income tax and the mine.

"Do you know Andrew Drummond?" says the immigration guy in the navy-blue hat with gold braid. "Father to you?"

Gordon said one word, "Dead."

And that seemed to be it. Reg and Gordon were put together in another room where they were asked where they were staying, and what their plans were. Reg did the talking. "We are staying here in the city for one week. We want to see the place my friend's father lived, so we will go to Valparaiso after one week. We are on holiday, but we look for family too. Is that okay?"

They are released into bright sunshine. Unshaven, sweating and eager for food and a shower. The taxi takes them to the Radisson, "But you didn't arrive," says the receptionist at the front desk, "your rooms are no longer available, we just have one room left."

"We were delayed," says Reg, "not our fault. Not yours either, we'll take what you have. It is for one week, yes?"

"Sir."

As the two men close the door on room 317, they breathe deeply. Almost in unison. "Never expected any of that," says Gordon.

"I should have thought," says Reg. "If there was any shady business going on, then your dad would be blacklisted, but I would have thought after more than twenty years..."

"Let's not worry about it," says Gordon. "Do you want the shower first?"

And with that they slip into an easy sharing of space. Making coffee and tea for each other at the room's kitchen bar area. Ordering room service and lying back on the two king sized beds in undershorts watching the news in Spanish on the TV.

By evening they are ready to take in some sights. Before they go Gordon sends Joslyn an email from his new iPad: 'Hi Jos, we've arrived. Bit of a delay and upset at the airport here but all okay now. We are at the hotel I told you about and gave you the numbers for. But you've got our cell phone numbers if something crops up. Kisses for Pea. G.'

He thought after he'd hit send that maybe he should have included kisses for her too, but it was too late and anyhow, Reg was raring to go hit the town.

They started in the hotel bar. Glitzy; mirrors, crystal chandeliers. Old, faded sepia photos around the wall in gilded frames. Photos of the British era when Chile was more English than England. Just like parts of India too. With street names like Cambridge Road and Hereford Boulevard. "I had no idea," says Gordon to Reg, "no idea that the place used to be so British."

"It does make you think, doesn't it," says Reg, "how much things have changed in the past, even over the past fifty years."

They sip their cold beers sitting out on the verandah on rattan chairs under the stars and marvel at the warm temperatures. "Of course, we are in the southern hemisphere, the seasons are the other way around, aren't they?"

Reg doesn't reply, he has his eyes closed and he's breathing deeply. Then he says, "You know, none of this would be happening if your dad hadn't died leaving you with this mystery, we wouldn't be sitting here now, would we? Makes you think."

"Indeed," says Gordon, "and we have tomorrow to look forward to, too. What time is the appointment?'

"Eleven," says Reg. "Time to start really taking the lid off. Do you still want to? There is always time to back right out now?"

"No going back," says Gordon. "And maybe we should just sit here for a while, not worry about looking for night life tonight. Tomorrow may turn out to be a big day."

9.

The offices of Snrs. Jose and Gladstone on Avenue Santa Lucia are old school. Reg said he was expecting all glass and steel. Instead, the colonial building has a facade of columns and mellow stonework like something out of a book of architectural history. The two men took a taxi, even though the law offices appeared to be close by, the concierge assured them the road was 'very very busy, taxi is best,' and so they were guided by him.

They climb out of the taxi and look up at the impressive building and then at each other. "Jeez Reg, how much is this going to cost?" says Gordon.

"Don't know, but we'll ask that early on. First one hour meeting two hundred dollars. It may be enough for us."

They are directed to the second floor, no elevator, but a gentle curved staircase with highly polished brass handrail and rich, dark red carpet on the stair treads held in place by Victorian stair rods. They remind Gordon of the rods his mother took up from the stairs back home. They have the same acorn carvings at each end. He has no time to wonder where they came from, or why she took them up. They reach the 2nd floor and are shown into a large office with French doors opening out onto a balcony with views across the city and towards the mountains. A man stands on the balcony with his back to Reg and Gordon.

He turns. "Good morning," he says in a perfect English accent. "Bill Gladstone, senior partner, so glad to meet you. Finally. You must be Reginald Conrad," he says to Gordon.

"No," says Gordon, smiling, relieved that he wouldn't have to resort to his meagre Spanish, "this here is Reg, my lawyer and friend, I am Gordon Drummond."

Bill Gladstone points to a seating area of the office with deep leather couches and a brass topped coffee table. "Shall we? And please, call me Bill."

As the three men settle into the leather couches, the door opens and a tray of teacups, tea pot and a plate of ginger cookies appears in the arms of a young man. "Thank you, Jorge," says Bill Gladstone. "Hope you all like tea, or would you rather have coffee or something cold."

"Tea is fine for us, ain't that right, Gordie," says Reg, winking.

"Yup, tea's good," says Gordon. "A touch of the old country?"

"Indeed," says Bill. "But I was born here, my parents too. It was my grandparents who were the settlers. I do go back to England from time to time. I went there to boarding school, then to Oxford and on to Law School after that. But I missed this place. It doesn't compare with England. Have you been?"

"What," says Gordon, "to the UK? Oh my, oh my, oh my, I've never been further than Halifax Nova Scotia. I had to get my first passport to come here and I'm sixty-two years old."

The three men laugh. A genuine laugh that indicates common ground.

"Oh yes, by the way," says Reg, "the immigration people have kept our passports, all tied up with our reason for the visit, can we ask you to look into that for us?"

"They'll be fine," says Bill, "I'll take care of that as part of this case file if that's okay. Now, maybe we should get down to business, then I'll take you somewhere really good for lunch. Don't worry, that will be off-tab, it is just so refreshing to meet a couple of fellows like yourselves. Maybe I'll take a trip to your part of the world at some point, and you can return the favour, I hear the lobster is very good."

"You can say that again," says Reg, "but the industry is suffering, just like everything else."

"Indeed," says Bill. "Now, let's take a look at what you wanted to see me about shall we?"

He pulls a mahogany cart towards him. It has three red box files piled on the top. Below is a cabinet with the door open. Inside is a wooden box about the size of a shoe box.

"I've been in touch with a small firm of lawyers up in Valparaiso," he says. "They sent these items down by courier last week, I felt I should do a bit of research on your behalf, in advance of your arrival. I've actually already run up quite an account for you."

Reg looks at Gordon, then back at Bill. "How much?" he says.

"We're already over six thousand US dollars," says Bill, "but you may not need much more than we have managed to collate already, this consultation is included in that amount and any of my time in the few days you are here, I'll be happy to answer questions."

Gordon nods at Reg. "Sounds good," he says. "We just don't want to break the bank; this project may turn out to cost more than it's worth."

"I think you'll be happy with what I've found," says Bill. "The only problem is people—there are people who may find this upsetting. Your father had two lives, Mr. Drummond, sorry, Gordon. Two lives. He kept them both separate, very cleverly, I might add."

"We've already gathered that much," interjects Reg. "With the information we found back home, passports, references to a mine. And photographs. Photos of a woman, or women and a child or children."

"I hate to tell you this, Gordon, but I suspect you may already be prepared for a bombshell. You see, your father was, in fact, a bigamist."

10.

The taxi takes the three men to the Aquesta Coco seafood restaurant on Andres Bello about ten minutes from the law offices. It is 1.30 and Reg's stomach has rumbled for twenty minutes. Bill took the hint, ordered the taxi, and now they are seated at a round table in a quiet corner, overlooking a tree-lined boulevard. The facade of the restaurant is not dissimilar to that of Bill's law offices. "Same architect," he tells them, in response to their quizzical expressions. "His work is everywhere; did some work for The National Gallery in London, too."

Gordon sips his tall green glass of bottled water, pushing the lemon slice out of the way with his tongue. He studies the menu, "Not exactly MacDonald's is it?"

Bill laughs. "It is good," he says, "everything is good. They do a sampler if you'd like."

Gordon orders the sampler for an appetizer, Reg orders the king crab, following Bill's lead. For their entree they each settle for catch of the day, swordfish, although Reg's attention is drawn to the eel. "We catch eels in Nova Scotia," he tells Bill, "down along the Eastern Shore. They have the seal of approval from Her Majesty the Queen."

Bill nods, "I will have to visit, it sounds an extraordinary place. Bet you fellows are missing it all ready."

Gordon hasn't thought about what he's missing, until Bill mentions the words. Pea's face jumps into his mind immediately and he says, "Can you excuse me for just one moment, I need to check something." He pulls his iPad from his attaché case and looks at the photos of Pea. Her dark brown eyes like melting velvet, her pink nose showing through her short white coat. He swallows hard, then looks up at the table as the appetizers arrive. "Sorry about that," he says, "just something I had to do."

"So, Bill," says Reg, munching his crab, "where do we go from here?"

"The mine is in trouble," says Bill, "not financial trouble, that is well secured. No it's all this new environmental stuff. The mine has been taken to court by the environmental department of the local government up there for non-compliance."

"What can I do?" says Gordon.

"Your father was the owner," says Bill, "but when he left, over twenty years ago, he signed over ownership to his daughter, Perdita Drummond and her son."

There is a stillness and a silence around the table. Gordon looks up from his plate. He sees the gilded framed mirrors around the restaurant walls, reflecting lights, blue skies, sun, dazzling him with images of himself. The table appears to rise and then fall. Reg and Bill look at him.

"I have a sister?" is all he can say. "Perdita? That's what Dad wanted to call Pea when we got her. So he called her Perdie. It all makes sense now. He gave all that up to come back home. Didn't he?"

Bill nods. He says nothing.

Reg reaches across for Gordon's hand. "We'll get it all sorted, Gordie," he says, giving his hand a squeeze.

The lunch is memorable in many ways. That's how Reg recalls it later, when the trip is over. He tells Gordon how remembers most of the words spoken with each serving of the five-course lunch. The dessert of Lucuma Cake, described as a traditional meringue lucuma or eggfruit frost cake filled with a crunchy and soft meringue and lucuma cream. He says he still has no idea what lucuma is but will always remember the feeling that he was transported to a different world. Thanks to Gordon. Thanks to Gordon's dad dying and leaving a mess to be sorted out.

They say goodbye to Bill back at the law offices. Bill has copied the documents onto a memory stick in addition to packing many things into one box file for Gordon. Reg keeps the memory stick as back up, "Just in case," he says.

Gordon understands. After they were split up in immigration, he wants to be double sure that nothing gets lost in translation this time.

They have five days to kill while staying in the Radisson before heading to Valparaiso. Gordon sees little reason to waste the time, "Let's be tourists, for the next few days."

Reg agrees, "But not today," he says. They spend what is left of that life-changing day in their room at the Radisson, sifting through documents and talking.

"Who would have thought it?" Gordon says.

"I reckon nine out of ten people have a secret life. You'd be surprised at some of the things I have to deal with in my job."

"I still wonder if Mom knew. I guess I'll never really find that out now."

There is a sadness in Gordon's voice, but also a new-found exhilaration. He is thinking that tomorrow, out in this city as a tourist, he could be walking the same streets as his father before him. That he's getting a taste of his father's other life. He wonders now why it had to be such a great big secret.

He also wonders who is this sister? Was she the woman at the funeral? Through the afternoon and evening of that eventful day, sitting on the sunny balcony of the Radisson Santiago, Gordon phones Joslyn, Reg phones the office, and they reassure themselves that all is well back on the icy south shore of Nova Scotia.

The following morning, they leave their valuables and the paperwork in the safe in the hotel room and head on out to explore Santiago. Bill has already given them some ideas, "If you're interested in art and architecture," he said, "you'll probably enjoy wandering the cobbled streets of Santiago's older barrios, but if you are out in the mid-day heat, then maybe Parque Quinta Normal would be a good bet, it houses over a half dozen museums within an incredible maze of greenery." He'd scribbled down a few places on a table napkin and Reg has it in his pocket.

But it's the Cerro San Cristobal that Reg and Gordon head for first. Reg has read aloud the description from the brochure over breakfast, towering over the Chilean capital, this hill-hugging park is a recreational oasis with public pools, botanical gardens, and breathtaking views of both the city and the Andean peaks—smog permitting. Santiguans come here to jog, bike, and hike. Tourists come to ride the rickety funicular up to the hilltop Virgin Mary statue and sip on mote con huesillo while taking in the panorama.

So that's what Gordon and Reg do, they ride the rickety funicular, a mountain railway rising steeply from the city until they reach the top. They get out, breathe deeply and look way down over the city partly cloaked in smog. They use their smart phones to take photos, of the view, of each other, and then like kids, hold out their phones to take photos of themselves, poking out their tongues like fourteen-year-olds do for Facebook. Laughing. Arms around each other in this new-found experience and friendship.

When they return to their hotel, just after sunset, they find a courier has delivered their passports to the front desk.

11.

Planning the trip to Valparaiso has not been without difficulty. Initially they were not sure why they are going, and why for so long. Gordon, felt, right from the day they decided to go to Chile, that if there were things needing his attention, then a couple of weeks would not be enough. They'd double checked the type of air tickets and felt confident that, if need be, they could cut the trip short and just go home.

Valparaiso is only seventy miles northwest of Santiago. Gordon and Reg, after a couple of days in the capital, wondered if a car rental would be a good idea. Bill visited them part way through the week and suggested it would be better taking a bus or even a van taxi and renting a car when they got there, that is, if they felt they really needed a car. "Valparaiso is quite a large city," said Bill, "you may find it's too stressful. If I could, I'd come along with you, really. But I have a big case coming up next week. If it gets an adjournment, I'll let you know. Now you have my cell phone number and I have yours. Let me know how you make out."

They opt for the bus. It turns out to be a comfortable long-distance coach with a washroom, but a luggage restriction. Bill comes to their aid at the last moment saying, "I'll get it sent out to you, let me know for sure where you will be staying."

"We've decided against an hotel, Bill," says Reg. "Because it's a long stay we wanted somewhere we could spread out, invite people round if need be. More a home away from home kinda thing."

"Yes," says Gordon, "there's this website called homeaway.com." He smiles, so glad he got himself up to speed on computer searching and the like. "The one we've booked has got three bedrooms and three bathrooms." Gordon and Reg begin to laugh. "So we'll have loads of space if you do want to join us."

"Wow! Where is it?" says Bill.

"Somewhere called Cerro Alegre," says Reg, reading from his printout, "apparently a world heritage part of the city, well placed, good views and plenty of parking. Looks nice. We've booked it for six weeks. Got a good deal."

"When did you book it?" says Bill.

"Just before we left home, we looked at hotels, and well, we are not really hotel kind of people. We want to do some cooking, shop in the local markets, get a feel for what it's like to live here. They are letting us have it for $500 a week."

"Yes," adds Gordon, "and if we feel like taking a trip to another area, we can leave our stuff there, and travel light. I'm hoping this new, yet to meet, family of mine will be able to spend time with us too."

Bill assures them that all will be well as he says goodbye. "If all Nova Scotians are as easy going as you two, it must be one lovely place to live. But enjoy Valparaiso. It used to be big in English heritage, many immigrants settled there. You'll see some of the traditions have lingered. There's actually an Irish Pub I think, that's probably about the closest to what you have back home. Still, enjoy, let me know if there's anything you need. And I will make sure you get these," he says, pointing to the suitcases at his feet.

The bus ride suits the two men perfectly, they stow their one bag each in the luggage hold and board the bus with small backpacks containing bottles of water, snacks, their passports and travel documents. They sit back and watch as the country passes by. It is eleven in the morning and the roads are busy.

"Bill was right about a car rental," says Gordon, pointing out the cars flashing by the bus at top speed.

Reg nods. He watches through the tinted windows. He stretches, finds the foot-rest under the seat in front. The highway running out of Santiago is hectic. There is much concrete and merging of traffic. "Yes, I understands now what Bill was saying. I'm so glad we didn't rent a car."

After about half an hour they leave the city and find themselves on a twinned highway, much like highway 103 back home. It is bordered by scrubland and then foothills of mountains. The distant hills are a pale purple and puffs of white clouds skit across the sky. Reg looks up through the Velox in the roof of the bus. He says to Gordon, "Can you believe we are doing this?"

"Funny," says Gordon, "I was thinking the same thing. Look we're at the road toll, does it remind you of the Cobequid Pass?"

After a couple of hours, with the two men watching the scenery, napping and sipping water, they begin to enter the outskirts of Valparaiso. The roads are lined with tall trees, tin shacks of a shanty town, rickety fences held together with torn tarps. As they begin to descend Gordon says, "Look. The sea."

"I see it," says Reg. "It's the South Pacific."

"Seems these little shacks have the best view," says Gordon, "can't help wondering now, if we've done the right thing. This family stuff is sure bothering me."

But as the get closer to the city itself they see pretty, pale pink fences. Houses painted pale gold and olive green.

"Wouldn't look amiss in Newfoundland, B'y," says Reg with a wink.

The road surface changes to old cobblestones and houses looking like those in the American Deep south, with ornate balustrades over tiny balconies.

"It's quiet," says Reg, "do you think it's siesta time?"

"Si, si," says a voice from the seat in front. "Siesta, si." And a shiny head pops up and smiles a wide white smile.

The bus drops them outside a small white church. They are thankful to get off, stretch their legs and retrieve their bags. Reg phones the number he's been given for the apartment. "Ye wait. Be right with ye," a Scots voice tells him. So they sit on a park bench by the small white church which also seems to act as a bus terminus. Gordon studies the graffiti on walls up and down the street. "It doesn't look very prosperous, does it?" he says.

"Hmmm" says Reg, "we may not be staying as long as we thought then." Within minutes a small white van pulls up beside them and a gaunt man wearing tattered shorts and a Tartan-Army football t-shirt.

"Guid timing," he says, "I'm Jock McLeod, I've got yer keys here. I'll tak yer to the flat. It's just aroond the corner here."

Set in an alleyway, between the old crumbling small stores and houses is a double iron gate. Jock unlocks the gate, "This is key number one," he says. "It's not complicated, there are only two keys, one for the gate, and one for the main door."

The apartments are modern and well equipped; not what Gordon and Reg are used to back home. Jock tells them, "Ye've got my number if ye need anything, there's a stack o' leaflets and that, telling ye what's what o'er there, and there's a little shop for groceries just across the road, it opens at aroond four, but ye'll find some stuff to get ye started. Bread, tea, coffee, milk, that kinda thing already here."

"Thank you," says Reg. "Is it easy to find out where things are, to get around, you know?"

"Och, aye," says Jock. 'If ye need the gay bars, ye've to go a couple of blocks over."

And with that, he was gone.

Gordon and Reg collapsed onto the large sofa in guffaws of laughter. "I'll get the tea kettle on," says Reg, still laughing.

"I'll get a load of wash going as soon as we've unpacked. Be good to get some of these sweaty clothes washed, won't it?"

"Listen to you," says Reg, "no wonder Jock thought we were gay."

"Ha, yeah, funny," says Gordon, "and there is internet, right?"

"Supposed to be," says Reg, "I'll check it out."

With mugs of hot tea in their hands and the washing machine underway, they still can't get an internet connection. "I'll call Jock," says Reg.

"Och aye," says Jock, "I should 'a' said, ye'll need the passcode, it's scotlandthebrave all lowercase. Okay?"

"Got it, many thanks," says Reg. He calls to Gordon, "I've got it, just connecting now."

Between them they've taken over three hundred photographs, mostly bright colourful street scenes, views from the bus, a couple of goofy ones of each other. Nothing spectacular. But Gordon wants to send a couple to Joslyn for her to show Pea. He also wants to email her.

A message comes straight back, "Pea still has fleas."

"So sorry" writes Gordon, "I thought we'd got them all, so sorry, did she give them to Louie?"

"Funny," writes back Jos, "I think she got them from Louie in the first place. Don't worry I'm taking care of them. How's things?"

"Things are good, we've moved to the coast, in an apartment now, very nice, better than a hotel, three bedrooms, three bathrooms, when are you coming? (joke) we can see the Pacific from here."

Joslyn doesn't reply. Gordon wonders if he's offended her.

Reg says, "The internet connection dropped out. Maybe we should try later. Are you aware that it's more than dogs have brought you two closer?"

Gordon shrugs, "I guess," he says. "I've also been thinking back to the funeral."

"Huh?"

"Yup, I can see more clearly now, black figures shuffling through the snow, like fleas through Pea's white coat. Reg, there was more than just one woman."

By four o'clock the world outside the apartment complex starts to come back to life. The small stores open their shutters, and a bustle of activity begins to hum. "What do you think?" says Reg. "Shall we go exploring?"

"Well, yes, why not," says Gordon, "but shouldn't I try and make contact with this woman first?"

"I thought you might want to catch your breath after the bus ride, get your bearings, look for some groceries for making supper first, then you might begin to feel more human, and be more able to handle this. You know this is something you have to do on your own, right?"

Gordon does know. He's still not sure how he's going to go about it, so for Reg to take a walk around the area, see what's what, get a few supplies might not be a bad idea. "Give me ten minutes, okay?"

When Reg returns, Gordon is waiting on the doorstep. Flushed. "I did it," he says.

"What?" says Reg.

"I phoned her. When I was all alone in there, it was absolutely quiet except for the swishing of the washing machine. So I phoned the number Bill gave us."

"What did she say?"

"She's coming over at ten tomorrow morning."

"Jeez, that's the worst bit over, I'd say, well done, Gordie, what did she sound like?"

"Soft spoken," says Gordon, "just like Dad. Now, where are we off to?"

"I'm impressed, really. How about we forget about groceries and head down to the waterfront? I'm really dying to see the Pacific."

It is more of a trek from the apartment than they first thought, after a couple of blocks they spot a line of taxis and ask the first one to take them down to the front. "Esplanade?" asks the driver.

"Si," says Gordon, more than happy to make use of the eight-week course in Bridgewater. "Si, por favor."

The taxi drops them at a wide palm-tree-lined road. Busy with traffic, tall, ornate colonial style buildings on one side and a promenade on the other. Valparaiso citizens were promenading; couples arm in arm letting the sea breezes cool them down, babies in strollers with their mothers in tight-fitting capri pants and bespangled t-shirts. Youngsters with school bags on their backs, kicking stones and delaying going home to do their homework. It is a busy spot.

Reg and Gordon take photographs then sit on a bench looking out over a glittering ocean and talk again about what is to come.

"It WAS her," says Gordon.

"What was?"

"At Dad's funeral, it was her. She said so. She said she was sorry she didn't speak. Sorry that she had returned here without seeing me."

"So what will you talk about tomorrow?"

"I don't know," says Gordon, "I know how foolish that might sound, but I honestly don't know."

"Will you want me to leave you to it?"

"I thought about that," says Gordon, "of course I don't. We are in this together. Well kind of, I wouldn't have done any of this without you. But I will not introduce you as a lawyer, just a friend."

"Not JUST a friend, I hope," says Reg, slinging his arm across Gordon's shoulder, "good friends I hope. I can keep ducking back to the kitchen, make coffee, put cookies on a plate, that kind of thing. If it goes well, we could take her to lunch, we can look somewhere up on the internet tonight."

"All sounds good, Reg, thanks, so we will still have to get a few things in for tomorrow then. But first let's find something to eat down here, then pick some stuff up at one of those stores near the apartment on our way back."

They find a small eatery. Reg practices his Spanish this time, but they don't get the pizza he ordered, they get battered deep fried octopus with French fries on the side. They laugh and decide to give it a try. "Not bad," they agree, washing it down with a cold beer that doesn't get lost in translation. They ask the waiter to order a taxi for them when they're done. The taxi takes them back to the corner near the apartment where the small convenience store is still open. They buy peaches and eggs and some kind of cookies that they think Perdita might like.

The internet is working when they get in. Joslyn has received some of the photos, she says they make her laugh and suggests that they could try Skype another time, then Pea could listen to Gordon, she thinks the dog is missing him. "Not as much as I am missing her," murmurs Gordon before his head hits the pillow.

It is their first night in Valparaiso.

12.

Gordon is up early. He makes coffee and sits on the balcony, watching the city come to life. Small delivery trucks rattle up and down cobbled streets dropping off cases of Coca Cola, milk and assorted fruits and vegetables. He smells freshly baked bread and is about to go in search of its source when Reg stumbles out of his bedroom door, "You up then already?"

"Ha, of course, couldn't sleep. This is exciting stuff. Don't you think?"

"Indeed, do you smell fresh bread?"

"Yes, I was just going hunting for it, do you want to go?"

"No, that's okay, you go, I'll get a shower and see what clothes are fit to wear."

Gordon grabs the keys from the counter and puts his wallet in his back pocket. Reg stops him, "I've been told it's best not to put your wallet there," he says, "apparently there are pick-pockets."

"Right," says Gordon, feeling the wind being taken out of his sails. "I'll just take a bit of cash. Ten thousand pesos should do it?"

"I should say so, I think five hundred is about the same as our dollar. You should take a bit more in case you see something else."

"I'll get used to it, we will need to find a bank soon though, I'd rather use cash, wouldn't you?"

When Gordon gets back with two fresh white loaves and a carton of mango juice, Reg is showered and has tidied up the apartment. "Gotta look nice for the lady visitor," he says. "Did you bring anything for her from home?"

"I did as a matter of fact," says Gordon. "I brought her a small bottle of maple syrup and a carved loon. I have no idea what she might like, but that's all I've got."

"Plenty, and perfect I'd say. Now we'd better get breakfast and clear away before she gets here. Is she coming alone?"

"Good question. Don't know. We'll soon find out."

As the clock slips around to ten, Gordon gets anxious. He stands up, walks the floor, out to the balcony, back to the chairs on the far wall. Stands and looks at the artwork on the walls—water colours of sail boats. Sits down again. Rearranges the tourist brochures on the coffee table. The time is now ten after ten.

"You did say ten?" says Reg.

"Yup, woman's privilege I suppose, either that or she's inherited the Nova Scotia time-keeping gene."

"You gave her the address?"

"Yup, and the phone number."

"What about the gate?"

"The gate?"

"Yes, you need the key to get through the gate."

"I think there's a bell, or a voice thing, isn't there?"

At twenty-five minutes past ten the access phone rings.

Gordon goes down to the gate. A pale metallic blue Mercedes convertible is parked awaiting admission. He opens the gate. The car doesn't move. Out steps a tall angular woman with long dark hair. She is wearing large sunglasses, a red striped cotton blouse and jeans.

"Hello Gordon," she says. He moves towards her. Slowly. She opens her arms. "I am Perdita," she says.

Gordon is not used to physical expressions of affection, but he is drawn to this woman and hugs her. "Hello," he says, "it is good to meet you."

She brings the car into the parking space, locks it and together they walk up to the apartment where Reg is waiting with tea laid out on the dining table. Cups, saucers with spoons. Small plates for cookies and a blue bowl of peaches in the centre of the table.

"Perdita, this is my friend Reg from Mahone Bay," he says. "Reg, this is Perdita. My sister." It feels strange to say the words. He looks at her and she smiles. It is his father's smile, and he has no doubt she is his sister.

"You've both got some catching up to do," says Reg. "I just have to go out for about an hour. Bank, Post Office, that kind of thing. I won't be too long. Then maybe we can all go for lunch; I understand the city is going through a culinary rebirth." Reg blushes, wondering if he's said too much, but covers it up by saying, "I was reading all about it in the Good Food Guide."

"I know a great place," says Perdita, "it is a little way out, and maybe if we could all get into my little car with no trouble, I can drive us."

With Reg out of the apartment an awkward silence settles over Gordon and Perdita. They sit opposite each other at the dining table. Studying each other's features. Looking for signs.

"You look like him," Gordon says.

"As do you," says Perdita.

"You must have missed him when he left," says Gordon.

"As must you, just a small boy."

The conversation is one of empathy and understanding. "I'm glad you are here," she says.

"I'm glad too, I have no-one now."

"But your friend?" Perdita points to the door.

"Reg and I were at elementary school together. We've known each other all our lives. He's not my partner or anything like that."

"Were you never married?"

"No, I looked after Mom. Then when she passed, it was Dad. I've never left home. How sad is that?"

"Not sad. It is good. You are a good son. I hope I was a good daughter too." Gordon refreshes the teacups and offers Perdita a cookie. She takes one and nibbles the edges. Gordon can see she is as nervous as he and wonders how he can help overcome it.

"Hang on," he says, "I have something for you." He goes into the bedroom and comes back with a gift bag. "Just small things," he says, not wanting to cause embarrassment, "a couple of things from home, I thought you might like."

Perdita draws out the bottle of maple syrup first. "You have brought this all this way? Thank you so much. Papa often talked about how he missed it." She put her hand to her mouth as if she'd made a blunder, "sorry, I did not mean…"

"It's okay you know," says Gordon. "It's absolutely fine. So he was Papa to you and he was Dad to me. Seems he was two different people. One foot in one world, and the other in another. I have his old passports; he wasn't just here in Chile you know."

"No? Did he not come home to you every year, at Christmas time? He left us here and said he had to go away."

"I think he was in New York each Christmas." Gordon says, shrugging his shoulders, not knowing what more he could say.

Perdita plunges her hand back into the gift bag. "Ah, this is wonderful. I know what it is. A loon," she says, "like Looniberg."

Gordon laughs, "Lunenburg, I don't think they are connected. But it is a beautiful bird. It has a haunting cry. It carries its babies on its back across the water."

"I have something for you too," she pulls a velvet bag out of her purse. Gordon recognises it as similar to the small bags in the suitcase on top of the armoire. "We found these recently, when going back through Papa's trunk. We never had the key before, then just before his death, it came by FedEx. Gordon draws back the silken strings of the bag and pulls out a silver watch on a chain. "This was his?" he says.

"Yes, open the back," she says in a whisper.

Gordon flips open the silver watch back and there lies a golden curl. His. He knows it is his. He cannot help himself as the tears tumble down his cheeks, he sobs. He turns his head away in embarrassment, then when he looks back, he sees Perdita crying too. Heavy mascara running down her face.

"We need to get out for a while," he says, "this is really quite overwhelming. It is actually almost unbelievable. But together, slowly, I think we can put the pieces together."

When Reg comes back, he finds the two sitting on the balcony talking about birds and bird watching, something Gordon has never mentioned before. "How's it going?" he says.

"Good, how did you get on at the bank?"

"Oh fine," says Reg, "good job I took my passport though, apparently I needed ID. Anyway, I've got cash, shall we go to lunch?"

Reg climbs into the back of the convertible and doubles his knees up under him, "It's a good job I'm a skinny guy," he says, laughing.

"It is not too far," says Perdita, but this not a good idea, I will call another car." She flips open a silver cell phone and rattles out rapid Spanish. "We wait, five minutes only," she says. "Other car will come."

The gold Mercedes limo glides around the corner without Reg or Gordon hearing a sound. "Here it is," says Perdita. "I will leave my car here and we will go together, she says to Reg and Gordon. "Gracias, José," she says to the driver. "Bella Vista por favor."

A ten-minute drive takes them to a higher level, a good residential area, and a boulevard of designer stores and high-class restaurants. José pulls up to a place set back from the rest. There are potted geraniums on the steps, sunflowers in the small front flower beds and the sign above the awning says 'Drummonds'.

Perdita sees the look on Gordon's face and smiles, tentatively. "It is my son's restaurant," she says. "He is a chef."

Gordon is speechless. He is not sure he can cope with many more surprises. But it is with a feeling of premonition that he enters the restaurant. He doesn't notice the 'closed' sign on the door, but Reg does. As they leave the bright sunlight and walk into the richly decorated restaurant, they see every table filled with people. The people stand and begin to clap, and say "Welcome Gordon Drummond, welcome, bien venidos." Perdita walks to the far end of the room, the people sit, and she shows Reg and Gordon to a table at the centre where her son, Eduardo, stands. Gordon is speechless, he is the spitting image of Andrew.

"Hi," he says, "at long last we get to meet. You are my Uncle Gordon."

Reg pulls out a chair and sits down, hoping to get everyone settled. This wasn't the light chatty lunch he had in mind, but 'when in Rome' he tells himself.

"Hello everyone," says Gordon, before he sits down, "it is lovely to be here. This is my friend Reg from Canada."

This starts a whole lot of 'welcomes' all over again and clapping until Gordon sits down with Reg on his left, Perdita on his right, and Eduardo opposite.

The food begins to appear. Gordon recognises so many dishes. Just like his father's suppers he had made ready each evening for Gordon coming in from work. The dishes with the eggplants, the fancy desserts with unpronounceable fruit. Deep rich wine and soft freshly made bread on the side. Gordon wonders if he'll wake up soon and find himself back at Indian Point surrounded by ice and snow. For a brief moment feels homesick, as if he has landed on some alien planet. But he also begins to get a stronger feeling of the life his father led, and what he had to leave behind to come home twenty years ago. These people, so colourful and exciting and obviously successful. So happy. Yes, that was the feeling in the room, one of happiness. No incriminations. No questions about why, or why not.

Gordon reaches for Reg's hand under the table, and gives it a squeeze. Reg grins at him and squeezes back. "Okay?" he mouths.

Gordon nods. "Okay," he mouths back. And he knows that for the time being anyway, things are really okay. He has no idea what tomorrow will bring, what affect the court case about the gold mine will have on him, or what other skeletons will drop from the sky, but for now, all is fine.

Perdita turns to him and says, "We go to my house after this, you may wish to Skype your friends back home. Talk to your little dog, yes?"

And Gordon wonders how in the hell she could read his mind.

<h1 style="text-align:center">13.</h1>

Gordon can't remember all the details of that first day of meeting his sister. The afternoon is as blurred as his dad's funeral and the weeks that followed were. A small group of the extended family went back to Perdita's house before Reg and Gordon returned to the rented apartment. He does remember the feeling of visiting her house for the first time. A mixed feeling of jealousy and pride.

The house stands high above the city with wide views of the Pacific from every window. The limo tires crunch the gravel driveway. Gordon watches the palm trees and other foliage he has only seen on PBS's nature documentaries. He feels that he is entering even deeper into another world. A mysterious, even wondrous, place from which there could be no return. He asks himself if his father ever felt the same pleasure in entrapment. Wanting to leave and wanting to stay. All at the same time.

Reg takes photographs with his smart phone, "Unbelievable," he says, "what do you think?" Gordon doesn't reply. He blots his watering eyes with a Kleenex, as if he's clearing them for a better view, using it as a pretence for his emotions. Still wondering if his mother ever knew about this life of Andrew's.

"It wasn't always like this," says Perdita once they are all seated and settled on the large verandah. "We started in a small apartment down there, in the barrios" she points to the ghetto area. The shambles of shacks on the far side of the city, now brightly painted with an air of defiance. "That wasn't always like that either. It was dirty. Smelled bad. But we survived and after all those years, now we are here."

While Perdita goes to the kitchen to organise refreshments Reg asks Gordon if he should mention the mine.

"I don't think, well maybe not today. I know we have to sometime; I don't want her to think that's why we are here."

"No?" says Reg. "Okay."

Teacups are laid out on the glass topped rattan table, with small side plates, "Royal Albert?" says Gordon. "We have these at home too."

"Yes, Papa sent these to me. He sent many things each month, just look around."

Gordon begins to understand the Fedex receipts now as he sees Nova Scotia art on the walls, paintings by John Neville and Barbara McLean, Inuit artifacts he recognises from the Houston North Gallery in Lunenburg—sculptures in soapstone of seals and Inuit seal hunters adorning ornate highly polished credenzas. Out of place but looking absolutely at home.

There were never many works of art in the Drummond house in Indian Point. It was enough to have a fresh coat of paint every six or seven years. And that Gordon always did himself. In fact, he has no recollection of ever hiring anyone to do anything. And now here he is with a sister who hired drivers and cars and had valuable works of art in her house. Mixed emotions can be dangerous things, until now he has kept a steady nerve. Looked for the positive. He takes a gracious attitude as his mother always taught him.

His mind wanders back to Maryanne, his mother, but he stops himself wondering what she would have made of all of this.

"It's a beautiful spot," says Reg.

"We like it," says Perdita. "We feel we can breathe here. The city feels closed in, until you get to the water of course. Tomorrow, would you like to take a sail?"

Gordon is taken aback with the offer. He imagined this busy fifty-something capable woman would have things to do, a business to run maybe, a gold mine even, and yes, a court case hanging around her neck. "Aren't you busy?" he said.

"No, I've told everyone I am on holiday, vacation as you say, and as our father always said, 'it ain't goin' nowhere' is it?"

Gordon laughs, "He taught you some local Nova Scotia phrases then?"

"Oh yes, 'holy suff'rin' lightnin' was always a favourite of his, I learned that by the time I was three years old. My mother was very cross."

"Your mother?" says Gordon."

"Yes, Mama. She died."

"When was that? How long?" says Gordon.

"Oh twenty years," says Perdita. "After that Papa left."

"So what about a sail then, Gordie, you up for it?" says Reg, always adept at dealing with awkward situations.

"It's been a long time," says Gordon, "I think I can remember how to sail, bit like riding a bike isn't it?"

"You won't have to do anything," says Perdita, "just enjoy."

They drink their tea in silence, letting the jagged elements of the conversation permeate. Looking out to the horizon on the Pacific. Beginning to understand that life is not simple. That people can be more complex than they seem.

"So, tomorrow, the car will come at eight o'clock, bring you to the dock, we can spend all day away from everything. We can talk as much as you would like. I have questions, of course. Eduardo will come with the food and drink. You need hats, sunscreen, long sleeves. Everything else will be there. The boat is called Drummond's Dream. You will like it I'm sure."

The car takes the three back to the apartment where Perdita says good evening and picks up her Mercedes convertible. "See you tomorrow, wear safe deck shoes, too," she calls as her car glides out through the iron gates and onto the cobble stones of the alley.

"Whirlwind," states Reg.

"You can say that again," says Gordon. "Is this all for real do you think?"

"We've got almost seven weeks to find out, I'd suggest we don't rush things. Let's enjoy the moments as they come."

"You're right," says Gordon. "But I can't help comparing. The modest life out on Indian Point—to all this." He opens his arms and points out through the French doors to the sky.

"I know," says Reg. "But this isn't you. And you don't know the story behind her at all, yet. Her mother for instance. The gold mine and all that. Dragging them from the ghetto to a high-class residential area. Setting up a grandson with training and then a restaurant. It all took money. Was it good money, Gordie? Do you really want to know the detail? And where does New York fit into the picture? Remember the passports?"

14.

Tuesday dawns golden and hopeful. By 7 am., Reg and Gordon have eaten a breakfast of fresh toasted bread with giant ripe peaches on the balcony. They have a backpack filled with sunscreen, bottles of water and spare shirts.

"It's a pity we didn't get to email home last night," says Gordon.

"Send a text on your phone," says Reg, "tell Joslyn you're running around like a blue-assed fly and will be back online tomorrow. Let's put tomorrow aside to catch up with some stuff I reckon."

"You're right," says Gordon, "I feel like I've had the wind punched out of me on the one hand, and some kind of exotic elixir pumped into me on the other. It really does feel like a dream. Oh look here, there's a message from Bill, he says he's coming down himself tomorrow with our other bags. When we get back from sailing, we should get that other bed made up. I'll email him back."

The car takes them to the Viña del Mar Yacht Club. The marina is resplendent in sail boats and ocean-going yachts of all sizes. Reg spots an orange West Wight Potter, "I used to have one like that," he says. "It was great fun, learned to sail in it. I called her The Saucy Sue, not officially, just my name for her." He waves to the young woman who is tinkering around on the small deck.

"Morning to you, "he says.

She waves back, "Hi," she says, "Americano?"

"Canadian," calls Reg. "Top of the mornin' to ya!"

They follow the driver to the end of the marina where Perdita is standing on the dock. She is wearing a navy and white striped cotton jersey with tight white pants and red deck shoes. She wears a red Roots Canadian Olympics ball cap and very large sunglasses.

"Good morning," she says. "All set?" She waves her hand towards the yacht. Reg estimates it is about forty feet. A sizeable cabin to the fore and three crew members busy with lines.

"Well, good morning to you, looks like we are all set. Nice boat. So this is Drummond's Dream," says Reg. "Is it yours?"

Perdita doesn't respond. Then, "I hope it still is," she says, "we may lose her in the case."

"Case?" says Gordon, "the mine case?"

"Better not to talk about it now," says Perdita, "but we will, I may need your help. Do you know any good lawyers, these guys here are playing with me," she points towards the city.

"Funny you should say that..." begins Gordon.

"What he means is..." says Reg.

"...Reg here is the very best there is, he's not just a good friend, he was Dad's lawyer and mine too."

"Is that why you have come?" says Perdita, her mouth becoming a hard gash in her face.

"No, not at all," says Gordon, putting his arm around her shoulders, "Reg is a friend first and foremost. He came with me because, well because this is probably the scariest thing I have ever done. I have never travelled. And I have never flown before. Tell her Reg."

"All true, absolutely true," says Reg. "Friendship first. Law—as and when."

Perdita takes a visible deep breath. "Sorry, I have just been so screwed lately. Papa left a bit of a mess to clear up."

"I know the feeling," says Gordon.

They cast off from the dock and motor out of the marina. The city of Valparaiso looks like piles of quartz jumbled on a hillside, sparkling in the early morning sun. A glass of iced mango juice is put in Gordon's hand by Eduardo, "Can I call you Uncle Gordon?" he says.

"If you like," says Gordon, "I've never had a nephew before. Or you can just call me Gordie, that's what my friends call me."

The sit opposite each other on the deck, sipping juice and looking out to sea. "Mama doesn't do this often enough," he says, "she is too busy taking care of everything. Always business. Always on the computer. Or the phone. I'm so glad you are here. She may relax now. This has been a very long time to come."

Gordon smiles at the occasional lapse from perfect English. "I have tried to learn a little Spanish," he says, "especially for this visit."

"Bueno," says Eduardo, "you are a real Drummond."

"And this," he pats the seat beside him, "is Drummond's Dream." It is not a question. If the boat is about to be repossessed Gordon is already thinking about how he can get it up to Nova Scotia, to the Lunenburg Yacht Club. He plans to talk with Reg about it later. But for now, he is content to watch the coast of Chile, with its backdrop of mountains. The coast is rugged and stretches forever. Waves crash against the rocky shores. He understands from Reg's summaries of his research that Chile is almost all coast and mountains, stretching for two thousand miles, from Peru to Cape Horn. When he thinks of Cape Horn, he realises that transporting the yacht that route could be hazardous. Panama pops into his head. And with that the passport entries in his father's passport. What in the hell was he doing in Panama? The same as New York?

"Reg?" he says when Eduardo goes below to prepare midmorning snacks.

"Hmmm?" Reg is kicking back with his eyes closed, looking more relaxed than Gordon has ever seen him.

"Would it be possible to sail her home?"

"WHAT?" Reg sits up with a start. "This? Sail this home?"

"Yes, and shhhhh," says Gordon, "it's just a thought, better than letting her be repossessed."

"Repossessed?" says Reg. 'I'm wondering if you're possessed! Seriously though, we could talk to Bill tomorrow."

The afternoon dreams on. It reminds Gordon of an old Australian movie, Picnic at Hanging Rock. He once rented it from Blockbuster Videos in Bridgewater. The story haunted him. The faded colours and pan pipe music lingered in his mind long after. It was a story of Victorian schoolgirls at an Australian boarding school, one with strict discipline, the girls take a day's outing to a remote area, a beauty spot, for a picnic. Gordon remembers it was ages ago, his mother was still alive, and she wanted to watch it again before Gordie took it back to the store. "It's supposed to be in by four, Ma," he said. "That's okay," she said, 'I'll pay the fine. I just want to watch it once more."

Gordon absorbed the atmosphere of the movie and that's how this afternoon out on the yacht feels now. Everyone dozing after the excellent grilled fish lunch cooked by Eduardo. They've drunk a chilled white Chilean wine with the fish and fresh salads, and afterwards Perdita pulls out an apple pie. "To make you think of home," she says, scooping ice-cream from the cooler, to top off the pie.

The crew quietly sail the yacht in a gentle southerly breeze about two miles off the shoreline. The movement of the boat and the occasional flip-flap of the sails lulling the four passengers into an afternoon sleep. Books slip off laps onto the deck, drinks stand on tables untouched, and no-one speaks.

Gordon surveys the scene as he wakes, aroused by a gull cawing overhead. He wonders if they are sailing into a black hole, like the one behind the hanging rock in Australia, never to be seen again. Always to remain a mystery. A mystery called Drummond's Dream.

But more gulls circle the boat, cawing and heeking and one by one, Reg, Perdita, and Eduardo wake, blink into the late afternoon sunshine, stretch, breathe deeply and murmur sounds that can only be good ones.

"Tea?" says Perdita.

"Coming right up," says Eduardo.

As Drummond's Dream motors into its berth in the Viña Del Mar Yacht Club, Reg and Gordon gather together their belongings.

"It's been so good," says Gordon, "thank you, Perdita."

"Tomorrow?" she asks.

"Tomorrow we need to catch up on things," says Reg, hoping he is not interrupting or being too pushy. "But maybe by seven tomorrow evening we can get together. Bill Gladstone is coming out from Santiago."

"Gladstone?" she says, "Why?"

"He is bringing the rest of our luggage, we couldn't put it on the bus," says Gordon. "He's planning to stay for a couple of days, probably until the weekend. But if you need me, Reg can keep him entertained, I'm sure."

Perdita smiles. "Yes, I think I will need you. The case needs looking at. But first I'd like for you to come with me to the mine."

15.

Perdita hands Gordon the file as they begin the long drive to the gold mining region. "It is a long way, bring a bag for overnight," she told him over supper the night before. Bill and Reg were silent as the Drummond siblings discussed the day ahead.

And now they swing out of the Valparaiso suburbs into open country and head towards the mountains. Gordon has little time to watch the scenery change from scrubland to breathtaking views as he reads the files.

It seems there is a Canadian connection. And it is through his father who still held a board position until his death. There is nothing to indicate that Gordon would step into his shoes.

Mining has stopped due to concerns over environmental issues and Perdita wants Gordon to see for himself. "Do you think Reg and Bill should come too?" he says before they finally climb into the limo.

"No," Perdita says. "Next time, but for now it should be the two of us."

It is early afternoon when they reach the Perdita Drummond Mine. Gordon has never seen such a blot on a landscape in all his days. "This is nothing on the Sydney Tar Ponds," he says quietly.

"What is Tar Ponds?"

"Oh, that was a huge environmental issue in Cape Breton, after the steel plants destroyed the land and the air around it, then closed down. Left something that appeared to be destroyed forever."

"And?"

"It's been addressed. Local people complained about ill health, cancer, many, many things. After all these years it has been transformed into a park."

"Could we look at such a solution?" says Perdita.

"No, but it is such a pity Reg can't see this, he might have a way out. Why is nobody working?"

The government has suspended all working here until the case is resolved," she says, "we are losing money every day it is closed; we need that money to put forward a proposal and win the case. In other words, we have to build a case. A good one."

"Are they worried about the water supply?" says Gordon.

"Yes," she says, "you seem knowledgeable about this."

"No, it's just that it crops up all over the world. I watch CNN. And PBS. All these cases have been resolved. You know the old saying?"

"What's that, Gordie?'

He smiles at her use of his name. "Money talks," he says.

"I've tried to tout for other investors," she says, "is that what you mean?"

"No, not at all," he says, "wait until we talk with Reg and Bill, You'll see what I mean. Reg has been involved in an ammolite mine in Alberta, he can show you the website with what they've done for the environment. The mines are shallow, just like this. Quite different to something like a coal mine, for instance."

Perdita takes Gordon on a tour of the mine. In the front office he dons protective garb and a hard hat. She gives him one that says 'A. Drummond.' "Yes," she says. "It was his." She pinches Gordon's cheeks; South American affection.

He looks at the photographs gracing the office walls. Photos of his dad cutting ribbons, smiling, surrounded by smiling Chilean miners. Gordon had no idea this was his father's former life. He tries to understand how he climbed from Cable Mechanic, as his occupation was described in the passport, to owning a gold mine. The tour takes them through an early part of the mine. Organised. Clean. A new experience for Gordon.

As they leave, he picks up a handful of gold dust from the ground. "May I?" he says.

"Of course, it's your gold too," she says.

"You know, we have gold in Nova Scotia," he says.

"Really?"

"Yes, the sort you go panning for, not mining. I often asked Dad if he wanted to give it a try, there is a place near us called Gold River, but he always said, 'I don't think so'."

They stay at a small bed and breakfast about five miles from the mine. "Hola Maria," says Perdita, to the owner who comes from the kitchen wiping her hands on her yellow pinafore.

"Hola Madame," says Maria with a sad smile.

She shows them each to the small bedrooms telling them that food will be ready in half an hour.

"Good," says Perdita, "time for a shower. See you down there in thirty minutes, Gordie."

Gordon kicks off his shoes and lies back on the knitted blanket covering the bed. It reminds him of the blankets he has seen on the Antiques Road Show and guesses this is an example of local Indian work. He would like to find something like this to take back for Pea. Maybe one for Louie, too. Yes, two blankets. He will ask Perdita on the drive back.

He doesn't shower, but drifts into a dreamy sleep. He wakes to find Perdita banging on his door. "Come on," she says, "the food will be cold."

They eat in a familiar silence now. So much has happened in such a short time. Gordon's mind is on fire with thoughts, problems, solutions. He smiles, reminding himself that he thought he was to face a boring retirement with no friends and nothing to do.

Now he has so many friends, family, and so much to do he doesn't know what to tackle first.

"Can I buy some of those nice blankets to take back?" he says, as they drink their strong coffee, watching the sun set over the mountains.

"What, the local blankets?" she says.

"Yes, don't laugh, but I think my little dog might like one. I was going to ask on our drive back, but…"

She does laugh, but not unkindly. "I will take you," she says, "before you leave for Canada, I will take you. You can choose and they will ship for you. Don't let me forget. With all these other things, I have much on my mind."

16.

Bill and Reg have a fruitful day with Gordon gone. After talking through the possible ways to get Drummond's Dream up to Nova Scotia, Reg fills Bill in on the gold mine case. "Yes, I do know all about the case, I've been watching it carefully. It's the same all over the world. The local Indians have made some really good points. This could be a perfect example of a solution for these environmental issues to the world."

"What are you saying, Bill, the solution could be a profitable business too?"

"You've got it, you and I think along the same lines, Reg."

"But the wheel is already invented," says Reg. "Take Alberta."

"Oil?" says Bill.

"No," says Reg. "Ammolite."

"Never heard of it," says Bill, "can you tell me more?"

Reg explains how ammolite is a unique gem accessed through shallow mining procedures. How after each kilometre of land is carefully scraped and dug back to reveal the strata of ammolite, the landscaping begins and the land is not just restored to what it once was, but with planting of trees and shrubs, it is being transformed into a beauty spot. A place for nature to take forward and become something it never was before. "The government will use it as an example for future projects, I guess," he says.

"Interesting," says Bill.

"Here, let me show you."

Reg logs onto the internet and finds the website for the ammolite mine. There are photos and video clips of the before and after. Bill is impressed and says so.

"You know, you two guys were destined to come down here," he says, "you are bringing ideas and knowledge that not just Gordon's family, but the industry as a whole needs."

They open a couple of bottles of beer and sit on the verandah and talk about more personal things, "Are you married?" says Reg.

"Nope. You?"

"No, not now, I was for a short time when I was young. Didn't work out."

"Gordon?"

"No, him neither. Looked after his mother. Then his father. Devoted his life to them. When his dad died, Gordie thought it was all over. He had nothing to look forward to. I'm the only real friend he's got. It helps that I'm his lawyer too." Reg laughs.

Bill laughs too. "Amazing what death can do," he says. "But this is a bit extreme. A father living a double life, two families, hidden assets and all that."

"It's been an emotional eye-opener for Gordie. In my job I turn up family secrets, but never anything like this," says Reg.

"Happened to me a couple of times too," says Bill, "but as you say, nothing like this. What time did you say they'll be back?"

"Not 'til after dark, fancy going out for something to eat?"

When Gordon arrives home, Perdita comes in with him, "Just for a few moments," she says, "I really do need to get back too."

Reg and Bill are back from the restaurant and are sitting at the dining table which is covered in paper, note pads, and the laptop is open, whirring away.

"Hey you two," says Reg, beaming.

"Hey?" says Gordon, not expecting such a welcome.

"Hi," says Perdita, "you must be Bill."

"Yes, sorry, how rude of me," Bill stands and shakes hands with Perdita. "We've never met, but I've heard so much about you."

She looks at Gordon and Reg.

"No, not through these two," he adds, "but you are well known in the business world. All good," he adds.

Over the course of two weeks, Reg, Gordon, Bill and Perdita meet to talk through the problems and solution options. Perdita wants to get Drummond's Dream out of the picture—she knows it could be the first thing to be seized by authorities. She transfers ownership to Reg who gets onto a guy he knows in Ottawa, an offshore qualified skipper. He can fly down with a small crew and sail it up the west coast of South America to the Panama Canal. Cross through the Canal and sail through the Caribbean Sea to Florida. From there they'll sail the inter coastal waterway into the North Atlantic, up the New England States coast, across the Gulf of Maine and then up the southwest coast of Nova Scotia to Lunenburg. "He thinks it would take about three months," Reg tells Bill.

The four settle for that and then get down to looking at how to handle the gold mine issues.

Gordon feels very much that Reg is in his element. Bill Gladstone and Reg work in tandem for hours, pouring over project proposals until it's agreed that they'll bring a consultant down from Alberta Ammolite. His name is Joel Zwicker, and they go into Santiago to meet him at the airport the following Thursday.

The apartment in Valparaiso is getting crowded. The owner, Jock, pops in one afternoon to ask if they'd like the one next door too as the booking for that has just been cancelled. Gordon snaps it up. That's where they put Joel.

"S'great this," says Joel. "The dining room is bigger in this one too, would it make a better meeting room?" This is Joel's first solution to a problem; solved before it became one.

By the court date, Reg and Gordon have been in Chile for three and a half weeks. It feels like forever. Bill trips back and forth to Santiago to keep his law business in check, but he has a good and loyal partner and much of their work is done on the phone or via the internet giving Bill all the flexibility he could wish for. He has explained that winning this case could be a real coup for the partnership and set them apart from the competition. With Joel Zwicker, descended from Canadian aborigines, as their expert witness, Bill is confident that the case is in the bag.

Meanwhile Gordon and Perdita deal with family concerns. Getting to know each other. Talking about the past. Trying to regret nothing but finding it difficult.

"What about your mother?" asks Gordon one day.

"She loved him," is her simple reply.

"He must have loved her too," says Gordon.

"Yes, very much. They did marry you know."

"But how?"

"I know, now I think it probably wasn't legal, they married in the church. Come, I'll show you."

She takes him to the Iglesia Anglicana, St. Paul's Church. It turns out to be the small church where the bus dropped them on their first day. In a way, it looks like an upturned boat, with no tower and no cross. It seems that it was built by English settlers and is now a national monument.

"Not Roman Catholic then?'

"No," says Perdita, "Mama was catholic, but Papa was not. Lutheran, he said, so this was a good solution. This area was part of the old British community, this church was built by a famous architect, Lloyd or a name like that."

"William Lloyd," says Gordon, touching a plaque by the door.

Together they admire the stained-glass windows and the paintings of the Ten Commandments on either side of the altar. Perdita points to 'thou shalt not commit adultery' and laughs. Her voice rings through the tiny church and Gordon feels a happiness he has not felt for many years. It is as close to euphoria as he can imagine.

"She is buried out here."

They walk through the churchyard among the graves with English names. William Thomson, Grace Henderson, Amelia Wright. And they stop at Maria Anna Drummond. There are fresh flowers. The grave is trimmed, the stone bright white and scrubbed.

"I come every week," she says. "You'll do the same for Papa, won't you?"

"I will, that's a promise, I'll send you photos. Right now it is high in snow, I talked with Joslyn last night. They've had a big storm."

"So cold," says Perdita, "to be lying in the ground, so cold like that." She shivers, then says, " Joslyn, who is she?"

"A work colleague," says Gordon, "she is taking care of my little dog for me. I miss her."

"Joslyn?"

"No, my dog, Pea—well, Jos too I suppose. She is just a friend. I have no girlfriend."

"Reg?"

"He has no girlfriend either."

"No," she laughs, 'I thought maybe you and Reg..."

Gordon laughs too. "No, we are not gay," he says, "two guys can be friends, can't we?"

"Of course, but I do not want you to be lonely, back in the cold north, I have seen what it is like. No colour, bare, white, dark."

"You will come in the summer?" says Gordon. "You can stay at Drummond, that's our house. We can sail the Atlantic. I will learn to cook pancakes and serve them with maple syrup. Bring Eduardo. I will show you the other side of life."

"You have said it all," says Perdita. "The other side of life. It is true all life has another side, and we will only find it if we look. It took courage for you to come."

"As it did for you to come up for the funeral. How did you know? I've never really worked that one out."

"He wrote," she says. "Sent with Fedex. A note and the keys to the trunk. He knew."

"Are you saying he knew he was dying?"

"Yes, he wrote something like 'I have reached the end now my Perdie, that's what he called me, I've reached my end. It has been good. Let there be no more lies.' I watched the internet for signs of a death announcement and as soon as I saw, I booked my ticket. I stayed in Halifax for four days afterwards trying to find some way to contact you. But I didn't have your braveness."

"I have something else to tell you," he says.

"Yes?"

"My mother was also Maryanne."

Perdita is silent.

"Coincidence? Maybe. Maybe that's all it is. There is just one more question," says Gordon, "then we can leave the past behind and move on."

"Yes?"

"Isn't there a husband? You? Are you married? You use the Drummond name."

" I never changed my name when I married," she says. "Papa said it would complicate the mine's paperwork. Then my husband died. Eduardo was just a tiny boy. There was an explosion. At the mine. It is not a happy place for me. He is not buried anywhere. Unless you count the mine."

Gordon takes his sister's hands in his. "We were both in a very difficult situation," he says. "I was already in shock; I didn't have the warning you did. In the end this has turned out better, I think. I have been able to take a look at my father's life without anyone getting hurt. When you come, we will do some of the things he did in the past twenty years in Nova Scotia. Quite different from here that's for sure. Now come back to the apartment, we'll make tea and find out how the guys are getting on."

17.

The initial hearing takes place in Santiago and the team, as that is how they now refer to themselves, check into the Radisson Plaza.

"Welcome back, how many rooms?"

"We are five, so we will take what you can offer, all together please," says Bill, "I could just go home," he says to Reg and Joel, "but I think it's best we stay secreted here, don't you?"

"Good plan," says Joel, "it's quite a country, I do hope I get chance for a bit of sight-seeing. The trip to the mine sure opened my eyes as to the place's versatility."

"If all goes well, we'll make sure you get the royal treatment," says Reg.

The Radisson gives them four suites on the top floor. "All for yourselves," the desk clerk says, "no-one to bother you. You are here for the case, yes?"

"How news travels," Perdita says in Spanish, "Si," she says to the desk clerk. "Here for the case."

"Good luck then," he says, "I hope all is good for you."

They sit around the large table in the bridal suite until 2 am., then Gordon says, "We should call it a night. We must be there for ten, right?"

"Yes," says Bill. "We are ready, well, as ready as we'll ever be. I'll arrange for room service breakfast for us all here at seven and we can go through everything one last time."

The court hearing is almost a non-event. The court room is not as packed as Gordon expects. He feels that somehow the information they were to present had leaked and found to be favourable. Joel speaks well as an expert witness. He shows photographs of the ammolite mine in Alberta; the beautiful park land with colourful birds in the trees and butterflies perched on large pink echinacea flowers. He is asked about timeframes and the water run offs and costs. There is no need for an interpreter either. The English spoken in the court room is impeccable. By 1 pm the hearing is over. Their proposal has met with approval. The panel asks for a project plan to be presented within ninety days. The sooner they have it, the sooner the mine can reopen.

"You may need to stay on," Perdita says to Joel.

"Not a problem," he says with a grin. "Can't wait to draw up the plans."

Reg and Gordon are in their final week in Valparaiso. Perdita is taking them to the weaving co-operative in Indian country. Reg doesn't question why but has a good idea that this is something to do with Pea. He hasn't ceased to be amazed that Gordon and Joslyn have spoken on Skype most evenings. Chile is just an hour ahead of Nova Scotia, so after supper for Reg and Gordon, is before supper for Jos.

Reg has watched as Gordon talked to Pea, telling her he will be home soon, and something makes him wonder if he should think about getting a dog, too.

"We could go for walks together. All of us, Jos with Louie, and you and Pea, and me with mine," says Reg. "I like the look of Louie; how do I go about adopting a retired racing dog like that?"

Gordon explains to him about GPAC, Greyhound Pets of Atlantic Canada, a volunteer organization that brings up retired racers from the tracks in Florida. "You should see them when they arrive," says Gordon. "All colours and sizes, all eager to have a happy retirement. You couldn't do much better than a greyhound."

"Are they old?" says Reg.

"No, not at all, although you could apply for a senior, Louie wasn't even two when Jos took him, he just wasn't a very good racer, that's all."

The two men begin to think about going home, about the journey ahead of them, not just physically, but the emotions involved too.

Reg and Bill have become firm friends. Arrangements for visits are talked through. Reg even looks into buying an apartment in the same complex as the one they were using. "Jock is the manager, he has the keys and lets people in and out etc.," says Reg. "You just block out the weeks you want to use it yourself and the rest of the time people pay rent, just like we have, and it helps to pay for it. Bill can get someone to take care of the conveyancing for me. What do you think?"

"I think you should sleep on it, in fact I think you should wait until you get home before making a final decision," says Gordon, "maybe we're all carried away with the sunshine and mangoes."

"Not like you," says Reg, "I thought you'd be all for it, in the circumstances."

"Well, I am, of course I am. I can't wait to get home now, but then I'll be looking forward to coming back, and you're right, for such a long visit, the accommodation has been the biggest cost."

"It's alright for you, you have family now you can stay with."

Gordon knows Reg is kidding, "I'd rather stay independently," he says, "tell you what, why don't we buy one between us."

18.

Air Canada flight AC093 takes off on time for Toronto. After a flight that seems to go on forever, they touch down and find they have four hours to kick around Pearson Airport.

At Tim Hortons they order a snack pack of chocolate glazed Timbits and two double doubles and watch humanity pass before them. But Gordon doesn't see them, already he is looking forward to home. To the wood stove in the kitchen, to seeing just what mail has piled up. And to Pea. He wants to hold her tight and tell her he will never leave her again, and of that he is quite sure now. Next time, she will go too.

He went to Chile in search of his father's past and found a family. He found a smart, vibrant sister who has business troubles as well as personal ones, and a fatherless nephew who has promised to visit in just three months' time.

"Bit of a roller coaster ride, ain't it?" says Reg, nodding at the people jostling by, pulling suitcases on wheels, adjusting backpacks, clutching papers, answering cell phone calls. "Not my idea of fun really. But hey, we had a good time, didn't we?"

Gordon looks at him, "We did indeed. We turned something that could have been a disaster into a trip of a lifetime. And if you ever find that your father led a double life, make sure the other was somewhere warm and sunny, Australia maybe, then I'll come with you to dig up the dirt."

"Old Murray? I don't think he ever left The Bay," says Reg, "well not to my knowledge anyway."

"Just look at what I didn't know," says Gordon, "I had no idea, no idea at all…"

"So what about New York then?" says Reg,

"New York? Dad? No, I thought we'd leave the rest of his story stay right where it is. Let sleeping dogs lie, so to speak. But Perdita and I talked last night, she wants to dig a little deeper."

The 5 am. flight to Halifax is called. Reg and Gordon board for the final leg of their journey home.

As they land at Stanfield International and taxi to the terminal, Gordon looks at the land. His homeland. And notices the birches' buds just starting to leaf out into a delicate lime green haze. Announcing a new spring. He knows that the pussy willows will be sporting their silken buds on the bank beside the house, his home. Drummond.

And there'll be masses of white, purple and yellow crocuses opening on his parents' grave.

PERDITA

I waved my big brother, Gordon and his good friend Reg off in departures. It was a sad day for us all, "I had no idea I would feel like this," Gordon said. Dabbing his eyes with a large white handkerchief. I'd given him a set of fine linen handkerchiefs after I found him using rough paper towels or Kleenex.

"You deserve better," I'd said the night I gave them to him. He pulled one out and admired the blue embroidered 'G' in the corner. "So much makes sense now," he said, "and yet…"

"Yes?" I said.

"So much doesn't. We're not finished are we?"

"Nowhere near," I said. "I'll be up in the summer, and we can pick up the threads of where we've left off, but for now, I am so very happy that you found me."

"And I you," he said.

"Don't worry," said Reg, "I'll keep my eye on him."

I watched the two elderly men work their way through security, smiling, being courteous, joking with officials. Turning for that final wave to me. No excess baggage either, I'd managed to convince them that shipping would be so much easier for them; for the hand-woven blankets and local pottery to arrive on the doorstep at the Drummond house without them having to lift a finger. I hoped Jos would appreciate the gifts and will see that she, not just his little dog, is never far from Gordon's thoughts.

I didn't drive straight home. I needed time to assimilate all that had happened. How this very traditional man demonstrated his love for family. A family he didn't know existed. Instead of being accusatory and thinking bad of his father, my mother, me and my family, he embraced us and I was able to see how Papa's good genes had blessed us both.

EPILOGUE

In spite of Covid restrictions, I'm here with Gordon now for another summer. I've been every year since Gordon's first visit five years ago.

We've taken Drummond's Dream out to the islands a few times. It has made me understand so much more about the extreme contrast of my father's life.

And we've talked. Jos comes too, she and Gordon are now what young people call, an item. I knew it would happen. And nothing to do with dog fleas at all. We joke about that. Very sadly, Gordon's little dog Pea died last year. I know he misses her all the time. He talks of her a lot and tells me more about how our father called her Perdy.

With the power of the internet, Eduardo (my son) and Jos, found out what our father did in New York all those Christmases years back. And it was nothing to do with other women as we were beginning to think, but for respite. It turned out our father had an aversion to Christmas festivities and found a silent retreat just outside New York where he could recharge before returning to the double life he led. I suspect the increasing challenges with the mine didn't help.

As a young man, he'd arrived in Chile as a cable mechanic. At the end of his business career he owned the mine. Juggling his family life must have added to the stress.

And while he never spoke of his other Canadian family to me. Nor vice versa to Gordon, he left the trail open for Gordon and me to find one another.

- end -

Acknowledgements

I must firstly give thanks for the ten years I had with Tilly (Hollowell Chantilly Lace 2012 - 2022), my much loved beautiful white and black whippet girl who lives on through Pea in this story. And by association, Alex and Diane for bringing her into my life.

Also Pierre and Rose who knew exactly how to sail a yacht from Chile to Nova Scotia; it was do-able after all. And by association, GPAC (Greyhound Pets of Atlantic Canada).

To Dennis, whose pop up antiques in Liverpool and the old cardboard box which held (at the bottom under piles of old photos) the dusty passports that gave birth to the story idea. And to the 3-day novel project (2013) in which the first draft happened.

Thank you to my loyal and oh-so-honest alpha and beta readers: Kat, Elke, Vicki, Marg, Pam (RR), Pam (S), Kimberly, J.P. Vincent, Bruce, Debbie, and John. Your eagle eyes are remarkable. Not forgetting the really early readers, Richard and Jan. And the most recent readers, Adam and Laura. Forever grateful.

To my flag-waver-in-chief, Vicki, for the hours, nay—days, weeks, and months when you've been there for me, FaceTiming on Sunday afternoons, extinguishing my doubts, cheering me on, and making me laugh. Non-stop showerings of love for you and for Jim for texting laughter at times when laughter is always the best medicine.

None of my books would exist without Arne. Thank you are words to small for your immense support, encouragement, astuteness and love.

And for dragging me off down the coast for fish and chips (to the very eatery in this story) when you knew I just needed a break.

To Summer Stewart for saying 'yes' again. And thanks always to all the team at Unsolicited Press for turning my manuscripts into books. For making them real. And for making the entire book creation process an absolute joy.

And finally, thank you always to this peaceful corner of the world, where thinking, observing, dreaming and creating can happen. You just have to give it chance.

Nova Scotia, Spring 2023

EVA MATSON

a novella

For Julia
my brave, bright, and beautiful sister
1955 - 2021

INTRODUCTION

Eva came to me in a brown paper parcel.

There is an elderly gentleman in Shropshire, England, who sends us curious packages. A few years ago, a large shoebox packed with many and all varieties of postcards arrived in our mailbox here in Canada. Back then he sent an abundance of these packages; I suspect he combed charity shops for such artifacts for us, but as busy people, we (my husband and I), while appreciating parcels from the old country, could only give them a quick flick through, dragging out one or two specimens with a 'hey look at this', and then the boxes were packed away in a cupboard until…

…a year or so ago, in an effort to de-clutter, one of these shoeboxes of postcards was brought out and an evening was spent poring over each and every one. Some were quite old, with interesting stamps. The messages also were curious: family members writing to each other with beautiful handwriting—on postcards—over a hundred years ago, greetings for birthdays, and 'wish-you-were-heres' from seaside resorts.

Then out dropped the photograph.

It's a profile portrait of a young woman. Probably in the early or mid-1920s. She looks somewhat tentative, nervous, but hopeful. The slump in her shoulders shows she is not comfortable having the photograph taken. Her hair has been waved for the occasion it seems and, except for a stray curl near her temple, not one hair is out of place. She has a strong face with a nose of aquiline tendencies. She doesn't smile or show her teeth, her lips are firmly closed in the straightest line imaginable. From the sepia photograph it is difficult to get a feel for her colouring, but I would say brown eyes and dark brown hair. Not a peaches and cream complexion.

She wears a double string of fine pearls, and a diaphanous georgette silk blouse with an embroidered bodice and a ruffle. It would appear the blouse is homemade, the right sleeve, nearest the camera, has not been set professionally into the blouse body. Is she the dressmaker? Or was it made by a family member?

The photograph has a thick backing sheet. I turn it over. On the reverse is a newspaper clipping. Firmly glued. It is an entry form for a beauty contest. The prize £2,500. An enormous sum for the 1920s, is my first reaction.

But I'm troubled by Eva. For Eva. What kind of life did she have? Did she make a difference? Was she happy? I want to make her so, but I also question my right to build a fictional life for this woman.

The name Matson rings bells. I remember now, a greyhound-rescue-group friend in England—her mother's married name is Matson. So I send her a message: 'Hi Sally, is this any relation of yours?'

Amazingly, she writes right back. 'I'll ask Mum.'

In the meantime, I do some more digging myself and find an Eva. In Dorset. A record of baptism. May 1900. I feel close to her even in her babyhood and, for some reason, I fear for her future. But I also want to be excited for her.

There's another note from Sally, 'Yes, there is a Dorset connection, I'll follow up when I can.'

And I'm grateful for that. I still wonder if it's OK to fictionalise this woman. I recently read Sean Michaels' Us Conductors—a novel based on the life of Leon Termin. If Mr. Michaels can do it—then, surely, so can I. I just don't want to hurt or offend anyone.

I'm Google-street-viewing villages on the Dorset coast. What a picturesque part of the world to be born into, to grow up, to fall from trees, to run on the beaches with hair flying in the breezes, to fall in and out of love, and maybe to die.

I feel Eva's photograph has come my way for a purpose: to give her a life. To explore a woman's life that transitions from the Victorian era—life without modern conveniences and where family ruled, especially by the matriarchs—through to a world approaching rock 'n roll and sexual freedom. I have a photograph of my grandfather's mother who would have been the age of Eva's grandmother. My Great-Grandma Cope looks strong. Forceful even. A woman capable of making decisions and doing her bit to further the causes of women at a time when changes were imminent. She also has a twinkle in her eye, so not without humour. And she must also have been quite a romper between the sheets with eleven children. Or was that, too, the role of women in that era?

I've already started to write Eva's story when I hear back from Sally: The family contact she was planning to get information from died in a car crash a few weeks ago.

I am speechless. I don't know the details of the crash, or who the man was, or what connection he was to our Eva, but it seems I now have to go it alone and fill in the gaps of her life as I imagine them.

And I am so sorry, Sally, for your family's loss.

I look again at Eva's photograph. Is this the young woman who once flung her leg over the crossbar of father's bicycle and pedalled like billy-o to fetch the doctor to her sick grandmother? I reckon so. I reckon she had all the guts she was going to need for what was to come next in her life.

S.B.B. 2015

Additional author's notes.

I've found a transcript of the memorial stones in the Chickerell graveyard. Eva's name is there. So is Grandma's. And that really sends me shivers. I had no idea in 2015 when I first wrote this story.

I look again at the only photograph I have of my great-grandmother, Grandma Cope. She has to be my blueprint for Grandma in Eva's story. Grandma Cope canvassed for a political party in Leicester. The story goes that her eleven children took care of each other, very ably, and when there were insufficient chairs, the young ones had to stand and let the older children sit: respect for elders. I met Grandma Cope, once, when I was very young. She had a kind but commanding air. She sent out for the cream cakes that day. The best I had ever tasted—given that I had never had a cream cake until that day it stood to reason it would be the best. I chose a meringue. Filled with fresh cream. Unforgettable.

Grandma Cope, like Grandma Matson was firm, commanding, but hidden underneath it all, a gentle caring kindness.

This is a work of fiction. Only Eva's photograph, its backing sheet, and the correspondence with Sally are real. Research regarding the wars that affected characters in this story was accurate at the time of writing. There is no evidence that Douglas Fairbanks visited Dorset, or had a smelly tobacco breath, but he is in the story because, well, why not? Any discrepancies are entirely mine and it is my hope that they do not adversely affect my story of Eva Matson.

S.B.B. 2021

Part I

1. Amy

The baby was born on May 24th, 1900. Queen Victoria's 81st birthday. It stood to reason that when she was baptised at the little Church of Mary Magdalene in Langton-Herring on August 9th, both May and Victoria would be chosen names. But Eva? Grandma Matson was the epitome of a family matriarch. Little Eva's father, George, was overwhelmed by his mother, always known as Grandma, even to her son, even to the villagers and tradesmen, she was known to rule the family.

"That baby will be named for me, of course," she said to George and Eva's mother, Amy. There was no question.

Amy really wanted to call her baby, Margaret Rose. But didn't offer her thoughts. She kept them to herself and on summer afternoons, sitting on the garden seat under the apple trees, rocking her little girl, she sang, "Margaret Rose with the sweet button nose..." and, more often than not, a single tear would fall onto the baby swaddled on her lap. Onto the hand knitted baby dresses in fine cream wool. Amy rocked back and forth, "You'll always be my Margaret Rose, no matter what," she said.

Little Eva gurgled and blew bubbles from her tiny, pursed lips, looking into her mother's deep brown eyes, looking above at the apples beginning to sweeten on their boughs, and beyond to the deep blue summer skies of rural Dorset.

Amy placed baby Eva gently back in her baby carriage, it was the carriage Grandma Matson trundled up the garden path a month before

Eva's arrival, "It was our George's," she said in her firm deep voice. "It was good enough for him. It will be more than good enough for yours." She pointed at Amy's baby bump, well hidden under her flowing smock. Amy blushed.

And so Amy had no choice but to accept that this would be the baby carriage for her new baby. She was hoping that she and George would take the charabanc into Dorchester before too long and choose one from the Co-op. But it was not to be. The one Grandma Matson insisted they use was good enough. It had to be. Grandma Matson was quite clear about that. The chrome shone; the hood worked just fine. The fitted waterproof cover had a tiny scuff in one corner, but Amy, being an accomplished needle-woman, was able to sew an invisible hedge-tear darn in fine black silk. There was no sign of a scuff having been on the corner at all. Grandma was impressed when she saw it, saying, "Very nice, Dear," making Amy feel, for once, that she'd done something right. Grandma followed her praise with, "but there was really no need, the babe will soon have it all kicked up. Just like our George. And you will be having a boy, won't you." It wasn't a question, more an order.

Eva's birth was a long and difficult one. Amy got the first signs of labour on May 22nd when she was hanging out all the blankets on the line. "Why have you done this heavy wash today?" George said. "They were all quite clean."

But Amy had scrubbed floors and polished windows until they shone like the chrome handlebars on the baby carriage. She rubbed with vinegar and newspaper until her fingers bled. "I don't know George," she said. "I just had to, I suppose, make ready for our baby."

The labour pains began that night around eleven. George rubbed her back to ease the aches and discomfort and made her cups of hot milk with a boiled onion until his mother arrived.

"I heard you'd started," she snapped while pulling a large starched white pinafore over her head and tying it around her ample waist. "Now let's see what we have." She proceeded to pull up Amy's petticoats, revealing body parts only George had ever glimpsed before. But there was no time for embarrassment.

"Shoo you," Grandma said to George, "make yourself useful, boil kettles, fetch clean towels. And bring me a pot of tea."

As George scuttled down the wooden staircase with a clattering not unlike a herd of horses, Amy quaked with fear of the woman known to all as Grandma. For a moment, just a brief one, she wondered why a woman of such ferocity was called by a name evoking gentleness and warmth. She looked again into the firm set lines of Grandma's face, the piercing brown eyes, the strong manlike nose, the hint of facial hair above the top lip and the chestnut brown hair pulled back into the tightest of buns. Amy had never seen Grandma's hair not in a bun. She wondered just how long it really was, and how wavy.

"Now listen to me, Girl," Grandma was saying, "I can see you drifting away with the fairies and that just will not do. You have a job to do, and I am going to be with you all the way." Grandma put a hand on Amy's shoulder. It was an uncharacteristically gentle touch and Amy knew she was on a journey for which there was no turning back. This baby would be born. And Grandma would make it happen. Amy closed her eyes, thought of England, and handed herself over entirely into the hands of George's mother.

It turned out to be a long and fruitless night. Grandma fell asleep in the rocking chair alongside Amy's bed. Amy's pain subsided to the point where she too fell into a sleep full of dreams. Dreams where she gave birth to ten little grandmas and awoke with a start, screaming, "God help us."

Grandma, too, woke up to the screaming, replying, "Indeed, Child, God help us. And he will. Let us say a prayer together. Amy had no choice but to sit with the large starched white pillow behind her, put her hands together close her eyes and stumble along with Grandma:

Dear Lord, you have helped us through this night. A night brought about by earthly sin. We beseech you to keep us safe as we bear the pains so rightly brought down upon us by you, Dear Lord, as punishment for the dirty sins we have committed. Bring forth this baby free from all blemish and blame for the sins of his parents, we ask you this in the name of the Father, the Son, and the Holy Spirit. Amen."

Amy was shocked into the final Amen. Shocked that her condition was being seen as the result of a dirty sin. Shocked that George's mother should see things this way. But she knew she'd married into a religious family, and accepted such in order to marry George, who she loved with all her heart.

On Wednesday, May 23rd, the pains had subsided to the extent that Amy managed a gentle stroll around the garden. Grandma had popped back to her own house next door to put wood on the fire, leaving Amy in George's hands. "On no account is she to get out of bed," she barked, as she strode out of the front door.

Of course, the moment she disappeared around the high, yellow privet hedge, Amy said to George, "Get me out of here, even just for five minutes. I need to smell the fresh mown grass and the salt sea air. Just for five minutes, Georgie."

Grandma would have had a fit, firstly to hear Amy call her son Georgie, something unheard of other than behind George and Amy's closed doors, and furthermore to see her in her bedroom robe, walking up and down the garden path. George and Amy talked. "I'm really scared, Georgie," she said. "Why did we let this happen?"

George smiled, "It's a natural thing," he said. "How do you think we all came into being?" It was a typical George response. George the thinker, the reasoner, the man who read and researched topics in depth. A man who spent his few spare hours a week at the library pouring over encyclopaedias.

"You are right of course, Georgie," said Amy, "I didn't think of it like that. Your mother keeps going on about how sinful it is." She hesitated to criticize his mother to him. "Of course we are not the only people ever in the world to have a baby. What a grand little family we are going to be, Georgie."

George took her hand and they stood together before slowly walking back into the house and up the steep, narrow wooden staircase to the bedroom, seconds before they heard the front door latch open and close and Grandma's footfall on the stairs.

"Out of bed, are we?" she said.

"Just to take a look out the window, Grandma, and at the sea," said Amy, aware she was lying. "How good it is to breathe in the sea air."

"What! Have you opened this window, George? Now you get it closed forthwith and get back down those stairs and make tea for us all. I think we are in for another long day." Grandma sat back into the deep grooves her ample behind had made in the cushions on the wicker rocking chair and picked up her knitting.

"Can I do mine too?" said Amy. "It might help to calm me."

Here was something that both women were in agreement on. Grandma handed Amy her knitting basket with baby jacket almost complete, the soft wool and the tiny needles holding the last sleeve to be knitted. Amy stroked the knitted item before picking up the needles and beginning the shaping for the armholes. "I should have this finished by dinnertime," she said to no-one in particular.

"Just be careful you don't get yourself into a ferdoodle," said Grandma, nodding as she worked the eyelet holes on the right baby bootee.

Twilight descended, casting shadows around the bedroom, with its mahogany tallboy topped with intricate lace doilies, highlighting the large painting of a mermaid. Amy imagined the white lace curtains could lift gently in the evening breeze if only the window were opened. But Grandma was booming down the stairs to George, "You'd better go for Doctor Wilson, I don't want us to get lulled away. Your wife is tired, and the babe is tired and I think we must do something."

Grandma's shouting brought Amy from her reverie. She sat up in bed bewildered, looking around her saying, "Where am I, what's happening, where are my daisies?" And Grandma knew Amy was delirious and a doctor was needed.

George headed off on his bicycle into the descending night. Gravel flew up along the road behind his wheels as he pedalled for Amy's life. And the baby's. It took more than twenty minutes for him to reach Doctor Wilson, who had settled down with his pipe and the evening paper and a glass of port after supper. But as soon as he heard he'd been summoned by Grandma Matson, he put on his light linen coat and his deerstalker hat, picked up his Gladstone bag and cycled along beside George at not quite the speed George had achieved on his outward journey.

It was dark by the time they arrived, almost ten o'clock, and the good doctor was at Amy's bedside before he'd removed his coat. "Now then young lady, what is going on?" he said.

Grandma told him, blow by blow, of the day Amy had had, Amy didn't open her mouth, just lay back and waited for death to descend. 'If they've sent for the doctor, it must be bad,' was the thought that jingled around in her head. The oil lamps were lit and shadows of Grandma and Doctor Wilson loomed high on the far wall. She couldn't hear what they were saying, but she began to pray to herself, 'Lord take care of my Georgie. Make sure he changes his vest on Fridays. If my baby lives, please take care of him and call him Victor, in God's name, Amen.'

The pain hit her with an almighty punch. She thought it was God's answer to her prayer. She closed her eyes and waited to be transported to heaven.

Eva was born at 2.15 am on May 24th. By 7 a.m., with the early morning sun streaking through the lace curtains, Amy could make out the shape of Grandma Matson in the rocking chair with a bundle wrapped in her arms.

"There you are, Dearie," she said. "Welcome back, it was a long, long night. But you will survive."

Amy was in disbelief. "I didn't die?" she said, tears gently falling to her hot cheek. "And I have a baby, can I hold him?"

"You do indeed have a baby," said Grandma, "but..."

"But...?" said Amy, more tears rolling down her cheeks. "Is he alright? Is there something wrong?"

At that moment George came through the bedroom door carrying a tray with tea and hot buttered crumpets. "For my girls," he said.

Grandma laughed, "Yes," she said, "for the girls, you have a baby girl, Amy. A beautiful little baby girl." And with that she handed the bundle to the tear-stained Amy. She pulled a shawl around the young woman's shoulders and said, "It was a bit tough for a while, you are going to feel quite sore and must stay in bed for at least two weeks, but everything is going to be fine. The little mite will need to be fed very soon, so once George leaves, I will show you how."

"What happened?" said Amy. "Why can't I remember?" The tears began to fall again. She looked around at the sheeting, rags, and towels, blood-soaked on the floor by the bedroom door. "What has happened to me?"

"It is nothing child," said Grandma, "You will heal. We had to save both you and the baby, it was necessary. George was here and Doctor Wilson. You will recover in time. Now let's look at your lovely baby girl."

Grandma placed the baby in Amy's weak arms. Amy looked down at the perfect head, the soft cap of dark hair and the eyes as purple as violets. She touched the tiny perfect fingers of her new-born girl, the fingernails, still soft, but perfect, minute, and kissable. She pulled back the shawl to show the baby's tiny feet, Amy counted the toes, one, two, three, four, five..."

Grandma laughed, a tired laugh but still a laugh, "You can check her all over, but she is perfect. And look we have bound her navel, a large copper penny has been placed to help it tuck back in and then we've bound her with bandages."

Amy mouthed, "Thank-you," to Grandma and said, "but we had no name for a girl, only Victor for a boy."

"Today is our queen's birthday," said Grandma, "but if you call her Victoria, it will for certain be shortened to Queenie. Do you want that?"

"I like Margaret," said Amy, "but it will be up to George."

"There is also May," said Grandma, "but don't you think May Matson sounds a bit of a mouthful?"

Amy drifted back into the fresh pillows. She didn't want to be desultory with Grandma after all she'd done over the past two days and nights. "We'll talk, George and me," she said, looking towards the tray of tea and crumpets.

Grandma helped her with breakfast. "Then we have to feed this little one," she said.

Amy had heard of mothers breastfeeding babies but had never learned how it could happen. There was a pamphlet Grandma had given to George a few weeks before. Amy had read it and was shocked. She had no idea that milk would come from her own body for the baby, no thought as to how she could put another human to her breast. She wondered if it would hurt.

2.

The little village of Lingwell St. Mary is on the Dorset coast. It is a village without a centre. People often say how lovely it would be if there was a village green, with a couple of park benches where they could meet up and chat. The nearest thing to that was a standing stone. A single standing stone like those at Avebury and in the highlands of Scotland. No-one had a clue as to where it came from or how it got there. It is not local stone, more like a Welsh granite. Once in a while someone left a message and pinned it down with another pebble or rock. Like a prayer to a heathen God.

The vicar of St. Mary's tried for many years to have the stone removed. "It is a pagan artifact," he said to the council who replied, "Sorry Reverend, it is of historical and archeological interest. It can never be moved."

People were posted behind the high yew hedge to see who was leaving notes, but no-one had ever been caught. Reverend Jones collected the notes in a large cedar box that he kept in the vestry at the church. He hoped to consult a hand-writing expert, to see if the scribbler or scribblers could be identified. So far no handwriting expert had been consulted. And therefore, no culprit had been named.

The nature of the notes bothered Reverend Jones. He wondered who in the village might have money worries, who might have problems with a brutal husband, and who might have an unwanted baby. As he walked around Lingwell, he nodded at passers-by. And they nodded back, "Good morning Vicar," in response to his hearty "Good morning to you folks this fine morning."

He strolled along The Tops. A string of terraced houses set on a hill outside of the heart of the village. From The Tops there was a good view of the coast, the rolling breakers hitting the cliffs, and the walkers picking their way along the beach, some hunting for fossils, some were couples looking for a cave to canoodle, some solitary figures walking for their health or to blow away the cobwebs. The Reverend Jones was calling on the Matsons, to talk about the new baby born two weeks ago.

Grandma Matson opened the door. "Hello Vicar, so good of you to come, Sir," she said, showing him into her own front parlour. She'd placed newly starched cream lace antimacassars on the chair backs and draped a clean dark red chenille cloth over the rosewood table ensuring the Queen Anne legs were well obscured. "I have the kettle on the hob ready for your tea," she said, "and then we can discuss the arrangements."

She bustled about with tea things, laying an embroidered tray cloth on the tray before warming the pewter teapot, adding the tea leaves from the caddy with the painting of Queen Victoria, pouring milk from the enamel pitcher into the tiny pewter cream jug and putting two tiny lumps of sugar into the vicar's saucer.

"Now then," she said. "We have to arrange for the new baby to be baptised and for the mother to be churched."

"We do indeed," said the vicar. "When do you have in mind? And shouldn't I meet the baby's parents for this discussion?"

"Not at all, Vicar," said Grandma. "Leave it all to me. They have plenty to cope with right now. Poor little Amy had a very rough labour which you do not need to hear about."

The vicar hastily sipped his tea and reached for a currant bun. Grandma's baking had a reputation for its goodness and he was not about to miss an opportunity to taste this day's results of her hard work.

"We will call the baby Eva, after me," stated Grandma, "then Victoria for our dear Queen, and May for the month she was born."

"Good, good," said the vicar. "Good names for a child who will be a model of goodness, but I didn't know your name was Eva. Everyone calls you Grandma!"

Grandma laughed. "I'm everyone's Grandma, always was, always will be. I think August is a good month for all this, give Amy time to recover and for things to settle down. The baby should have regained her birth weight too, which is important if she is to wear the christening robe that I wore when I was christened."

The vicar raised an eyebrow.

"Yes, I was a big child," said Grandma, as if that explained all. "Would you like to visit them now?"

The Reverend Jones crammed the last of his currant bun in his mouth and washed it down with the excellent tea before following Grandma through the back kitchen, along the adjoining garden path and straight into the kitchen of Amy and George next door. "Shouldn't we knock?" he said.

"Knock? Knock? Why on earth do we need to knock?" said Grandma. "It is family."

George was stoking the coal fire of the back range when his mother arrived with the vicar. He put the brass poker back into the stand holding the rest of the fire irons, nodded to the vicar and pulled his braces up over his shoulders.

"Where is she?" asked his mother.

"Who?" said George.

"Who? Who? You great lummox," said Grandma cuffing George softly around the ear, "why the baby of course, the baby and your wife."

The Reverend Jones breathed deeply; he didn't believe in physical abuse and George could see from the frown that Grandma could be out of favour if he didn't laugh it off, so laugh he did, "Hey Ma, shall we box again?"

"Stupid lummox," said Grandma. "But very proud father, Vicar, can't you tell?"

And the vicar certainly could. George had been busy constructing a cradle from willow cut from the edge of the bank. Fresh willow strips that would stay curved once dried. The cradle would provide a soft place for the new baby to sleep. The rockers were made from larger strips and it wasn't difficult to see how talented young George was and what love he had for his new daughter. "See this?" he said to the vicar and held up a small baby blanket carefully crocheted in a fine wool. "While Amy's been resting, she has made this for our little girl."

The vicar nodded with approval, gently fingered the edges of the shawl, stroked the smooth willow of the cradle, "Let us meet our new villager then?"

Grandma took the vicar upstairs to Amy and the baby, who were ready and waiting for the visitor, their first. The coverlet of Amy and George's bed was smoothed and tucked in the corners, the baby was swaddled in Amy's arms. "Good afternoon," he said to Amy, "what a wonderful gift from God." He softly touched the baby's head in the sign of the cross, closed his eyes as if in prayer. "And you are naming her Eva."

Amy looked up startled, "Eva? I've been thinking she would suit Margaret, Margaret Rose. What did George say?"

Grandma butted in, "We think Eva is a good name for this little girl. It is my name."

Amy opened her mouth. No words came out. Then, "Fetch George, can you?" she said. "Did you choose her name without me?" she said as George stumbled through the door, pieces of willow in his hand.

"Name? Did we choose her name?" he said.

"Looks like she will be Eva," said Amy. "I liked Margaret, but Eva is Grandma's name and I agree it really suits her and carries on the tradition. Can we have Eva Margaret Rose?"

The vicar interrupted, "I have written down here on the forms ready for the baptism, Eva Victoria May."

George and Amy looked dumbstruck. Grandma looked satisfied with herself and beamed from ear to ear. "Very very nice too," she said. "So that's it settled. The christening will be in August, we will need to let everyone know. I doubt if Alfie will be back from the war, but we can hope."

And everyone nodded in acquiescence at the sound of George's father's name. There had been no news from South Africa and the Boer War for weeks. Now was not the time to raise any objections to the baby's name. There were much more important things to worry about.

"I will write to him," said George. "Tell him he has a granddaughter and her name is Eva. Eva Matson. That will be something for him to come home for, won't it? Something for him to hang onto."

"Yes," said Amy, "and I have two pair of wool socks knitted too in that charcoal grey that he likes. We can put another parcel together."

George, Grandma, and the vicar took their leave of Amy as the baby began to snuffle. "It's four o'clock," said Grandma, time for her four o'clock feed." She nodded sagely at Amy who nodded back with a tremble of a smile and waited until the bedroom door was closed before unbuttoning the front of her chemise and placing tiny Eva's rosebud mouth on the breast.

She was beginning to enjoy the feeding process. Yes, it had been painful at first and her nipples were sore, so sore to the touch, but slowly as each day passed she felt the thrill of providing her baby with sustenance from her own body. The pains and discomfort in her nether regions had her in tears for the first ten days, but they too were beginning to fade, and she was able to walk around the bedroom and even make her way to the privy rather than use the chamber pot without looking as if she'd just climbed off a horse.

Grandma came in each morning and evening and gave her a saline douche: salt in warm water gently sluiced through her private parts, easing the smarting and helping the healing. Amy's embarrassment at her private parts being revealed had been overcome after the night of Eva's birth and she appreciated all Grandma had done. Another reason not to kick up a fuss over the fait accompli with the baby's names.

Eva suckled hard on the breast, her little hands clutching each side almost like the kittens that Amy had watched when they all suckled from the mother cat. Amy took one of her daughter's tiny hands in hers and said, "Nothing is ever going to harm you my daughter, whatever happens in this world, I will be there for you. I will protect you. I will fight for you. I will love you."

And then she began to sing,

The Lord's my shepherd,
I'll not want, He makes me down to lie
In pastures green; He leadeth me
Beside the still waters
And in God's house forevermore,
My dwelling place shall be.

At the bottom of the stairs the vicar, George, and Grandma heard the sweet, gentle voice and smiled.

3.

August 5th promised to be a fine day. Amy woke early when she heard Eva snuffling in her cradle. She lifted her gently, wrapped her in her shawl and carried her over to the bedroom window, whispering so as not to wake George. "See," she said to Eva, "there is the sea. And there are the fields, and the little houses. Nobody is yet awake, but soon the church bells will ring for you."

Amy held the baby to her breast and let her suckle. The past three months had been a giant journey for Amy, giving birth, becoming a mother and learning all there was to learn about being one. She was amused that she'd been so bewildered to begin with and accepted that it was all quite natural now. She enjoyed letting little Eva cling to her breasts and suckle whenever she wanted, in spite of Grandma's admonishings. Eva was Amy's baby girl and if Eva was hungry, Amy would let her feed.

She carried Eva gently down the steep wooden stairs, creaking open the latch door at the base of the staircase and into the kitchen. For an August morning the kitchen had a bit of a chill and Amy added sticks to the embers of the hearth and waited for sparks to bring the kitchen fire and hob back to life.

George had brought the baby carriage into the kitchen when Grandma gave it to them, and Amy tenderly placed Eva in, while she attended to the fire and the kettle. She rocked the carriage back and forth with one hand while filling the kettle from the large water pitcher with the other. Eva snuffled softly, not letting out a cry that would disturb her father. While the kettle bubbled on the hob Amy removed Eva's napkin, allowing her to lie free of encumbrance. It was a private occupation, neither George nor Grandma were aware that Amy allowed her baby girl this freedom. Eva waved her chubby legs in the air and gurgled.

Two hours later, all scrubbed and in their Sunday best, George, Amy, Grandma, and little Eva made their way to St. Mary's. The bells rang out for the morning service and the only dampener on the day was that Alf Matson, little Eva's grandfather, would not be with them. No word had come back from the army and the Matson family had no idea if Alf was alive or dead. They prayed constantly for his safe return and were convinced that prayer would bring him home in one piece.

The organ played an adagio voluntary, the strains of which could be heard from the church walk as the family approached. "Herbert's very fond of his tremolo," stated Grandma with a sniff. "Got no backbone that lad. Pity we couldn't have had Raymond this morning, but Raymond has gone off to fight the Boers with Grandpa, so there's not much we can say about that. Is there?"

No-one replied. Amy secretly thought the organ sounded like dragonflies hovering over ponds and streams, she liked the delicacy of the tune and thought it perfect for her baby's big day. On the church steps stood Aunties Ethel and Grace Matson, and Uncle Arthur. All from Weymouth. They would be Eva's godparents. Grandma's suggestion. No one quibbled with Grandma.

Aunty Ethel wore a grey silk dress with a myriad of silk-covered buttons down the back, reaching from her neck to her hips, another long line of buttons along the seams of her sleeves to her cuffs. Amy thought Aunty Ethel looked most elegant. Aunty Grace was in blue. A costume of fine wool with a cream silk blouse with embroidery on the points of the collar and again on the cuffs. Amy had never seen either outfit before. Uncle Arthur wore his best Sunday suit and dress shoes in place of his usual hobnail boots. He wore his military tie from the Hussars. Since he'd been invalided out, he was permitted to still wear his military colours.

Amy looked at George beside her in his navy suit with his white starched shirt collar and black tie and wished they could have afforded more. She wore her homemade cream dress in georgette with a fine lines, embroidered in red silk, around the collar and buttonholes and while it wasn't made by a dressmaker or bought from a gown shop, she did feel quite smart. Grandma proudly wore her regular church-going clothes.

Little Eva was wearing the christening robe that Grandma had suggested in the first place. It had been hers when she was christened. It was long, flowing down in fine muslin with a fine silk embroidered scalloped hem, neck, and cuffs. The muslin had darkened with age, but it still looked just the job and everyone in the Matson family thought it was perfect as they had all worn the same robe for their own christenings. Amy did wonder, for a brief moment, how much longer it could be worn, and if Eva's children, whenever they came into the world, would have to wear it too.

As they entered the church, the organist began to play, 'Sheep May Safely Graze,' and Amy felt the hint of a hot tear of joy as she gathered with the family around the font at the back of the church. She'd come a long way from the back streets of Dorchester, to being part of this fine family in this picturesque village, a house of her own, a faithful husband, and now a baby. She indeed felt blessed and caught herself drifting away from the order of service, wandering with the grazing sheep as she gazed at the stained-glass window before her. She was twenty-two years old and felt so grown up and responsible. A mother. If only her own mother could see her now and be part of this day. But she had never divulged to the Matsons where her own parents and siblings were. She dreaded the thought that George's family could outcast her, she would lose her baby Eva. And George, too.

The service was short and full of sweetness. Eva cried, just a little, which the Reverend Jones said was a very good thing, this as he made the sign of the cross with the holy water on Eva's pink forehead. The choir sang All Things Bright and Beautiful. The sermon was all about Jesus saying, Suffer the Little Children to Come Unto Me. And with much praying and bobbing up and down in the pews, the service came to an end with a very pompous organ rendition of Jeremiah Clarke's Trumpet Voluntary.

"Really," said Grandma. "Was that really necessary?"

But Amy thought it was all quite wonderful and ceremonious and said as much to George, "So much more glorious than our wedding, wouldn't you say, George?"

George nodded but was looking to the edge of the churchyard, where a dark figure lurked behind the large elm tree. "Who is the land-loper?" he said to Amy.

"No-one I know, or at least I don't think I do," said Amy, squinting her eyes against the noon August sun. The man was dressed entirely in black. His clothes appeared to be more rags than clothes. He had a beard that was mostly black or dark brown and Amy couldn't tell if it was going grey, but by the stoop of the man she expected it to be greying. In spite of the stoop, he was tall and wore what was once a Homburg hat. As he saw the couple looking in his direction, he saluted and ducked behind the tree.

"Tell your mother," said Amy. "I think it is someone from the war."

George hesitated for a mere moment. He wanted nothing to mar this special day. But if this was someone who had been sent by his father, he felt he should alert Grandma. Grandma was in deep conversation with the Reverend Jones and together they called across to Amy, "Come back into the church with us child, for you must be churched."

Amy had not forgotten. She adjusted her small veiled black hat, handed little Eva over to George and together with the vicar, Grandma, Ethel, and Grace, she re-entered the church. Where throughout the christening her head had been held high with pride and her face glowed, she now bowed her head and took on a solemn and devout look.

She had consulted Grandma about her dress and it had received a nod of approval, in spite of the red embroidery adorning the collar and buttonholes. "Yes," said Grandma, "you are decently apparelled according to the scriptures. Bow your head low child and we will rid you of all sin." She removed Amy's hat and replaced it with the parish's churching veil. A long grey/white muslin veil that had seen better days. For a moment Amy allowed her thoughts to consider what other heads the veil had been placed upon and hoped they had no nits.

She was completely shrouded by the veil from the top of her head to her hips as she knelt at the altar. The Reverend Jones began the churching with:

"I AM well pleased: that the Lord hath heard the voice of my prayer;

That he hath inclined his ear unto me: therefore will I call upon him as long as I live.

The snares of death compassed me round about: and the pains of hell gat hold upon me.

I found trouble and heaviness, and I called upon the name of the Lord: O Lord, I beseech thee, deliver my soul."

Amy felt her stomach heave with fear at the words 'snares of death' and held her breath. The vicar's hands were firmly placed on top of her head at this point, she could feel the heat from his sweaty palms.

He proceeded with:

"Lo, children and the fruit of the womb: are a heritage and gift that cometh of the Lord.

Like as the arrows in the hand of the giant: even so are the young children.

Happy is the man that hath his quiver full of them: they shall not be ashamed when they speak with their enemies in the gate."

Amy shuddered at the words. Imagined George's quiver full of arrows and tried in vain to put the image from her mind.

Finally, she could tell from the tone of the vicar's voice that the ritual was coming to an end:

Let us pray.

"O ALMIGHTY God, we give thee humble thanks for that thou hast vouchsafed to deliver this woman thy servant from the great pain and peril of child-birth: Grant, we beseech thee, most merciful Father, that she through thy help may both faithfully live and walk according to thy will, in this life present; and also may be partaker of everlasting glory in the life to come; through Jesus Christ our Lord. Amen."

Still with head bowed low, the vicar and Grandma leading the way, the aunties on each side of her holding her by the elbows, Amy was led from the church into the August sunshine once more. Into the bright blue skies. Into the arms of her husband. Free from sin.

Traditionally it was not considered proper for the husband to be present and George was aware that he must wait outside while Amy was blessed and forgiven her sins that had brought about the gift of a baby. It didn't occur to him that a loving marriage was not a sin. Or that he had no part in the coupling that produced Eva. This was just something that had always taken place after the birth of a baby.

"Was it alright?" he asked.

"Not really, but I suppose less painful than giving birth," she said.

He could see her flushed cheeks and the hint of a tear in her eye. But said, "Now we must find out who this fellow is."

The figure emerged from behind the elm tree as George approached. He tipped the brim of his hat then gave a tentative wave. As he got closer, George could see the man had been living out in the wilds; his skin was as wrinkled and gnarled as the bark on the tree. His clothes were mere rags; tattered and torn and encrusted with mud.

"George," he said, "is that you?"

George cocked his head in recognition. "Pa, Papa, can it be?" And then he ran. Ran into the frail arms of his father. "I must get Ma, Grandma will want to take care of you," he said with tears streaming down his face. "We are here for the christening of our baby. Your granddaughter, little Eva Matson. Come."

The two men, one upright and proud, the other bowed over in humility, hunger, and exhaustion, made their way to the christening group who were all standing on the steps of the church, straining their eyes to see just what George was playing at with a scoundrel over on the far side.

"He knows him," said Amy. "George knows who that is, look. Look how he is helping him walk, the poor man."

Ethel, Grace, Arthur, Grandma, and the vicar, watched as George and the pathetic figure drew closer. "Surely not, thank you God in heaven," said Grandma. "I don't believe it. It is my Alfie. But where is his grand uniform of the Hussars?"

She marched rather than ran towards George and the man. "Is it really you, Husband?" she said, showing little emotion. "What in the Dickens has become of you, where is your regiment, why are you not in Africa fighting the heathens?"

"Lord in heaven woman, you haven't changed one bit," said the frail old man. "Yes, it is I, your husband, home from the wars before I could get myself shot to smithereens like the rest of them poor buggers."

"Alfie Matson wash that mouth with soap and water," said Grandma, and then, more gently, "come on let's get you home and bathed and some good hot food inside you and you can tell us all about it. You need to get cleaned up for the christening tea for your new little granddaughter, Eva."

Amy held Eva up for Alf Matson to see but drew no closer for fear the baby could catch some dirty disease from Africa. "Evie, this is your Grandpapa," she said and smiled at the unrecognizable wretch standing before them. "George, you'd better go and help your papa, the rest of us will take care of the tea this afternoon, won't we?" she said to Ethel and Grace. Uncle Arthur had moved to join George and Alf.

"I thought as much, I didn't want to tell them," Arthur said to Alf. "I always hoped and prayed you would show up. And here you are. My word Alf, it is good to see you home. Let's hope there will not be trouble ahead."

The following Friday, Grandma found Alf slumped across the kitchen table. "What in the Lord's name is wrong?" she said.

"Oh Ma," said Alf. "I think they'll be coming for me as a deserter. This letter came in the morning post."

Grandma saw the buff envelope in Alf's hands. Hands that were still covered in sores and scabs from the weeks he'd lived rough on the Transvaal. Each night before bed she'd rubbed a salve made from goose fat and eucalyptus into the sores all over his body, not just his hands. Each night she said, "I'll need to fetch Doctor Wilson if they don't get better."

"No Ma," said Alf. "It's best if no-one knows I'm here yet. See what the letter says."

Grandma read aloud from the single sheet: Alfred George Matson deserted his post on June 19th, 1900. If the corporal can appear at Dorchester Barracks immediately leniency may be shown for his crimes.

"I must go Ma," said Alf.

"Go!" said Grandma. "You can't go to the camp in Dorchester, you'll be shot."

"No Ma," said Alf, "I mean go right away from here. So that you are not involved. You can say you haven't seen me."

"I haven't seen you? Of course I've seen you. As have Ethel and Grace and Arthur and the Vicar, not to mention Amy and George. Baby Eva doesn't count, of course. But there's plenty has seen you, Alf Matson."

Alf shrugged his shoulders. "What's left to do then?"

"I'll get Doctor Wilson, he'll fix you up and you can get off back to Africa and tell them you got lost." said Grandma.

Alf looked through the window at his son, George, playing with the baby Eva. "And miss this," he said. "It may mean I never see them again. Never see you again."

"You tell them just what happened," said Grandma, "Tell them how you were captured, how you woke up to find yourself on a boat to Holland and how somehow you walked from the Norfolk coast to home here in Dorset with barely soles left in your shoes. And that you fully intended to find your regiment and carry on doing your job. You do that Alfie and they may well see reason."

"You think, Ma? Well, best fetch that doctor then. And that will make one more who knows."

Grandma called to George on the lawn, "Bring little Eva to me George, and run and fetch Doctor Wilson to attend your father's sore tired body. Don't tell him who or what or anything. I'll greet him on the door stoop and tell him myself."

4. Eva

Eva's baby years were filled with sunshine and joy. Amy made sure of that. Hand-knitted toys with button eyes and stuffed with rags were her favourite. Mostly knitted by Amy, but Grandma, once in a while, found time to make little finger puppets in different colours. If you looked closely, you could tell they were fingers from old gloves, but Grandma embroidered whiskers and noses and little eyes and when pulled onto fingers and peeking over the kitchen table they took on lives of their own.

Eva cooed and giggled as Grandma, waggling pink knitted fingers, recited 'This little piggy went to market, this little piggy stayed home...' and then the brown fingers for Goldilocks and the Three Bears. She combined the pink with the brown fingers for her tale of The Three Little Pigs and the Wolf. "I'll huff and I'll puff and I'll blow this house down..." said Grandma as the wolf. Eva cried at the thought of the poor little pigs losing their house, until Grandma pulled off the fingers puppets and placed them on Eva's own tiny hands.

Amy saw little of these antics, but she could hear the gurgling and the giggles. She hung the washing on the line, Eva's baby napkins as she still wasn't trained for the po despite bribery and threats and gentle cooings. "It'll all come when she's ready," was Grandma's advice, "George was a late developer too," she added. Amy didn't think much of hearing this about her strong, handsome husband, but smiled anyway saying, "Thank you Grandma. That gives me hope."

The sad thing for Amy was to realise she and George probably wouldn't have a brother or sister for Eva. Eva's birth, for which Amy was not fully conscious, meant that her childbearing organs were damaged. She knew how much George wanted a son, a little boy to hold high on his shoulders as he walked across The Tops and down to the seashore. He had started to do these kinds of things with Eva, but Grandma kept telling him that little girls don't behave like that. "She's more lad than a girl though, isn't she, Ma," he said in reply. "But you're right Ma. She should be who she is, a happy little tomboy of a girl. I'm going to teach her football as soon as she can run without falling over every five minutes."

"She'll need a pair of trousers then," said Grandma, "I'll see if I still have a pair of your rompers from when you were a baby."

5.

Summer turned into autumn. Five-month-old Eva watched the leaves fall from the trees from her baby carriage parked outside the front door. She lay back and gurgled at the birds gathering in the trees, getting ready for their flight from winter. Eva reached and grasped the toys strung across the hood of her carriage, making them jingle and whistle. It was as if she was trying to join in the birds' chatter and squawkings.

Amy hung the washing on the line. It was early Monday morning and George had left a good couple of hours earlier for work. He had recently been appointed to the police force and issued a new bicycle. Amy was puffed up with pride to wave him off each morning in his new uniform.

"You take care of my baby girl," he said each dark morning as he kissed Amy's cheek and chucked little Eva under the chin. "I'll be back at dinnertime."

Grandma too, had gone. To Dorchester on the early charabanc. She hadn't heard a thing from or about Alf and was getting more and more worried each day. There was another letter from the Army, just like the previous one.

"Does this mean he never made it back?" she muttered out of earshot of George and Amy. "Oh Alf, what have you done?"

Amy was alone with Eva for the day. George would come home at noon and Amy had a good lamb stew already bubbling on the hob, she would add potatoes and carrots mid morning. But for now she was content to be with her baby and the soft autumn breeze. She put down the washing basket, now empty of wet sheets, and picked Eva from her baby carriage, "Look," she said, "see the birds."

Eva burbled and cooed and, as a five-month-old, made noises unlike any of the words Amy had started to teach her. Amy pointed to the sea. And the sky. Then the birds. Eva chuckled and blew bubbles down the front of her winceyette nightdress. Amy dabbed at the dampness with the hem of her own pinafore and said, "Come on, let's get you inside and cleaned up."

By the time George arrived home for his midday dinner, Amy had the home as smart and shiny and sweet smelling as a new pin, the plates and knives and forks were on the table and Eva strapped into the highchair Grandma had dragged out of the attic. George had sanded it down and painted it in fresh cream paint, and they had only begun using it for Eva since she began to sit up.

Over dinner George said, "Did Ma go? To Dorchester?"

"Yes," said Amy. "She went very early, before you."

"I hope everything is alright," said George.

"I hope so too," said Amy. "They always say no news is good news, but I would have thought your Pa would have let her know. Something anyway."

"It is a recondite situation," said George.

Amy raised an eyebrow. "Pardon?" she said.

"Recondite," said George, "we learned it at the station this morning, it means beyond understanding. What happened to Pa is most surely beyond understanding to me."

When Grandma eventually arrived home, the twilight was setting in. George still wasn't home from work, and Amy was bathing Eva in the tin bath in front of the fire. Grandma removed her black wool coat, her leather gloves and her felt hat.

"Well, that is that then," she said, her eyes blazing steel, "I sent him to his death."

"What on earth are you saying?" said Amy. "Why did you send him to his death?"

"I told him to go back to Africa and tell them he was lost," said Grandma, her pale face turning even whiter. "They picked him up at Dover. He has been shot for being a deserter. What will I tell George?"

"Oh my dear Lord," said Amy. "Poor Papa. Poor Papa. Poor you. Poor George. We will tell him everything. He is a policeman after all. He told me at dinnertime there is a military warrant out for Papa's arrest. The force has been quizzing George too."

"We must stick to our story that he wasn't here," said Grandma. "None of us have seen him. We sent the letter back saying he was in Africa. We will need to live with this lie all our lives."

With that, she collapsed. Amy ran to fetch the Sal Volatile smelling salts and by the time George came in from work, rubbing his cold hands before the fire, Grandma was getting some of her colour restored.

"There you are Ma," he said, "how was it?"

"Not good, George. I am now a widow. And you are half orphan."

George rushed to his mother's side and took her ice cold hands in his. "No," he said, "tell me it is not true. Please tell me."

"It is true my son," said Grandma. "He was shot at the barracks in Dover after he was caught trying to get a ship back to Africa. They have given me this." She reached into her capacious pockets and drew out a few miserly possessions that belonged to Alf. "It is all we have of him now," she said, "that and the awful memory of those sores and the sight of him in rags under the giant elm tree. Even putting a note by the standing stone didn't help. How will I remember the funny young man I married, the man who played the squeeze box with so much gusto I thought we would laugh ourselves silly?"

"I remember those days Ma," said George. "Amy didn't know him back then, but those are the memories we will hold onto. Those are the stories I will tell little Eva about her Grandpappy. Stories and tunes. And my word, if it kills me, I will learn to play his squeeze box so that we can share those same tunes once more."

6. EVA

Going to school was a daily adventure for Eva. At four and a half she was taught to knit dish cloths. She loved the feel of the string-like yarn as she, with her tongue between her teeth, and a furrowed forehead, slowly wound the yarn around the big wooden knitting pins. And then with a beaming show of accomplishment, complete each stitch.

She was taught to cast on using her thumb. Grandma wasn't sure if she should correct her granddaughter and show her how to do it with two knitting pins. But teachers knew best, she said to Amy, and let Eva continue with the method being taught in school. Eva's first square garter-stitched dish cloth was brought home at the end of the Michaelmas term with great ceremony.

"Why don't you wrap it in brown paper and give it to Grandma for Christmas?" said her mother. "I would really like to save it as a keepsake as your first piece, but I know Grandma would love to have it. I don't expect she'll use it either, but keep with all her treasures."

Grandma's treasure chest was always a source of great intrigue to Eva. She would climb into Grandma's big bed and look across at the great dresser with the top drawer always locked. "Do you have the key?" she asked.

"Oh yes, child," said Grandma, showing Eva the key that hung on a silver chain around her neck. It was a small brass key, no bigger than Eva's own thumb nail, Eva had never seen such a tiny key. "It never leaves my person," said Grandma.

Then she told Eva, "In that drawer there is another key, one for the trunk."

Eva had often climbed atop the strong leather-covered trunk to look out of the window, to see the sea and the sky beyond. She'd never give much thought to the trunk itself. "What is in it, Grandma?" she said.

"Oh my word child, all these questions. That was my going away trunk."

"Going away?" said Eva. "Where were you going Grandma?"

"I once thought I was going to America," said Grandma. "Grandpa was going to get tickets. That was before your Dadda came along. I was just a young slip of a thing then."

Eva tried to imagine Grandma as young. As a slip of a thing, but no matter how hard she tried, the image just wouldn't present itself. "Did you go?"

"No child," said Grandma. "Grandpa changed his mind. I haven't opened the trunk from that day to this."

7.

Eva grew into a gawky girl. "You're all arms and legs, Girl," said Grandma, "and no chest yet, no bosoms, a chest like a board you have."

Eva grimaced. She knew that other girls at school had breasts and were wearing corsetry. At twelve years old she looked like an overgrown eight-year-old. And what made matters worse were her activities after school. She walked home dawdling along the lanes, climbing over stiles, rummaging through brambles for juicy ripe blackberries. Letting the staining purple juices drip on her grey school pinafore. She forgot about the admonishments she would receive when reaching home, how she would have to change her pinafore and soak it in vinegar to get out the stains. She was always just happy to be out in the open air and free.

When she was fourteen, in late June as school closed for the summer, she knew she needed to come up with a plan. She talked with her teacher about helping at the hospital. "Ma'am," she said, "after the hospital visits we've done this term, my friends and I would like to volunteer to help more."

The matron hired the girls as helpers on the wards. They were to arrive at seven o'clock each morning and help until dinnertime. After a month they were able to stay all day if their work was good enough.

Eva thrived. She wore a pink and white striped blouse with dark grey skirts reaching the floor. Her best black-laced boots were polished to a gleam each evening when she got home, and her mother and grandmother couldn't be more delighted that she seemed to have found her calling. When the school summer holidays finished, Eva asked the hospital if she could stay on as a nursing assistant rather than return to her studies; that's how keen she was.

But Matron advised her to return to school for another year, to matriculate and then apply to their school of nursing. This was to be a turning point in Eva's life.

In July 1914, the world went to war. And that included her father. As a police sergeant, he had all the makings of a good soldier. Grandma was beside herself with worry, "Don't go the same way as your father," she said over and over to George around the kitchen table the day before George had to leave for the barracks in Dorchester for training. "You will come back to us, you hear me now, George."

Amy said little in front of the family. But Eva knew she'd been weeping. She could tell from the swollen eyes and tear-stained cheeks and the fact that her mother could hardly get two words joined together without running from the room.

George took his daughter aside. "You will look after them for me," he said. It wasn't a question. Eva nodded. "You are more like the man of the house than you'll ever know," said her father, his voice gentle and soft.

Eva didn't find this a strange statement from her father. Over the years she'd spent many hours with George learning all about repairing things around the house, planting vegetables in the back garden, and repairing the one and only family bicycle. "You will use my bicycle too," said George. "It will save you time going to and from the hospital, and you may need to pick up provisions for your mother and grandmother."

Eva smiled at this last one, she had no idea that her father took care of that chore. For some reason she thought her grandmother took care of food for the family. But she nodded and said, "Don't you worry, Dadda, I will take care of everything."

As the weeks and months passed, Eva's mother, Amy, received just one letter from George. It was the first letter he had ever written to her. She said to her daughter, "Look at this, I wonder who it can be from," when she saw the handwriting on the envelope.

"Why, it is from my Dadda, of course." Eva had seen George's handwriting many times as he helped her with her studies and wrote out labels for the vegetables in the garden at the back. Eva had a relationship with her father that was almost unknown to her mother. Amy knew that her mother was quite happy about this, she saw her mother watch them through the kitchen window. Amy always smiled and waved. Eva wondered if she was taking her mother's place with her father and if she should go inside and send her mother out, "Should I?" she asked George.

"Of course not," said her father, "your mother doesn't like getting her tiny smooth pale hands dirty." He said this in a kindly manner, as if he just wouldn't want her to get her hands even slightly dirty.

Eva considered this. Her mother was in her mid-thirties now, but her hair was turning grey and scraped back into a tight bun. Her once smooth skin was beginning to get the ruddy glow of living in the seaside country setting, and her love of needlework and sewing kept her busy in the house. She was also very much a companion to Grandma, who was still handling the execution of Grandpa, and not always too well. Grandma was going to church more and more frequently, Eva noticed. Sometimes early in the morning she'd be gone before the morning crepuscular sky broke with light.

Every morning, early, Eva watched from her bedroom window as Grandma Matson made her way down the front garden path, her head bowed low, and her hands clasped together as if already in prayer. Eva knew where she was going and knew that within thirty minutes Grandma would be back expecting the fire lit and the tea kettle bubbling along with the porridge on the stove. She hastened to dress, pulling on her black wool stockings and her navy blue nursing cardigan. Tiptoeing down the wooden staircase so as not to waken her mother. She knew her mother had been up until almost dawn sewing shirts for soldiers. And one soldier in particular, her George, Eva's father.

Eva was no expert seamstress, her forte was knitting, so she whiled away the long evenings knitting socks for the soldiers in strong grey wool that had come straight from the spinners at Sheeplake Farm not four miles away. If she held the knitted socks to her face, she could feel the sheep's bellies and the smell of their wool. She hoped the Dorset soldiers, on the front in France, would get a sense of home from the smell. She knew it would never wash out, not even with carbolic. And that was all part of her intention with the knitting. To weave into the work something from home. A message. That the women back home were thinking of their men and boys. Not merely leaving notes at the village stone.

Eva was pleased she hadn't a boyfriend or man friend to worry about, it was bad enough worrying about her father and all the men from the village who had gone forward at the beginning to offer their help to fight for what was right.

Grandma came into the warm kitchen. Eva stood at the stove stirring the porridge. She put a large bowl in front of Grandma and the jam pot beside it. She moved the large brown teapot from the hearth and placed it on the table with cups and milk and butter. Grandma touched her granddaughter's hand saying, "You are a good girl Eva, please stay that way and don't go the way of others. I pray to the Lord every day to keep you pure."

Eva was not sure what Grandma meant, she hadn't learned what goes on between men and women. She had begun to read penny dreadfuls which touched on romance and Eva thought that all sounded very nice, comforting and exciting at the same time, but she knew nothing of the coupling of two people, or, in fact, how babies came about.

On a late summer evening, with her chores done, Eva sat under the apple tree dreaming of a time when the war would be over. She was interrupted in her reveries as Amy called from the window, "Get Doctor Wilson, dear, Grandma is taken poorly."

Eva retrieved her father's bicycle, and wheeled it from the shed, only to find the tyre was as flat as her mother's Yorkshire Puddings. The pump was on the top shelf of the shed, so hoisting her skirts into her pinafore belt with one hand and the other on the stepladder, she nimbly climbed and grabbed the pump. Within minutes the tyre was inflated. Eva had no time to check for an actual puncture, she just hoped it would be enough to get to Doctor Wilson's.

The sea fog was rolling in from the horizon and without a bicycle lamp Eva found it hard to see just where she was going. It was not easy for other road users either, especially horses. A bit of a skirmish with the milk dray, leaving Eva sprawled in the lane, was the worst that happened. She quickly climbed back on her bicycle, dusted off the mud and horse manure that was clinging to her hem, and pulled into Doctor Wilson's home. "Come quickly please Sir," she said. "It's Grandma."

Doctor Wilson had a fondness for Eva, having brought her into the world and watched her grow into this strong young woman. He replied, "Eva, get into the buggy while I hitch up Sammy, throw your bicycle into the back and we'll be off the moment Mrs. Wilson brings me my bag."

Doctor Wilson, his Gladstone bag on his lap, and Eva beside him, trotted with Sammy along the darkened foggy lanes and up to The Tops. "Tell me what's wrong with your grandma?" he said.

"I don't know Sir," said Eva, "Mama just called from the window to bring you home, so I didn't wait, I just pedalled hard to get to you." Eva was still breathless from the pedalling but was glad she had a cart ride back up the hill, especially as her tyre was flat again.

"I presume you have a repair outfit," said Doctor Wilson, "being the able young woman you have become." Eva coloured slightly. Not used to receiving compliments. "Yes, Sir. I have Sir. I will attend to it the moment I know Grandma doesn't need me."

The brief conversation lasted until they drew up to Eva's home. Amy was waiting on the doorstep. "I'll tether Sammy for you, Sir," said Eva.

Doctor Wilson tipped his hat to Eva, making her feel very grown up indeed.

"She's a credit to you Mistress Matson," said Doctor Wilson to Amy. "She should have been a boy."

Amy raised one eyebrow. Eva didn't hear the remark, which would have amused her as she often felt that she should have been a boy.

8.

With Grandma taken to her bed with pneumonia, it left Amy and Eva to carry on, to hold the home together for when George came home. There was very little money. Occasionally an envelope came from George, but Amy's sewing was what put food on the table. And Eva's nursing assistant's nominal wage supplied the heat to keep them warm.

Eva planted the potatoes according to her father's instructions. Rows of kidney beans were now climbing the poles and looking promising. Amy had a fondness for her chickens and while they really enjoyed the eggs, only Grandma had the strength to kill one for to eat. But now, Grandma had no strength. She lay back as white as a sheet one moment and as red as a beetroot the next. Amy made her a gentle custard to help keep her strength up and Eva made a raspberry vinegar with the berries she'd picked along the hedgerow down the lane. As the vinegar cooled Eva watched the vermilion liquid puddle in the bottom of the bowl. She thought about her morning at the hospital: the poor man who had his leg amputated, the brightness of the blood. The large amount of blood. It made her own blood run cold, and then it was as if she had a revelation. She found it exciting; the fact that the removal of the man's leg was to save his life. 'A life with just one leg—but better than being dead,' the surgeon had said.

Eva thought about this. Would it be better to live with one leg than be dead? What could you do if you couldn't walk? Would you just sit and let everyone do things for you, bath you, wipe your bottom after doing your business?

She was so deep in thought pondering the situation that she hardly heard her mother call from the top of the stairs, "Eva, do you have the vinegar? I think it may help Grandma's cough."

"Coming Mama," said Eva, "it is just cooling on the window sill, maybe another five minutes."

She looked across at the glass bowl, the liquid redder than the raspberries from whence the juice came, the village could be seen encapsulated within the glass. And there too was the sea and sky above. "This is my world," thought Eva, "my world, right now soaked in blood, and there will be more before this war is over, and I will do my best to heal people and staunch this flow, take all redness from this place until we are serenely bathed in golden sunlight once more." She wondered if she should try her hand at capturing these thoughts in a poem. But, for now, she was needed for more urgent business.

She carried the bowl carefully upstairs to Grandma's room. A small silver spoon in her pinafore pocket. Amy opened the door for her and took the bowl until Eva was seated alongside her Grandmother's bed, slowly giving the old lady small sips of the vinegar, watching her mouth purse at the sourness, at the fruitiness and waiting for a glimmer of hope that the pneumonia was passing.

As Grandma drifted in and out of sleep, Eva stopped giving her the vinegar, and gently patted Grandma's blue lips with a soft flannel and, with another dipped in icy water, pressed it against her hot forehead.

"I'm going down now Evie," said her mother, "can you stay with her a while, I'll get our supper started?"

"Yes Mama," said Eva. "She'll be just fine with me. Look at the experience I'm getting at the hospital now, I know the signs, I'll call you if she worsens. If you hear nothing you'll know she is in a peaceful sleep and the fever is lessened."

9.

Grandma's fever broke at dawn. Eva had fallen asleep in the rocking chair by the window. Her unread book had slipped from her lap along with the shawl her mother had wrapped across her knees when she'd crept in to check on the two of them at four.

Eva had finished the chapter in her book about Hawaii as she dozed off. The people of the island go mauka, towards the mountains at certain times of their lives, and at other times they go makai. Towards the ocean.

Eva had looked through the window and seen the ocean in the moonlight and pondered the two expressions, but there were no mountains. She had never seen a mountain. Of course there was Cerne Hill with the giant carved into the side, her father had taken her there when she was about six years old in a borrowed horse and buggy. But she didn't feel that was really a mountain. She imagined high peaks with snow caps and people skiing down the slopes in warm clothes with big smiles and ruddy faces. Of a country called Switzerland.

Eva wondered if she would ever travel to such places and with that thought she drifted into sleep, dreaming of jolly times on mountain tops with friends she was yet to meet.

She woke to the smell of breakfast cooking and didn't feel quite as if she'd come back to earth with a big bump. She took Grandma's wrist and felt a pulse, weak, but still beating. Touched her forehead to find it was cool and not even clammy and whispered, "I'll be right back Grandma with a nice bowl of tea for you."

Grandma squeezed Eva's hand in acknowledgment. With a smoothing of her rumpled skirts and pulling the shawl around her shoulders, Eva tiptoed down to the kitchen to find her mother humming.

"There's been a letter," said Amy. "And a small parcel, for you."

"A letter?" said Eva, "from Dadda?"

"Yes," said Amy, "from Dadda, and he is doing fine."

"Oh Mama," said Eva, "I am so glad, it's been such a worry. What does he say?"

"I'll read it to you," said Amy, "but first your parcel."

Eva took the small box that had been wrapped in a hessian and stitched around the edges. It bore no postage stamps, just seals and frank marks. She gently unpicked the stitches, wound the string into a ball for reuse. She peeled back the hessian wrapping and folded it for future use. Inside was a small cardboard box with French writing, and, on top, a note. To my daughter Eva, with love from your Dadda. Keep the lanes alive with your ringing.

Eva looked up at Amy with a puzzled but excited frown. "What can it be, what does he mean—ringing?"

"Open it child," said Amy trying to contain her excitement. "I wonder why there is no package for me."

Eva opened up the box to find a bright, shiny bicycle bell. She pressed the little lever with her thumb to hear the foreign sounding tinkle. Then she laughed, "He remembered," she said, "he remembered Is-a-bell-on-a-bicycle."

"What are you talking about, child?" said Amy.

"It is a little joke Dadda used to say," said Eva, "like T-ree-s-are Green. Teresa Green. Isabel on a bicycle. We used to make up names for girls that had two meanings."

Amy nodded, and then a minute envelope dropped from the base of the bell box. 'For your mother,' it said on the outside.

Eva handed the envelope to her mother. She could feel the small bulge in the envelope. "For you Ma, you see, he didn't forget you."

Amy pulled back the seal of the envelope, slowly so as not to tear the velum. She wanted to cherish even the envelope, the first real sign that there was still love in George's heart for her.

At that moment the two women heard a bump overhead. "Grandma," shouted Eva, "are you in need of something?"

Amy left the half-opened envelope on the kitchen table and together daughter and mother ran up the stairs to see if George's mother was in trouble.

"I heard you laughing," she said, "can I hope the news is good?" The old lady was standing by the window, looking out over the garden and beyond. She still had on her chemise, but with her fox fur coat over the top. Both Eva and Amy began to laugh.

"Oh Grandma, it is indeed all good," said Eva. "Dadda has written. He is fine. And he has sent a bell for the bicycle."

"A bell?" said Grandma in the strongest voice she had used in quite some time. "What the use is a bell, we cannot eat or wear a bell." But she too laughed and announced, "I think it is time for me to leave my bed and see what messes you two have made of the kitchen."

The three women sat around the kitchen table with the large brown teapot before them, the lardy cake that Amy made last week, and the envelope which she'd placed beside her plate. Lardy cake was a traditional English tea bread enriched with lard, sugar, spices, and dried fruit. It originated from Wiltshire and was commonly found throughout the West Country. Historically, lardy cakes were celebration cakes and only made during special occasions as sugar, spices and dried fruits were considered luxuries.

"Why are we having this?" said Grandma, "It ain't Christmas?"

"It's Eva's birthday," said Amy. Eva is 15 today. She has received a parcel from her father in France." She looked across at her daughter. "You thought we'd forgotten, didn't you?" she said.

"No Mama. It just didn't seem right that's all, with Dadda away fighting the war and all."

Grandma looked forlorn, "I have nothing ready to give you child, but as soon as I am really back on my feet, I have something saved for you."

"It is of no importance Grandma dear," said Eva, "You just need to get well and strong, that is gift enough."

Three slices of the aromatic cake were laid on their plates and there was a quiet in the kitchen, each woman lost in their own thoughts. "What about your envelope Mama," said Eva. "You haven't opened it yet."

Eva and Grandma watched as Amy took up the small envelope. They smiled as she fingered the small raised centre. And then watched her face as she looked inside the envelope rather than opening it right up. They saw her eyes open wide and her mouth form a perfect 'O'.

"What is it Mama, show us. It is from Dadda isn't it. It has to be, it was in the same parcel."

Amy slid the gold locket and chain out of the envelope. There was the sound of combined breaths being caught. She opened up the small catch on the side and saw the tiny image of George on one side and her own picture on the other, when the locket closed they joined together. There was an inscription: Amy Sarah Matson, my dear wife with all my love, George.

Eva saw the tear that fell from her mother's cheek onto the clean blue tablecloth and rushed to put her arms around her shoulders. "It is beautiful Mama," she said, "it is as if Dadda is with you always."

"You are right child," said Amy, "and I thought he had forgotten me when I saw your bicycle bell, I felt left out—but it is not so, I hope and pray he will come home safely to us."

"He will Amy," said Grandma, "my George is made of stern stuff, he will outwit the Hun and come home. It will not be long now."

10. AMY

Amy lay in bed fingering her new locket. She held it close to her heart and felt George's presence. "Thank you, my sweetheart, for thinking of me," she said to the other side of their big empty bed. She felt badly that she'd misjudged the gift for Eva, that she'd felt a twinge of jealousy.

Amy had noticed that George and Eva spent a lot of time together as their daughter got older. How he involved her in things that she, Amy, had no personal interest in. Things in the shed, things to do with fixing the bicycle, were just two that came to mind. And now the guilt. She should be happy that George loved his daughter, not feel that there was a contest.

She stretched and got out of bed, running her cold feet into her carpet slippers with their pink pom-poms, and wrapped her thick wool dressing gown around her. She needed to go to the privy in the back garden.

It was barely daylight as she opened the back door and stepped guardedly along the garden path to the privy. She was surprised to see a candle glow coming from under the privy door. She wondered who could be in there at such an early hour. Both Eva and Grandma used the gazunder until daylight.

"Helloo-o…"

"Mama," called back Eva, "something's happened and I'm frightened."

"What?" said Amy, "what can you mean, have you hurt yourself?"

"No Mama, nothing hurts, just a bit of a belly-ache, but I am bleeding."

"Open the door, child, and I will see."

Eva opened the door to her mother, who wore both a frown and a smile. "Why are you smiling?" she said.

"Oh Eva, I'm smiling because it is nothing to worry about, it is your monthly visitor. We will get you the rags you need, that's all." said Amy.

"Visitor? What visitor?" said Eva, and why the blood, oh Mama, what is happening?"

Amy helped Eva back into the kitchen where she gave her warm wet flannels to clean herself, warm towels that had been hanging over the range, and she filled her a hot water bottle. "You are becoming a woman, Eva," she said. "This is what happens to women, it happens every month like clockwork. The time to worry is when it doesn't happen. Now you go up to your bedroom and change into clean clothes, use these rags to stop your clothes getting more blood, and then lie on your bed with this hot water bottle for the bellyache. I will bring you some broth to make you feel better."

Eva climbed the stairs. Bewildered. "Don't worry, Eva," said Amy. "It is just the curse of being born a woman and not a man."

Amy busied herself in the kitchen. "Eva has the curse started," she said to Grandma.

11. George

George was at Vimy. A letter he'd written to Amy was in his battledress, top left pocket, 'by my heart,' was his way of putting it. He'd developed a croup type of cough and the sergeant kept barking at him to put a sock in it, "The enemy will hear you from the other side of hell," is how he put it.

George tried to suppress the cough as best he could. His best friend Jim from back home had a small amount of brandy in a hip flask and offered George a sip.

"But I don't drink," said George.

"This ain't no drink, Georgie boy," said Jim. "This is medicine."

George took his first sip of brandy. The first in his life. He coughed as if he was coughing his heart up and then felt the warm glow begin to spread through his body. "That's good Jimmy." he said. "Don't tell Grandma."

They both smiled, they dared not laugh for fear the sergeant would bark at them again. But later in the day George was called to the last bunker to see the captain, "We're going to invalid you out Corporal Matson," said the captain. "If that cough of yours spreads we'll be in deep shit, as deep as the pig pens back home."

George knew the captain from the big house in the village. "Grandma will be glad to see you, and young Eva can nurse you back to health. I hear she is doing good work at the hospital. If this isn't finished, once you are strong enough, you can come back."

George felt a mix of emotions. The cough began again and with it the trembling and the fever. He coughed into his hand and was not aware that both the captain and the sergeant had seen the blood he was coughing up.

"We're sending you home tonight, Corporal," said the sergeant.

12.

Amy received the letter in September. "He's coming home," she announced to Grandma and Eva. He has a bad cough and a fever. They are sending him straight to your hospital, Eva."

The three women held hands and said a short prayer, "Thank you Lord, for sending my son, my husband, my Dadda, home to us, we pray that, with your help, we can make him well again."

"You let me know when he reaches the hospital, our Evie," Amy said to her daughter. "I wish to be there."

"I will Mama," said Eva, "I'll send the hall boy with an immediate message."

Amy scrubbed the house from bottom to top. She washed all the blankets in the boiler with the Reckitt's Blue, heaved the heavy, wet, sogging items through the hand mangle and had them blowing in the sea breeze, on the line, all the way from the kitchen door to the hedge. Her back ached but it didn't stop her. The moment all the washing was blowing on the clothesline she began a long baking session with breads and cakes until the pantry no longer had any ingredients.

Only then did she sit and have a small bowl of soup with a bread crust. And her reward—her tea in a large enamel mug.

Grandma put her hand gently on Amy's shoulder, "You have worked too hard," she said, "I know why you've done it but you mustn't make yourself ill, too. You'll need all your strength to nurse him."

"I want to make sure I am doing everything right for him," said Amy, "I love George more now than ever."

"I know," said Grandma, "and I bless the day you came into his life and ours. Our lives are so frangible, we should make sure we take care of each other every day."

Amy was touched by Grandma's sudden outpouring of personal feelings. She'd softened towards the woman she originally thought of as bombastic and bossy. She knew that she had gone through much with the execution of Alf, and now her son George—sick and away on the continent somewhere.

"I'll make us some more tea," Grandma said, "I could do with a cup, and I know you could drink another. Maybe, just maybe, we could cut into one of these cakes, George couldn't possibly eat all of them." They both laughed, tension eased by the thought of tea and cake. The release of the pent up energy made Amy feel like crying, partly with sadness for what had gone before, and partly with joy for her husband returning home, no matter what the gas had done to him. He would be home and safe.

George arrived home three weeks later. He was overcome with total inertia. 'Lassitude', the specialist at the hospital had called it. "You need rest and the love of your family," were his words, "and you will slowly get better. There is no rushing this." This is what George recounted to Amy when at long last she threw her arms around his frail body.

"It is more good than you will never know, to have you home," she said. That night Amy looked around the table as George, Grandma, and Eva all sat with a good hot plate of meaty stew before them. She said, "Before we begin, we should make thanks to the Lord."

They all bowed their heads and listened to Amy's gentle voice, "Our dear Lord and Father, we thank you for bringing my husband, Grandma's son, and Eva's Dadda home safely to us. We pray that you will heal his weakened body and spirit and make him well again. We thank you for these foods before us that have been brought in by all the folks in the village in celebration of George's homecoming." Amy stopped and looked across at her daughter's face, serene, thoughtful and filled with love, "and we thank you for helping our Evie to pass her matriculation exams with flying colours. Amen"

George and Grandma looked up with the final "Amen." They looked across at Eva. "You passed," said Grandma, "I had no doubts at all. You are a very clever girl," and smiling, she said, "I wonder which side of the family you get it from."

George rose on his fragile legs and raised his mug of porter, "To our girl Eva, who is becoming a good young woman and clever to boot, may you go far, my daughter, and make yourself and us all proud. And Ma, she gets it from both sides." He sat down with everyone laughing.

"Why didn't you tell us?" said Grandma.

"We wanted to keep it a surprise, didn't we Mama?" said Eva.

Amy nodded. "Tonight is a celebration of many things. Grandma who has been so poorly is now much better, we have George home safe, and Eva, with a bright future ahead too. And," she added, "we have these." She opened a brown paper package and held up many small envelopes. "Seeds," she said, "vegetable seeds for us to expand the garden. I have been around everyone in the village and asked for a handful from each garden. We will have produce to share with them too. Beans and peas and onions and cucumbers and so many things. George, when you feel better we are going to build a greenhouse."

Doctor Wilson had told her that a project was what George would need the most. Something for him to feel some self-worth. Something to get out of bed for in a morning. Something to get him out into the fresh air. And something for him and Amy to do together. The greenhouse was Amy's idea and she had already acquired some bricks for the base. The rest would be up to George to find at the timber yards and the like.

That night as George had Amy help him undress, she saw how wasted her husband had become, how his chest caved in, so unlike the brawny man she'd waved off on the chara. She heard his breath rattle and saw his sunken face, his eyes bulging from his head like a scared deer. "We'll need to feed you up," she said. "Get you back on your feet."

Deep down she had no idea how she would do it, but later in the kitchen she talked with Grandma and Eva. Eva because, even though she was just a young girl, had nursing skills and experience that would need to come into play. "We'll do it Mama," said Eva. "I'll talk with Matron and see just what we can do. I think rest, and fresh sunshiny air is a good start though. Tomorrow, I will find a way to get him down to the sea, let him breath in the sea air. Then when they tarmac the roads in Lower Town we can go and breathe in the air from the tar boilers, they say that is good for lung problems too. And…" she stopped.

Amy knew Eva didn't want to show off too many of her skills; she nodded to her daughter. "Go on," she said.

"There's something called Friar's Balsam, you have to put it in a bowl and pour a kettle of boiling water over it, then Dadda will need to sit over the bowl with a towel over his head and breathe in the steam. Matron says it works. I'll ask Doctor Wilson where we might get hold of some.

13. Eva

With her Grandma and her Mama deeply involved in restoring her Father to health, Eva had time to reflect on where her own life was to go. She hoped there would be an end to this war, but the war itself had given her the opportunity to learn. To learn about things normally reserved for men. When there was no-one to drive the ambulance, Matron said, "Eva, you ride your bicycle so very well, my dear, do you think you can take the ambulance over to the barracks?"

Without hesitation Eva jumped into the driving seat and with a grinding of gears, double de-clutched the new vehicle down the hill. She drove so slowly there was hardly need for braking, but as she pulled up at the guardroom at the Dorchester barracks, the guardsman saluted her and said, "For a girl, you are doing very well."

Eva was tickled pink by this and felt very much that this was a skill she'd like to perfect. At the barracks, there was a young soldier to be taken back to the hospital. His stretcher was slid into the back and the doors closed with two slaps of the hands and the stretcher bearers called, "Take him away Miss, and take care of him."

Eva was worried that the bumps and jolts could do harm to the injured soldier. If he'd had stitches she didn't want the wound to burst open. Keeping the ambulance in second gear, she drove the speed of a funeral hearse. People walked along the pavement faster than she drove. But she kept her head and pulled up to the hospital where Matron and two staff sisters waited to receive the injured man. "Well done, young Eva," said Matron.

Eva blushed and said, "Sorry it took a long time Matron, the road was a little bumpy and I didn't want to cause further injury."

"Absolutely, the correct way," said Matron, "more haste less speed I say." They unloaded the soldier and Eva went to park the ambulance. Matron said, "Why don't you practice for half an hour before you go home. We may want you to take it out again tomorrow."

Eva was thrilled. She worked through the gears, stepped on the brakes slowly and then tried an emergency stop. Stalling more times than not. She got out and cranked the motor and had no trouble getting the vehicle started up again. Finally she parked it in the shed and went to say goodnight to the hospital staff. "See you tomorrow," she said.

Her bicycle felt clumsy and light at the same time, after driving the ambulance with all its power.

George was in the kitchen sipping a hot broth when Eva arrived home, ringing her bicycle bell, just to let them know she'd arrived. She burst through the door all breathless smiles. "Dadda, you are looking much better," she said, removing her coat and putting on her evening pinafore so as not to sully her hospital attire.

"You like the bell?" said her father, "I heard it ring, it sounds very French."

Eva laughed, "I thought there was a difference," she said.

"Vive la différence," said her father and then, "forget I said that, Evie, that one is for grownups."

"I don't think I could feel more grown up," said Eva, "I drove the ambulance today."

Amy turned from the range where she was adding vegetables to a chicken stew. "You drove the ambulance?"

"Yes, indeed, it wasn't too difficult. I brought a wounded soldier from the barracks to the hospital," she said.

"But who taught you to drive an automobile?" said her father.

"No-one, Dadda," she said, "it all seemed most logical, after all I can ride a bike, that propels one forward using a method of chains, brakes, and gears, the ambulance was not too different other than I had to crank the motor, but then I didn't have to pedal, merely use the gears and the brakes—and steer of course," she added with a grin.

"You will need proper instruction if you are to drive again," said her father, "I will not have a daughter of mine endangering herself and others."

Eva looked crestfallen, "Oh Dadda, I was perfectly safe. I didn't move more than five miles an hour," she said. "People were walking faster than I was driving. I slowed for all the potholes as I didn't want the soldier's wounds to burst open. He had only been stitched up at the field hospital. Everything was just fine."

She looked up at her parents and her grandmother, "Isn't it the most wonderful thing? I loved it, I could feel the propulsion through my hands and feet. Matron is arranging for me to have lessons but she needs your approval first."

"I suppose we have little choice," said her mother, "and at least you are doing something towards the war effort which is more than I am."

"You are doing aplenty," said George, "and you are taking care of me right now. I approve, Eva, I think it is a wonderful thing that you do. Many girls your age still play with dollies."

Eva laughed. "I don't think that is something I ever did, did I?" she looked up. All three adults shook their heads, "No," they said, "you would rather be planting potatoes in the garden."

It was a major turn of events for Eva and her family. Eva had shown them how she had grown up and was responsible for the safety of others. For a girl of her age to be driving was something her mother could barely comprehend, but she accepted that Eva was in command of her own destiny.

Eva couldn't be more excited. In her room, by the light of the oil lamp, she looked at her hands, backs and fronts. Strong hands with long fingers, the kind of fingers a pianist would need. She touched the muscles in her wrists, the wrists that needed to be strong to crank the motor of the ambulance. And her arms—not delicate like a young woman's in a penny dreadful, but muscular like those of a young man. Eva stood before her mottled chevalier mirror and flexed her muscles like Charles Atlas—these were the muscles needed for doing strong manly things. And Eva had them. She didn't need to be pretty to get on in this world, she told herself, she just needed to be strong, to not have to ask any man to do anything for her, whether it be to open a bottle or a jar, or to crank the handle on an automobile. Eva knew that she just did not merely have the skill, but the strength. She reminded herself to ask to learn about how to change a wheel, too, when she had her lessons. After all, an ambulance with a flat tyre was neither use nor ornament, was it?

It was Doctor Wilson who remarked on her driving when he visited George the following week, "I hear you've found your niche?" he said.

"Niche?" said Eva.

"It's French," said George, "it means speciality, or some such thing." He smiled though. He was proud of his daughter and glad that Doctor Wilson had noticed how well she was doing.

"You mean the ambulance driving?" said Eva.

"Indeed," said Doctor Wilson, "I am thinking of getting myself an automobile once this war is over. I understand the Wolsey is a nice looking vehicle."

"I think the ambulance is made by Austin," said Eva, drawn into the male conversation like a natural, "I am taking proper lessons, but I still do the run to the barracks and back to the hospital, it is a fairly straight run, no real hills, or bends, and someone has been along and filled some of the potholes with sand—that was tricky with my patient this morning."

Both men look up, their mouths open. Eva suspects they are surprised to hear her speak with such authority on the subject.

"Was that young Neville?" said Doctor Wilson. "He has gangrene in both legs, a very sorry tale, you remember him George. He was in your regiment too. Were you at the Somme together?"

George nodded but said nothing. Eva suspected it was bringing back memories he could do without and hastily changed the subject.

"What about Dadda's greenhouse then?" she said. "Isn't it going to be the most wonderful thing? I can almost smell those fresh tomatoes now."

"Indeed, young Eva," he said, "Your mother's idea was excellent, to say the least."

PART II

14.

"The world has gone to hell in a handcart," said Ed Durrell, his pipe clenched between his teeth, with no sign of smoke from the briar. "I sometimes wonder if we really did win the war."

His reporting staff look up from their desks. The newspaper business had been busy enough for them, but obviously not profitable for their editor, who had the owners on his back. "What more can we do Mr. Durrell?" said Nigel Thomas, the youngest reporter on the team, the one looking after births, marriages, and deaths. And Women's Institute cake sales, jumble sales and garden parties. "I'm out there all the hours that God sends and then there are the reports to write up at the end of it all."

"Not good enough," growled Ed Durrell. "We've got to increase sales. Boardroom—one o'clock—come with all the ideas you can muster or we'll go under and you'll all be out of work."

Nigel Thomas nodded, but looking around, saw that his senior colleagues were not too impressed with him. He also knew they judged him for just missing the war by a few weeks.

"Trust him to open up his big gob again," said Bob Clarke, senior reporter, so senior he spent most of his time in the Rose and Crown listening to the locals and then writing heart-rending stories about their combined predicaments. Human stories they called them. Stories that made people want to buy a newspaper, to read all about the lives they think they are leading. Their lives according to Bob Clarke anyway.

Nigel reckoned that pictures with the stories would make them better and decided that would be one of his ideas at one o'clock. He also thought serials would work too; something for people to want to buy the next copy, to see what happened to their now favourite character. He put on his hat and coat and lighting a Park Drive cigarette, announced, "I'm off now then, have to catch the commotion in Market Street, something to do with a woman and a motor car."

"Hey, wait up there young whipper snapper, that should be my bag, I'm on the human angle stories remember, you go and report on the flower show in the Town Hall, why don't you?" Bob Clarke's words fell on deaf ears as Nigel had already left the office, clattering down the dusty stairs of the old building. He had a smirk on his face, he was determined to climb this career ladder as fast as he could, he wanted to be the editor, or at least the editor of the news pages before Christmas, he was only 23, but that didn't mean a thing. He had all his faculties, all his arms and legs and a perfectly good set of lungs, eyesight like a sparrow and a nose for a good yarn. He'd been too young to go to war and emerged from Dorchester Grammar School with his matriculation in first class honours and a bursary for University. His chosen subject was English and editing the college's newspaper was pure genius as far as he was concerned. It was his stepladder to the career he had set his sights on.

There was already a fuss in the centre of town. Crowds had congregated around the memorial, and he could see why; they were getting ready for Remembrance Day the following day. Barriers had been erected to prevent people from getting close to where the wreaths would be laid and the dignitaries would stand. The route for the parade was mapped out and he felt duty bound to be there bright and early the following day. But for now he was following a young woman dressed in trousers and a wind-cheater.

He knew who she was. It was that Eva Matson. The woman who did things like a man; she was known for it. She'd driven an ambulance during the war at only 15 years of age. He'd known her through school, too.

She'd matriculated two years early—something unheard of in his part of the world. He felt a little awe-struck by her as she stood beside a new Austin automobile. How he wished he had a camera with him. That would clinch the story for him where the paper was concerned. "Every picture speaks a thousand words." He had heard that saying so many times. He really had to get hold of a camera.

In the High Street was a new photographic shop. In the window was a small range of Kodaks. Recently the owner had his window smashed when he'd displayed the new range of Leicas, German cameras, made beautifully, Nigel was sure, but so soon after the war, they didn't sit well with the locals. He had ten minutes to spare before Eva Matson would do the drive around the town centre for all to see the new car on behalf of the local garage.

Nigel thought, "If she can do that to help sell cars, why can't I do it for cameras." and with that thought he popped into A.A. Black Photography with a beaming smile.

"Mr. Black. Sir." he said. "Good morning on this bright sunny day."

"What do you want, young Nigel," said Andrew Black. "You didn't do a very good job reporting on my smash and grab last week."

"Not I, Sir, that was my colleague, but I'd like to do something better for you, something that might boost your business."

"What's that then, Mister Good Ideas?" said Andrew Black.

"Just lend me that little Box Brownie for the morning. I'll report on the woman and the car and I'll give you and your business and the Box Brownie credit for the photographs. It'll be free advertising for you and will help me no end. What do you say? The event kicks off in…" he looked at the clock on the wall, "…less than five minutes."

Andrew Black hesitated for just thirty seconds, popped a film into the camera and handed it to Nigel. "You break it, you pay for it," he said, "I presume you know how to take a picture."

Nigel didn't really know, but he had a fair idea. He nodded, shook hands and thanked the man and flew through the doorway just in time to see Eva climb into the car. "Hold it Madam, Hold it," he yelled, waving the camera in the air, "a nice smile for the birdie please, that's it, say cheese." The crowd turned to look at Nigel and seeing the camera, all yelled "cheese" grinning like cats that had indeed got the cheese.

Nigel glimpsed Bob Clarke seething on the pavement. Bob scribbled stuff in his reporter's notebook. Nigel hoped it would be a scoop about the rookie who was going to get the scoop this time. He waved at Bob. Bob didn't wave back.

Eva posed for Nigel on the running board of the Austin. She nervously held one end of her cream silk scarf—that had been loaned to her by Austin—aloft—very Amelia Earhart, Nigel thought, and snapped away with a fury, hoping the spool of film would hold out. "Just one of you in the driving seat," he said.

Eva settled into the seat and with her hands on the steering wheel, smiled shyly into the camera. "I have to go now," she said, "they want me outside the Town Hall at eleven."

"Okey dokey," said Nigel, "have a good spin, I'll see you when you get back."

"Not on your nelly you won't," shouted Bob Clarke, "Mr. Durrell wants to see you back in the office."

"All in good time," said Nigel, touching the peak of his cloth cap, "all in good time."

By the time Eva had done her circuit of the town and was back at the town hall in a shower of fumes and dust, Nigel was ready for her.

She alighted from the Austin, the managing director was keen to have his photograph taken with her and called to Nigel, "Can you take one more young man, for posterity so to speak."

"Certainly, Sir," said Nigel, "and if there is chance of a few words for the caption, that too would suit us both very nicely indeed."

It wasn't much of an interview. Nigel took two more photographs of Eva with the man from Austin and the mayor, asked them a few questions, mostly to Eva, and explained that he wasn't much of a logophile. For him the photographs were worth many thousands of words and all being well, they would see them in Friday's Echo.

He dropped the roll of film off at the photographic shop to be developed and printed saying, "Quick as you can Mr. Black, if this works out there'll be lots more business for you down the road, I'll put in a good word at the paper."

He was loath to leave the camera and Mr. Black said, "You know you could buy it on the never never." And that was how Nigel Thomas got to leave the photographic shop with a new Box Brownie and two rolls of film. He dropped in to see the tail end of the Women's Institute talk on how to make children's coats from their mothers and fathers old coats. Wrote a funny little piece that he was sure would suit the editor and headed to the Rose and Crown for a pie and a pint before going back to the newspaper's office for the one o'clock meeting of being heckled by the seniors and the editor. But of course, Nigel had a few trump cards up his sleeve.

The office was so filled with pipe smoke as he pushed through the swing doors he thought he would choke. Either that or he would take up the pipe himself.

Mr. Durrell sat at the head of the table. The staff leaned against the walls, hands in pockets, mostly looking glum. Nigel slunk into a chair at the side about halfway down the room, a good spot to study faces and get an idea of how things were going to go.

"We are in trouble," said Ed Durrell. "Financial trouble and we've been threatened with closure if we can't make more revenue. Either from selling advertising space or selling more papers. Probably both, I reckon. Ideas?"

Ideas were few, and what were put forward were not going to save the paper.

Bob Clarke said, "Fire some of these young whippersnappers, they are just a drain. They don't do anything worthwhile, anyway."

Mr. Durrell looked up and squinted his eyes at Bob. He couldn't see much further for all the blue smoke. "How much would we save, Bob?" he said. "I am talking about making money, not saving it."

"Same difference in my book," said Bob.

"Actually it's not," said Mr. Durrell. "You don't know how much we pay them do you?"

Bob had to admit that he didn't, but smirked at young Nigel anyway, just to push home the point.

"What do you say, Nigel?" said Mr. Durrell. "Would it save us money, or how do you think we could make more?"

"Two questions, Mr. Durrell, Sir," he said. "And I think I can answer them both."

"Oh yeah," jeered Bob and a couple of the other older reporters. "New ideas is it?"

Nigel ignored them, removed his tweed sports jacket, rolled up his sleeves, and moved down towards the blackboard next to Mr. Durrell. The reporters all cheered. "Going to draw pretty pictures, are we?" said Bob.

"Not quite," said Nigel, "but you are warm. Question one, Mr. Durrell, you could save a little bit of money by getting rid of us younger men, but then the older ones would have to work overtime—at what? Time and half, double time? So, no, I take that back, it would cost you more in the long run." Nigel wrote an equation on the blackboard that had most of those in the room scratching their heads.

"Secondly, I have an idea that would sell more papers, and also a service that could be sold along with advertising."

"I'm all ears," said Mr. Durrell, "keep talking, young Nigel."

Nigel produced the camera from his satchel. "Photographs," he said. "I've just taken photographs of the mayor and the Austin fellow, and the young woman driving the car, down by the town hall. The roll of film is being processed right now at Blacks. He hopes to have them ready to show you tomorrow. If we can put pictures in our papers, especially on the front page, people will be drawn to The Echo rather than any other paper."

"Keep talking." said Mr. Durrell. The rest of the staff in the room had gone silent.

"We can also offer a photo-taking service to our advertisers—they will need more space for their adverts too."

"Nigel," said Mr. Durrell, "this might well work. Bring me the photos as soon as you have them in your hot little hand."

When Nigel left the editor's office, walking on cloud nine, he breezed through the outer office of reporters all banging on their typewriters, trying to look busy. He grabbed his hat and coat and waltzed off down the stairs whistling, When April Showers Will Come Your Way. He didn't do it to rub it in with his senior colleagues, he just felt as if he was getting somewhere with his aspirations. He also had another, much grander idea to put forward but told himself, 'Baby steps old fellow, baby steps, let's just get this one under way first.'

He headed back to the town square in search of Eva Matson. He wanted to tell her all that had transpired, maybe over a cup of tea in a café. When he spotted her, he whistled until she turned around.

But it was not a happy face that he saw. He could see that Eva's eyes were red rimmed, as if she'd been crying. He felt the urge to console her but held back when he saw the crowd of officials patting her on the shoulders and he heard them saying, "There, there, Dearie, we can do it all again next week."

Eva did eventually manage to tear herself away from the men in suits, and when she saw Nigel across the street, she managed a half smile and gave him a tentative wave.

Later over a sweet sherry—she'd declined the cup of tea invitation—in the Rose and Crown, she told Nigel what had happened, "Someone was supposed to be taking pictures," she said, "apparently something had gone wrong with the camera and they want to do it all over again next week. I may be gone next week, I have been posted."

Nigel's heart almost stopped when she said 'posted' but brushed that aside to tell her he'd taken many photos and that he would be picking them up tomorrow. And maybe they would be good enough to get over the problem.

"You are a Godsend," she said. "My Grandma always says things happen for a reason, and you taking the photos for your newspaper may solve many problems all in one swift shot. Do we need to tell Austin? And the mayor?"

"Why not wait until we have them," said Nigel. "Let's see if they are any good, after all, it was only with this," he pulled out his Box Brownie. "I have a new film in, we can take some more this afternoon if you like."

"Actually, I do have to have some portraits taken for an application," said Eva, "but not wearing clothes like this. Maybe we can arrange something for another day. I didn't know how I was going to get them done, and now, yet again, there was a reason for us meeting."

They ordered bread and cheese and pickles and munched their lunches together in a companionable silence. Nigel ordered another glass of beer and Eva, showing how grown up she was, declined another sherry. "Mother is expecting me home, she'll want to hear all about this," she said. "Well the car driving job anyway."

15. EVA

It was five o'clock when Eva arrived home on her bicycle, flushed and excited about her day.

"You're so late," said Amy, "we've been worried about you. Thought you might have crashed the automobile. Thought you would be home hours ago."

"Oh Ma," said Eva, "I am so sorry. It has been such a big day, some things went wrong, some things went right. And I have met a young man."

Amy stopped slicing bread. The bread knife poised in midair. "Young man, you say? Who is he? What is his name? Who are his people?"

"He is someone I knew once through school. He used to go to the grammar school until he went off to university in Durham." Eva knew that Amy would be, at least a little, impressed with the mention of school and university. "He took photographs of me driving the car, and me with the mayor."

"Photographs? Oh that is good, very good," said Amy. "Will we be able to show Grandma and Dadda?"

"I'll know better tomorrow Ma, when we see how they turn out. Blacks in the High Street are doing them."

Amy set a large cup of tea before Eva, "Drink this and warm yourself then, what is his name?"

"Nigel, Nigel Thomas. You know the Thomases from down by the coast."

Again, Amy went quiet. The Thomases were moneyed people, living in a big detached house with a garden, "Will you be bringing him here at all?" she said. "To our humble home?"

Eva laughed, "Maybe, at some point Ma," she said. "He hasn't asked me out or anything like that, but he could I think. This is just business for now." Eva didn't tell her mother that she needed some personal photographs. She didn't tell her mother she was on the brink of going away, either.

16. George

George had no desire to speak of his wartime experiences. And Amy knew he hated having to go and stand at the memorial in the town while the band played It's a Long Way to Tipperary. He wanted to tell them they never sang songs like that when they were fighting. That most of the songs were far too rude to sing in public. And that in the trenches with your mates around you, no song was too rude if it made you smile or shiver. It made you feel alive. Just a little.

But he put on his polished black boots and his dark overcoat and stood in the rain and the fog with his one medal pinned to his left breast. He kept his head down and swallowed hard when the prayers were said by the chaplain. He held his head up when they sang, For those in peril on the sea, because he couldn't even imagine what it had been like for those out at sea. At least he had been on terra firma, his feet planted firmly on French soil, as wet and soggy as it was.

Amy stood by his side, but the moment the formalities were over they headed home and not to the Rose and Crown as did the others from his old platoon. The moment they got through the door they could see that Grandma had a hot pot of tea all ready and some freshly made scones. It was good to have fresh food again after all the hardships of war. And here George was, four years after the war was over, still trying to forget.

He bit into his scone and tasted the plump raisins his mother had managed to acquire. He spread the salty butter, the butter from Edmond's farm up the lane, and let the flavours and tastes linger on his tongue. He closed his eyes and knew exactly what was in his mouth. The raisins from Jamaica, his mother said, came into Liverpool on a ship, and he tasted the sunshine and the sea breezes, the palm trees and he heard the steel drum band playing.

Food was becoming George's way of escaping his dreaded reality. The taste of honey making him think of the French farmhouse where they had found chickens and eggs and a farmer's wife scared shitless for her life. How they had smuggled her along with them behind the front and how she had a pot of honey hidden in her skirts, which she allowed them each to dip a finger into. He could remember sucking on that finger so hard it brought back memories of when Eva was a baby sucking on Amy's breast.

And as he thought about Amy and her breast, he thought about the life they had before the war, how they'd lain back in the fields of buttercups and once made love in the open air.

George was letting his mind wander. It was probably his only way of coping with what he'd seen and experienced. He could still smell the rot and the mud, the rat droppings and the cordite. He had tried to replace those senses with fresh baked bread, with fresh mown grass and the perfume of his wife. The only strong sense that stayed with him throughout was that of the ocean and that's what he longed for at that moment.

"Can you take me to the sea, our Evie?" he said.

"The sea, Da? Now?" she said.

"Yes, my dear," her father replied. "I need to fill my nostrils with something good and strong. We could try the bicycles."

Eva looked at her father with one eyebrow raised, "Are you sure, Da? The hill back could be a problem."

"I've dealt with bigger problems than a Dorset hillside," he said. He sounded stern, but he was smiling at his daughter. "Come on, what do you say? We can get your ma to pack us a picnic."

Amy did just that. She hard-boiled eggs and packed them in a small hamper that fitted on the bicycle handlebars, she cut thin slices of brown bread, spread them with butter and potted meat. She placed two home-grown tomatoes from the greenhouse in the basket along with a bottle of beer and a bottle of lemonade. "I wish I could come with you," she said, "but we only have the two bicycles."

"Ma, I have an idea. Be ready in half an hour," said Eva.

"Now what's the girl up to?" George said to Amy with a half smile. "She's a good girl, clever too."

Amy nodded and busied herself with cutting an apple pie from the larder. She cut four slices and laid aside one for herself and one for Grandma, then began packing up the picnic basket for George and their daughter.

"You should put other shoes on George," she said, "those are your Sunday best."

George looked down at his feet and understood perfectly what Amy meant, but the soles were out of his work boots and he had not enough money to repair them, "I'll keep out of the sea with them," he joked with his wife, "and give them a good polish when I get home, those others hurt my feet," he lied, not wanting Amy to know that the other boots were no longer wearable. "But I will wear my serge jacket, I know it is sunny out, but you know what doc said about my chest."

When Eva returned, she returned with the Austin automobile.

17. EVA

It didn't take Eva long to persuade the manager of the automobile garage to let her borrow the car for the day, "I'll try and get photographs of the picnic on the beach," she told him with her fingers crossed. It would all depend on Nigel Thomas for this ruse to work. She drove the car to the newspaper office and ran inside asking, without missing a beat, "Is Mr. Thomas here? He took photographs yesterday of the automobile demonstration in the town."

As she spoke, Nigel came in behind her. "I saw the car," he said, "I thought it might be you. I have the pictures."

"No time now, Mr. Thomas," said Eva, "I don't mean to be impolite, but time is of the essence, please can you come and take further photographs. We may be gone all day," she added to the editor who had come out of his office to see what the commotion was. Why was this tall, angular woman dressed in a two-piece dress suit gesticulating in the outer office? She cut quite a dashing figure in the tan coloured linen outfit with its self belt and large buttoned straps. So he told her, "You cut quite the dashing outdoor figure today, Miss Matson," he said. "And where are you luring my young reporter today?" He nodded at Nigel that it was certainly alright for him to go. "We had hoped to see the photographs from yesterday. Nigel, please can you leave them in my office while you are out?"

"Certainly, Sir," said Nigel, and when he saw Eva's look of disappointment, "I have two copies of each. I can take the second copies to show Miss Matson while we are out."

"Off you two young people go then," said Ed, "try and be back before we close the paper at 6 though. I have something I wish to speak with you about." The rest of the newspaper office fell quiet amid the blue cigarette and pipe smoke.

"Come on, Nigel," said Eva, "we don't want to lose the best of the light."

When Nigel got into the car, he said, "So the garage lent you the car for the day? It was very magnanimous of them."

"No need to be clever with the big words grammar school boy," said Eva with a laugh, "I went to college too, you know."

"I know," said Nigel. "Once we left school we didn't see each other again. We should make up for lost time."

Eva didn't reply. She felt a quickening of her heart and then settled into cranking the automobile. "We are taking my parents for a picnic on the beach," she said. "I hope you have your camera."

"You are taking me to meet your parents?" he said.

"In your professional capacity only, Mr. Thomas," she replied. "We can look at the photographs from yesterday first too."

When Eva pulled the car up to the front of the house, both her parents came to the doorstep and looked with their mouths open. "We are all going," she announced, Grandma too, if she would like."

"Oh my Lord," said Amy, "I've only boiled two eggs."

"Boil some more Ma," said Eva, "we are going to look at yesterday's pictures first anyway, and," she said as Nigel stepped from the car, "I'd like you to meet the photographer and reporter, Mr. Thomas."

A great deal of handshaking took place before Nigel entered the humble but cosy and clean kitchen and laid his large packet of photographs on the fresh white linen tablecloth.

"Aren't you young Nigel from Evie's school days?" said George.

"One and the same, Sir," said Nigel, as he poured out the twenty or so pictures and spread them across the surface. "Let's have a look at what Mr. Black processed for me yesterday."

Grandma came downstairs and stared at Nigel. "What's he doing here?"

"Hush Ma," said George, "he has brought the photographs from Eva's job yesterday."

"Has he indeed," said Grandma, taking her seat at the head of the table, "let's hope they are decent and there are no ankles showing."

The photographs were indeed revealing. Not of ankles. But in Eva's photogenic demeanour, the way she held her head for the camera, her half smile, her look of concentration when driving.

"Some aren't very clear," explained Nigel. "It is my very first film and I was not quite sure how they would turn out. Mr. Black at the camera shop has given me some tips. I hope I can take more today using that information." He patted the notebook in the breast pocket of his Norfolk tweed jacket.

The five people scrutinised each photo in turn. Picking them up, ooh-ing and aah-ing. "I really like this one," said Eva. It was the image of her gripping the steering wheel, tongue between her teeth in determination.

"I think that is the one I'll recommend for the front page," said Nigel. "Look out for Friday's paper."

"Now we must be off," said Eva. "You too Grandma."

"Not on your Nelly," said Grandma, "I'll never climb into a contraption like that. No, you young people go, I'll stay here and stoke the fire and water your tomatoes, George."

And so the four set off in the Austin automobile with hats tied to their heads and the picnic hamper in the back. Nigel sat beside Eva as she drove and Amy and George sat in the back. As Eva glanced back to make sure they were comfortable, she saw they were holding hands, George's leather gloved hand around Amy's white lace. It made her heart swell with love and she wondered, for the briefest of moments, whether that feeling would ever be hers too.

It was a short drive to the beach, but slow with the dirt and sand roads and the huge potholes that had never been repaired since before the war. "Hang on," said Eva each time a pothole loomed before her, and she gently eased the car with its hard wheels over the hollows and bumps.

"We could have walked faster, and even faster on the bicycles," said George, with laughter written all over his face. "But it would not have been an experience like this."

"You two go and find a good and sheltered spot," said Eva. "Mr. Thomas and I will carry everything."

George said to Amy, "Where did she get this bossiness from all of a sudden?"

"Probably your mother," said Amy, "but seriously, more likely working in the hospital." They spread the old army blankets on the sand between the dunes and waited for the two youngsters to bring the hamper and more blankets and a thermos with hot tea.

Before they laid out the picnic for dinner, Amy and George took a gentle stroll along the beach. It was deserted but for whooping gulls and the waders pecking for grubs in the wet sand where the tide had gone out. They walked slowly, arm in arm. "It is a long, long time since we did this," said George.

"It is indeed my, Georgie," said Amy. "All made possible now by our Evie."

Eva could see them looking back at her, "I think they may be speaking of us," she said to Nigel. "There is nothing to speak of, is there?" It wasn't a question, but a statement of fact.

"Do you need a response?" said Nigel. "I think we can work together, maybe we have a future in business. But I suspect not personal, unless you would prefer we go courting."

Eva laughed so loud she thought her parents would hear and she clamped her hand over her mouth and began to giggle. "Oh, Mr. Thomas, how could you be so forward," she said.

Eva spread out the picnic on the blanket. Nigel prepared to take photographs. He took one of Amy and George; their back views as they walked along the shore arm in arm, heads bowed towards each other. He already had a caption, Now the War is Over, and began already to think about a story of how people coped with what the war had done to them. He took another of their return to the picnic spot, capturing the look of calm upon their faces, and realised it was something else between these two people, and the becalming effect of the sea and fresh air that had brought this about. Not the words passing between the couple.

He turned and snapped three pictures of Eva as she sat upon the sand, one hand resting on the blanket with the picnic laid out so beautifully, "Pick up an apple as if to eat it," he said.

Eva picked the shiniest of red apples and raised it to her mouth. Snap, then took a bite, snap, and then another, snap. Again Nigel had a caption, Eva and the apple, and hoped that someday he could publish a collection of photographs through the decades, starting with his studies of Eva and her family.

The four sat around on the blanket, eating the good fresh food, eggs, triangles of smoked ham sandwiches, laughing while sucking pears, dripping juices. Then hot tea from the Thermos jug.

"I do declare that the most soporific meal I've ever had," announced Nigel, "Mrs. Matson, I congratulate you," he gave a little exaggerated bow.

"Go on with you, young man," said Amy. "Flattery will get you nowhere." Eva suspected she was flattered. She appreciated Nigel complimenting her mother. It was something that should be done more often, she thought.

The four didn't hurry to pack up the picnic. The sun was beginning to dip in the sky and the tide began to come in when Eva roused herself from her drowsy state in a panic. "Oh my goodness," she said, "the tide is coming in, we will get cut off, and the automobile, oh my goodness we will lose it in the sea if we don't hurry."

Nigel said, "You go with your parents and move the car back, I will pack everything up and bring it."

"You are a life saver," said Eva, as she stood and helped her father with his jacket, and her mother with her shoes. The three walked as quickly as they could to the car, climbed aboard, and waited while Eva cranked the motor.

She cranked and cranked, but the car just spluttered. The tide was coming in far too fast for her fancy. Nigel arrived with the hamper and threw it into the back, saying, "You get in, I'll do it." She gave him the starting handle and, on the second try, the car jumped into life. Eva reversed the car about a hundred yards with Nigel running after her.

Nigel hopped in beside Eva. They looked at each other and laughed. They looked behind at Ma and Pa, breathless in the back seat. They were laughing too. "Oh Evie," said Amy, "it has been far too long since we had a day out like this, do we really have to go home?"

"Indeed we do not, Ma," said Eva, "we will go for a spin around the town, Nigel can show the manager of the automobile company the photographs, and, if Nigel agrees, we can stop at the Willow Tree for tea and cakes. We can take a box home for Grandma too."

Nigel nodded in agreement. "I also have to drop into the office before six o'clock, remember?" he said to Eva. "My editor wants to speak with me."

It was indeed an afternoon never to forget. Eva got the approval from the automobile garage to hang onto the car a little longer. "We are glad you are showing it off around town," said the managing director, "we will have to come to some arrangement for your valuable services. In the meantime, we will have some remuneration ready for you when the car is returned. How about tomorrow morning? We will be closing shortly, and we know you haven't yet completed this wonderful excursion for your parents. Mr. Thomas, would you take a picture of us all together beside the automobile?"

Nigel obliged, then pulled out the packet of pictures from the previous day. The board of the car company gathered around the boardroom table. Eva hung back with her parents but listened to the reaction of the men in their morning suits and top hats. "You know young man," they said to Nigel, "we really think you have a talent; will you take more photographs when the new automobile collection arrives next month?"

"I certainly will, Sirs," said Nigel. "It would be my honour. I will talk with Mr. Black about a more superior camera once I have enough saved up."

"Tell Mr. Black we will finance the equipment. In exchange you could take the first set of pictures gratis."

Nigel was lost for words. Eva thought this was so uncharacteristic but kept her thoughts to herself.

Flushed with success, they then called into the newspaper office to find a riot taking place. The senior reporters had barricaded the editor in his office. When they saw Nigel appearing through the double doors, they stormed him. Until they saw George, wheezing and coughing through the blue smoke. They bowed back out of respect for the war veteran. "Mr. Matson, Sir," they said in unison, "to what do we owe this honour?"

"Out of the way young whippersnappers," said George. "My daughter and her young man have an appointment with your editor."

Amy had pride in her husband written all over her face. Eva blushed to hear Nigel described as 'her young man', but the crowd did disperse and made way for the four to enter Ed Durrell's office.

"Phew," he said, "you've saved my bacon, Nigel Thomas. And you've brought the star of the show with you too, and—well—I'll be blowed, George and Amy, how are you, you old buzzard?"

Ed Durrell popped his head through the open sliding window and called to his secretary who, until ten minutes before had been hiding behind the filing cabinet, "Sarah, a tray of tea and biscuits please, Dear, the good cups."

Over tea and biscuits, Ed Durrell laid out his plans. He kept nodding at George saying, "What a clever, smart daughter you have, George."

George made no reply, just puffed up with pride even more and nibbled on a chocolate digestive while sipping his hot strong tea out of Royal Albert china with gold rims.

"I've been looking at the mechanics of printing photographs in the paper, Nigel," said Ed Durrell. "I understand it is being done already in America, and there is no reason we cannot be at the forefront of things here. I've made a few calls. It looks as if we need to investigate this process—just like our advertising drawings, it will use different tones as patterns of small dots varied in size and spacing. I'm sure in time it will get more sophisticated. Hand-engraving would give us better quality but it'll also require considerable artistry and time—and therefore expense. The same with photogravure. I think we'll try and go with halftones."

Ed continued, barely stopping for breath, "They are made like this: the original printed photographs are re-photographed through a glass screen with a pattern of tiny apertures, onto a film or a plate. This will then be developed at very high contrast, resulting in dots that vary in size according to the intensity in the original. This, in turn, will be used to make a sort of contact print on a sheet of metal using a material which would harden when exposed to light. The rest of that material is then washed away, and acid etch used to dissolve the bare areas between the dots. This results in a plate to be used in the printing press. It will be fastened to a wood block and locked into place along with the type on the page. I've already discussed the entire process with Black, who is going to oversee the whole thing. You take the photographs, Nigel, we will get them in the paper. Let us see if this won't increase sales and put our paper back on the map."

Eva got lost about a quarter of the way through the conversation. Amy and George most certainly did. But Nigel hung onto every word Ed Durrell said.

They shook hands as Nigel said, "I've taken a series today, of Mr. and Mrs. Matson out on the beach, a good reflection of post-war recovery I think. I may have a longer story for us, even a serialisation and if that doesn't sell more papers I don't know what will." He didn't mention the deal with the automobile garage.

Ed slapped him on the back before the four made their way back to the car and off to the Willow Tree Tearooms. Amy said, "I am awash with tea, do we really need to go?"

"Yes," said Eva, "we just need to all catch breath and finish off this perfect day with a perfect cuppa. Don't you agree, Nigel?"

"Perfect," said Nigel. "We had one or two skirmishes, but all in all I don't think it could be more perfect, and it is all thanks to you." He looked at Eva with admiration and just a hint of affection.

18. Eva

"What kind of music do you like?" said Nigel.

"Music?" replied Eva. "Oh my gracious, I've never thought about it. Grandpa played the squeeze box, and I tried, but was never much good at it. Why do you ask?"

"There's a concert next Friday, I wondered if you'd like to accompany me."

"Oh, my word, Nigel Thomas, you are very forward," she said with a giggle, an unusual sound for Eva as she wasn't one of the world's gigglers, Eva was a woman of outright laughs, from the heart, from the belly. "What kind of concert?"

"Jazz," said Nigel. "It's not a concert in a concert hall though, I think you'll like it. Are you game to give it a try?"

"Me?" said Eva. "Game for anything me. Is it very formal?"

"There may be a little dancing too," said Nigel, blushing from his roots, the first time Eva had seen him blush.

"Why, Mr. Nigel Thomas, I do believe you are talking about courting. I have one dress to my name and that will have to suffice."

When Nigel arrived to collect Eva on the Friday night, he had with him a package which she opened in the kitchen before her parents and grandmother. It was a silk stole with long fringes in a cream silk satin; she put it up against her cheek to feel the softness.

"It goes perfectly with your green dress our, Evie," said her mother.

"You take care of her, my boy," said George, "and be sure and have her home before midnight."

The dance hall was busy. As Nigel and Eva mounted the steps people pointed and Eva heard, 'there's the girl who drives a car. There's the photographer who took all the photographs.' Eva began to feel like a celebrity and felt quite uncomfortable. "Can we find our seats quite quickly?" she asked Nigel.

"We have to hand in our coats first," said Nigel, "and get a cloakroom ticket. You may then want to powder your nose."

"What's wrong with my nose? You beast," said Eva; she had always been conscious of her strong profile and was not happy with the remark.

"Oh my golly," said Nigel, "it was just a figure of speech, many ladies like to go and apply more rouge before the show."

"I'm perfectly fine, thank you very much," said Eva, "but thank you for explaining."

Eva's green dress was once her grandmother's. It was a fine silk taffeta. Her clever mother had remade it for Eva some weeks before, predicting that her daughter would be needing more clothes for formal occasions since her career was taking off on a social level.

The bodice had a V-neck with tiny pearls sewn in parallel rows about half an inch apart. Encrusted was the word Amy had given it when she had finished. From the V-panel fell tiny pleats all drawn together in a high-waisted band that pulled the back into place. The skirt of the dress had two layers, the over layer was in panels and had rows of tiny pearl buttons along each edge.

George had been to town the week before and found a pair of patent leather Colonial Pump shoes, at least that is what the salesman had called them; they were most certainly for dress wear with a jet trimmed tongue and a bow in the Louis XIV style. A shapely French heel with a metal service plate and leather soles. He paid the princely sum of five shillings for them and went without his tobacco for two weeks in order to afford them. "But she is worth it," he had told Amy when he brought them home and showed them to her.

"Of course she is," Amy had said, "but I am a little worried that this is all happening rather too fast for my liking."

"She has a good head on her shoulders," said George, "as long as that Nigel doesn't introduce her to the demon drink, she will be absolutely fine."

Eva took off the wool velour burgundy coat she had saved for it for months. It was a superb fabric and exquisitely tailored embodying long graceful lines. It had fancy pockets and cuffs and a shaped over-collar of soft silk and button trimmings. The back was laid with tucks to the waist from which the skirted bottom fell in gathered folds. It was unlined and perfect for the balmy evening. Perfect over the green silk dress, and perfect with the handmade Cossack turban which had a deep brim and a crown top of lustrous satin. With a rose ostrich feather flagging the front, it was a remarkable hat, "For a remarkable lady," pronounced Nigel when she emerged from the kitchen door for her night out at the jazz club. Eva thought the deep rose colour might not go too well with the green dress and burgundy coat, but Grandma said, "Of course it goes, as with everything, if you like it, it goes. This fashion nonsense is just that, nonsense."

Eva was glad that her newly stocked wardrobe was getting Grandma's seal of approval. She'd been nervous when she returned from her shopping spree in Dorchester, wondering if the family would think her extravagant.

The music had started when they found their way down the dimly lit staircase into the jazz club. Eva was curious rather than fearful. Nigel took her arm in case she tripped on the loose carpeting on the steps.

The group playing was The Seven Spades. The pianist, Dan Kildare, had centre stage and was running his fingers rapidly, as if by magic, up the keyboard with Maple Leaf Rag, "It is a Scott Joplin number," whispered Nigel in Eva's ear.

Eva nodded, her eyes blazing with giddiness, her heart pounding in time to the music. She felt as if she'd entered a new world, a world she had no idea existed until now. Dan Kildare was then joined by Louis Mitchell, the drummer. Eva had never before seen a black man, except for

Al Johnson at the picture house. She gasped at the drummer as he rattled out riffs like she had never before witnessed.

And then the remainder of the band joined in the ragtime numbers. The bass player, a tall thin man with blond hair over his eyes, looking as if he was in a trance, a world of his own. A saxophonist and a trumpeter. Eva clung to Nigel's arm with excitement as they were shown their seats at a table for two front left of the stage, right on the edge of the dance floor.

As the number finished, the pianist looked up and into the audience, he spotted Nigel and announced, "And now, by special request for our favourite news reporter, a new song we have only recently perfected and featuring our very own bassist, Patrick Cairns 'Spike' Hughes, we give you, Everybody Loves my Baby,' take it away Spike."

People clapped and looked at Nigel and his beautiful companion. Nigel stood and said to Eva, "Shall we?"

Eva could hardly refuse, not with all the fuss, and so she took Nigel's arm and together they swung around the tiny dance floor as if they were made for each other. "I didn't know you were a dancer," said Nigel very closely into her ear.

Eva laughed, quietly, and said, "No, neither did I."

And with that they swung into a foxtrot and after the first sixteen bars, the rest of the club took their partners and joined them until the floor and the air throbbed with music and the hot breath of dancers and bodies all joined in one motion. One lovely motion; Eva felt on cloud nine.

When the music finished and they got back to their table there was champagne and two glasses waiting. "Gosh, for us?" said Eva.

Nigel looked to the back of the hall to the manager, who nodded and gave the thumbs up. "I suspect so," he said, "Now go easy Eva, if you haven't had it before, it can go to your head."

But Eva was thirsty from the dancing and the excitement and had knocked her first glass back as if it was homemade lemonade.

The evening had Eva in a whirlwind. It wasn't just the attention from Nigel; it was the music, the musicians, the smoky atmosphere, the hints of debauchery going on around her in the background. Then a tap on her shoulder.

"May I," said an American voice. Eva was quite taken aback and looked at Nigel for approval. She didn't know why, but as Nigel had brought her, it seemed only right. Nigel nodded but didn't smile.

"But of course," he said to the in-comer. And then to Eva.

The tall older man swung Eva onto the dance floor and it suddenly cleared of all other dancers. "You dance a tango?" he said.

"Do I?" said Eva. "I don't know. Is it the dance from South America?"

"From my country, yes," he said.

"But I thought you sounded like you were from New York," said Eva. "I've heard that voice on the films."

"It is indeed my voice you have heard young mistress," he said. "I was born in Argentina, but I star in films in North America. I am here now to make another." The rest of the audience clapped in time to the frenzied rhythm as the film star whirled Eva around the floor. Eva had neither the time nor the right angle to catch Nigel disappearing through the red velvet curtains at the back of the hall. She was so caught up in the moment, in the dance, in the film star, in the music and, of course, the fact that she had hurriedly swallowed two full glasses of potent champagne just moments before.

As the music slowed and she caught her breath, she felt the beads of perspiration across her brow and chest and then saw the empty seat at her table. "Nigel, where is Nigel?" she said. "He is my companion…"

At that moment the manager appeared and said to Eva, "We are fetching your hat and coat now, Miss. Your companion is waiting for you in the foyer. He is ready to take you home."

Eva nodded at the handsome film star, allowed her coat to be draped around her shoulders, firmly anchored her hat with an enormous hatpin of Grandma's and let the manager guide her gently by the arm to the foyer, where Nigel was waiting.

"Oh, there you are," said Eva, "you had me worried for a moment."

"And I you," said Nigel. "The clock is about to strike midnight and your father asked me to get you home safely. Before we go, we will take coffee in the back room, here." He pulled back the red velvet curtain to reveal a small ante-room set with a table and chairs and a coffee pot and cups. "We don't want to ruffle the old man just yet, do we?" he said with a hint of a grin.

"Oh, you think we will at some point do you?" she said. Then, "thank you so much," to the manager who retreated after pouring the coffee. "How is it that you get such preferential treatment?" she asked of Nigel.

"They want me to do a write-up for the paper," said Nigel. "They've also heard about the photographs and see an opportunity to get some publicity. But what do you think of this place? What do you think of the music? Isn't it wonderful?"

19. GEORGE

George sat in the front parlour, all stiff and starchy, with its antimacassars and aspidistras. The grandfather clock in the hall had already struck midnight and he was more worried than he'd been in the war about anything. His dear daughter, Eva, had gone out with a man and still was not home.

His imagination ran riot; was she in an accident? Had white-slave traders abducted her? Had that young man got his daughter drunk and had his wilful way with her? For some reason, this last option upset George more than the rest. 'He'd promised to take care of my girl,' he muttered to himself. 'He promised.'

Amy and Grandma had gone to bed hours before. Once the twilight had faded to dark, they left George with the only decent oil lamp burning saying, "We are sure she is alright. Our Evie is a very sensible girl." Amy added, "And she is no longer a girl really, we seem to forget that she is a responsible woman earning her own living, she will not do anything to jeopardize her reputation, I'm sure."

George could only nod, then shake his head.

He heard Eva and Nigel before they even opened the door. His dear, precious daughter burst through the door flushed with the evening and all it had brought. It made George's blood boil.

"Where in God's name have you been until this hour?" He blurted out. Loud enough to wake the entire row of houses, let alone his wife and mother asleep in their rooms above.

Without waiting for a reply, he slapped Eva across the face. The moment he'd done it he was filled with regret, with remorse and wished more than anything in the world he could take it back.

Nigel moved into the space between Eva and her father, "That's enough Mr. Matson," he said, "she has done nothing wrong. She has been a model of purity. I swear."

"Get out," roared George, "get out of my house and do not return."

With all the commotion Amy and Grandma came down the stairs just in time to see Nigel beat his retreat and Eva standing in all her finery, her hat askew and tears streaming down her face. The evidence of a red slap mark was indisputable. They stood in horror, looking at George, a man who had never shown violence in his life. "What have you done?" said Amy. "What have you done to our girl? What have you said to her young man? George Matson, have you lost your mind?"

20. Eva

Eva packed a bag that very night. She had no idea where she would go, but she knew she couldn't stay home if her father was going to get violent. She had never seen him like that. He was like a man possessed.

Her mother protested, "Where will you go, please don't leave just because of this one thing."

"I must, Ma, I am a woman in my own right. He doesn't own me and there is no excuse for what he did." She reached up and felt the bruising beginning to appear across her cheek, and the indication that she would have a black eye. "I have a photo shoot on Wednesday. What the dickens will I look like for that?"

Eva loaded the small carpetbag onto the back of her bicycle and, on her mother's instructions, took the lane to Doctor Wilson's. "He'll know what to do, both for your bruises and for your father's outburst," she said. "Tell him I sent you."

All was in darkness when Eva parked her bicycle by the hedge in front of Doctor Wilson's home. But, intrepid as she was, the fear pounded more fiercely in her head, and she knocked with the brass knocker on the front door. The black gloss paint gleamed in the moonlight and Eva could see the whole series of events of the last twenty-four hours pass before her eyes. When Doctor Wilson's wife, Aggie, opened the door to her, Eva collapsed.

She came to on the chaise in the front parlour. Doctor Wilson was kneeling beside her and listening to her heart with his stethoscope. His fingers on the pulse of her wrist, he looked into her eyes with a little torch and made her open her mouth and say 'aaah'.

"I think you'll live," he said. "Now, how about some tea? And some rest and you can tell me all about it in the morning. I see you've brought a bag." He didn't ask why. Eva was glad of that for now.

She slipped into the bed that Aggie Wilson had made up for her in the back bedroom. The linen sheets were cool and starched and made her imagine she was in a grand hotel. She had drunk her tea and nibbled on a digestive biscuit before being told that 'all would be put right tomorrow.'

She didn't think so herself; she had decided that this was a turning point in her life, a time for her to strike out for independence, to have an income of her own, and not to trust men. She was shocked beyond belief at the behaviour of her father. She felt sorry for her mother having to handle it at home by herself. She couldn't count on Grandma; George was her son and she would have a different attitude towards the situation, that was certain.

Eva dropped into a fitful sleep. A sleep filled with jazz and tall handsome film stars and Nigel's protectiveness, or was it possessiveness? That was something to get sorted out too. But first and foremost, it was a dream of automobiles and where they could take her. She, Eva Matson, would have to own an automobile before too long, that was certain.

And then she jolted back into the present, to that moment of her father striking her. Something that had never happened in Eva's life. No-one had ever lifted a finger to her. The shock of that, had her crying and fist-fighting the bedclothes, bringing the doctor into the bedroom. He gave her a sleeping draught. Eva fell into the most tormented sleep she had ever had.

Doctor Wilson and his wife were indefatigable in their pursuit of Eva's safety and well-being. Before Eva was even up and about the next day, the doctor visited George and Amy to try and find out what had happened. At least that is what Aggie told Eva when she crept down the stairs, her eyes red rimmed and her cheeks flushed and swollen.

Aggie made her eggs and toast and a pot of tea, and together they sat in companionable silence at the kitchen table. Eva had never met Aggie Wilson before. Yes, she had seen her walking down the street, going about her domestic shopping. A quiet woman with curly light brown hair showing hints of grey. Her bright blue eyes twinkled as she smiled, a very gentle smile that broke slowly and finished up with a beaming wide mouth full of bright white teeth like Eva had never seen on anyone before. Most of the people she knew had yellowed twisted teeth, or worse, no teeth at all. She knew Grandma's teeth went into a glass beside the bed each night. She remembered Grandma telling her about Grandpa's teeth being carried off by rats. They found them in the lining of the wall of the house when it was repaired years later. It had become a family joke. A story to be told over and over and exaggerated just a little each time.

And then she began to cry. The thought of family and what she might have caused, brought on a sobbing that had Aggie on her feet, and a cup of tea brought closer to Eva. "Drink," she said, "a cup of tea cures so many ills, and you are a healthy young woman. We'll sort this out. All of us, Doc, me, you and your parents and Grandma. We'll get together and sort out the problem."

Eva hoped so. She didn't want bad feeling with her mother or grandmother. But she was horrified still at what her father had done. She questioned whether she had provoked the outburst. Was it her fault? And what of Nigel? Where was he, and what did he feel about the whole thing? What a great shame that such a wonderful evening, her first real night out as a woman, should have turned so sour.

Doctor Wilson had his talk with George and Amy.

The Reverend Jones had collected another curious message at the village stone too.

21. George

When George came downstairs in response to Amy's calling, it was to find Doctor Wilson sitting in the front parlour balancing a cup of tea, in the best Royal Albert, on his tweed-trousered knees.

Doctor Wilson was a tall bony man, with an angular face and bushy greying eyebrows over his deep brown eyes. His Norfolk jacket hung from his shoulders and he sat with crossed legs revealing Argyle socks and light tan Oxford brogues.

George appeared in a collarless shirt, braces dangling over his thick woollen trousers. On his sockless feet were green plaid bedroom slippers with pom-poms. They were the slippers Eva had given him last Christmas. He hadn't shaved and the bags under his once blue eyes looked like burst purple plums.

"Good God, man, what the hell happened?" said the doctor.

"I don't know, Doc. It was dreadful. I have no idea what came over me. I cannot blame this on the war. I blame it on my love for the girl. If I could only take it all back."

"I should have stayed up with him and waited," interrupted Amy, "then none of this would have happened. How did you know Doctor, how did you know something was wrong?"

"Eva stayed with Aggie and me last night," said Doctor Wilson, "she is quite safe. You have no need for worry. She is safe but most unhappy."

"Do you think she will come home?" said Amy.

"Do you wish her to?" said Doctor Wilson. "Now Amy, I need to talk alone with George, can you give us half an hour?"

"Certainly doctor, I will bring you more tea then," she said, picking up the tea cups and placing them on the best silver tray, the one she and George had been given for a wedding present that sunny day, oh so many years ago.

"Now, George," said Doctor Wilson once the door was closed and the donkey brown woollen draft curtain rattled across on its pole. "What really did happen? To you I mean. I know Eva was out late. Was that really what it was all about?"

"Oh Doc, she was out late. I worried for her. The longer and later it went, the more my mind played tricks, and I just wanted her home safe. You brought her into this world, Doc. You know how precious she is to us."

"Indeed, George. I have known you all your lives, more or less. But why did you hit her?"

At the word 'hit' George visibly flinched in his chair. His knees came up to his chin and then down again, numerous times, thumping the turkey carpet so much that dust started to puther up. "I began to boil," he said, "just boil inside. We don't know that young man. We don't know where she goes with him. We don't want anything to happen to her. Then when they arrived at past midnight, they were all laughter and smiles and her face so flushed and rosy I just knew that something had happened."

"George," said Doctor Wilson, "Eva is not your little girl anymore. She is a woman—your grown daughter. She has begun to make a life of her own thanks to all you and Amy, and Grandma have done for her. She has had an education and is about to put it to good use. She is also very very sensible. And strong. Young Nigel Thomas is no threat to Eva. I've known him from birth too—I brought that smart young boy into the world just a year before Eva was born. He is more likely to look after Eva on your behalf than let anything bad befall her."

George was silent. Then, "I couldn't help myself," he said. "How can I say I am sorry? How can I tell her it wasn't really directed at her? It was just me wanting to keep her safe."

"I will have a talk with her George, maybe she will come and see you. But I suspect this is a turning point in her life and probably will be the initial cause for her to leave home and find her own way in the world."

"It was just seeing her in the fancy clothes with the light shining through the diaphanous dress, the thought that others, men especially, may have seen the same. I lashed out. Lashed out at the world. Not at Eva, my beautiful Evie. How could I?" George slumped in the chair, his head in his hands, and sobbed.

22. EVA

On his way home, Doctor Wilson spotted Nigel with his camera in the town centre; he was hovering outside a well-known fancy restaurant. He slowed down and called to Nigel, "What happened last night with Eva?"

"Oh Doc, it was all a misunderstanding. If only her father would have given us time to explain. Is she alright, do you know?"

"She stayed with us last night," said Doctor Wilson. "I've just been to see the Matsons. It is not a happy story. The war did terrible things to people's emotions you know."

Nigel nodded. "Can I see Eva?" he said.

"I'm on my way home now. I'll talk to her. Why not call round in about an hour, and either she will, or she won't. She's a strong-minded young woman. But I suppose you already know that, don't you." It wasn't a question, but Nigel nodded.

"Thank you sir, I will be there at four o'clock. Right now I have an assignment for the newspaper, and Ed Durrell will have my guts for garters if I don't get the photographs of the film star."

"Film star? What film star is that then, Nigel?"

"His name is Douglas Fairbanks. He danced with Eva last night. He is quite the Romeo, I'm afraid. But," he added hurriedly, "I took care of her, and made sure she did not succumb to his advances."

"Glad to hear it. Maybe when the dust has settled you can recount the evening to the Matsons. It may help them to understand this new world we have moved into, Nigel. Best of luck with the photographs. Better let me have a copy for my good wife."

Nigel laughed. A nervous laugh, but a laugh it was.

Doctor Wilson told Eva all about it over tea and scones in the front parlour. "Bumped into your young man on my way home."

"He's not my young man," said Eva, "I hope that's not what he thinks, I really don't want a young man right now, not really, I have plans you see."

Doctor Wilson raised one of his bushy eyebrows and winked at Aggie. "My word, these are nice scones, Aggie," he said, then, "do you bake Eva?"

Eva knew it was Doctor Wilson's way of changing the subject, but she was not prepared to let the matter drop just yet. "Did you see him?" she said.

"I presume you mean your father," he replied. "And yes I did see him. He is filled with remorse for what he has done to you. He really does love you, you know, Eva, and that is why he lashed out. He is worried for your safety."

Eva said nothing. She sipped her tea and buttered another scone, spooning some of Aggie's homemade strawberry jam on the butter. Her mouth watered for the first time since the upset. She didn't think about it, but the feeling was one of positivity.

"Should I go home and visit them?" she asked.

"I wouldn't go quite yet," said Doctor Wilson. "Nigel Thomas is coming to visit you first, here. Then I think it might be better if I get a message over to your parents for them to come over. Neutral ground it's called. We might stand a better chance of curbing everyone's emotions."

Eva said, "I'd better finish these, help Mrs. Wilson with the pots, and then go and tidy my hair, can't have anyone seeing me in this state." She touched her cheek where the slap had left bruising. "I didn't bring any powder with me to hide the marks," she said.

"I have some you can use with pleasure," said Aggie, "but is that alright, Andrew? To cover the bruises with powder? Might it hold back the healing?"

"A little won't hurt," said Doctor Wilson. "On the other hand, it won't hurt, either, for your father to see just what he has done. I recommend you stay right where you are. Let me help you to relax. Have you heard this?"

He turned to the gramophone in the corner, a large polished mahogany box, with a huge, shiny trumpet emerging from the side. He put on a thick black record, cranked the handle and lowered a needle to the record. "It is Aida, the opera," he said. "This the triumphal march, listen. Quite different from your jazz band last night, isn't it?"

Eva sat back in the horsehair-stuffed armchair and listened to the orchestral strains of Verdi. As the violins began the overture, she felt hot tears slowly trickle down her flushed cheeks. Doctor Wilson handed her a large, white linen handkerchief. "That's right, Eva, let the music help you heal. It is even better than all this tea. Better than face powder and rouge, and it won't hurt at all for you to let those tears flow."

As the music rose to its first crescendo, Eva felt a welling of joy on top of all the sorrow. A feeling of strength and she began to see that there was this thing called future. And it was just waiting for her to seize it. And live it.

23. Nigel

There was a commotion on the steps of the town hall. Nigel was torn between going to visit Eva at Doctor Wilson's house. Or the scoop. Nigel was a newspaper man through and through, so the scoop won.

It was a visiting unionist standing on the steps of the town hall with a megaphone held to his mouth. He wore a flat cap and overalls with hammers and screwdrivers slotted into the side pockets. His big fluffed out moustache wobbled as he talked, louder than necessary, into the megaphone.

Nigel arrived five minutes into the oration. The speech was urging working people to take action against their member of parliament, against their mayor and against their parish councillor.

"The end of the world is nigh," he began. Nigel had to muffle a snigger; he had heard this one before. "Take action now before it is too late." The crowd gathered closer to hear what this great orator had to spout.

Nigel eased his way back and out of the crowd. 'Take action now before it is too late...' echoing in his brain.

'I will indeed take action,' he muttered as he swung his leg over his bicycle and pedalled like billy-o to Doctor Wilson's house.

Aggie was standing on the doorstep, shaking the tablecloth. "You're too late, young man," she said.

Nigel's heart plummeted. "Too late? Has she gone? I came as fast as I could," he said through rapid breaths.

Aggie laughed, "No, I meant too late for tea, we've just finished and put everything away, but I may still have a cucumber sandwich and a jam scone left in the kitchen. Come along in."

Nigel let out a long breath of relief. "Phew, I thought I'd missed her. I would have died," he said.

Eva sat in the front parlour alone, her hands in her lap and her tear-stained face more thoughtful than Nigel had ever seen. He burst through the open door, "Eva, there you are. I've been so worried. What did the brute do to you?"

"I'll thank you not to talk about my father like that," she snapped.

Nigel had never heard her talk in such a tone. He was quite, quite shocked. "But he struck you," he said.

"And not without cause," replied Eva, "if we hadn't stayed out so long, if I hadn't drunk the wine, if, if, if…"

"You are not to blame yourself," he said. "It was all my fault, and that Douglas Fairbanks."

"Douglas Fairbanks," she said, sitting bolt upright, a flush of interest passing across her face, "was that the film star I danced with?"

"It most certainly was," said Nigel. "I've been to take photographs of him in town this morning. He did ask after you. But that is not why I am a little late. There was an activist on the steps of the town hall spouting forth like God Almighty, too. I've got both scoops, I may be heading for the big papers in London at this rate."

Eva looked straight into Nigel's eyes. He had never really experienced how piercing her deep brown eyes could be. She held her chin high, saying, "London, eh? So that's what all this was about."

"Not just me, Eva, both of us. That's what I came to say, Let me take you away from all this." He pointed through the window at the land outside Doctor Wilson's, the May blossom in full bloom, the poppies in the fields. Beyond looking out towards the hillside on which was carved the famous Cerne Giant.

Eva followed his pointed hand. She looked at the place with a fondness. It occurred to her then that Nigel possibly might not feel the same love for the place.

"Ma and Da are coming in half an hour," she said. "Will you stay? So we can sort this out? I don't want to live at home with them anymore."

Nigel saw this as his opener for his big question, just as Aggie popped her head around the door saying, "Young man, I have your sandwich and tea all ready for you in the kitchen."

24. Amy

George and Amy were summoned to Doctor Wilson's house by messenger just after breakfast. 'Come for tea,' the message said.

Amy thought it was a step in the right direction, and said as much to George, "We have to try and put things right, George. It is good of Doctor Wilson to be so kind. And to be invited for tea? How about that? We haven't ever been inside his house, let alone for tea. We should get the tin bath out and have a good scrub, both of us. Let's try and do our Evie proud. What do you say?"

It was the longest speech Amy had made since the devastating evening George had struck his daughter. She had held her own counsel and kept her mouth shut. Grandma had been much the same, which surprised Amy, but then she was probably ashamed of her son's behaviour. It was a family who had never known violence, and then there were the wars. Wars had changed everything.

Grandma got the pots of water boiling on the range. George kept pumping water by the bucket loads and eventually there was enough to fill the tin bath by the fire. "I'll take mine first if you don't mind," said Amy, "I'm not as grubby as you. Why don't you get the bowl and jug and set about a good shave while I bathe, then you can hop in?"

George was in no position to argue. He quietly went about doing as he was told, while Grandma had the flat iron out on blankets on the kitchen table. She ironed Amy's Sunday dress, and George's only white shirt, the one he kept for weddings and funerals. She lifted the iron from where it was heating on the side of the stove, and spat on it, waiting for the hiss that told her it was good and hot. The kitchen was a hive of activity that morning as all three prepared for what was to come.

As luck would have it, the rain began in earnest, right after dinner and Amy worried they would get their good Sunday clothes and polished shoes ruined in the mud. Grandma found galoshes and heavy waterproofs in the hall cupboards, but the waterproofs smelled of mould, and Amy flatly refused to let that ruin things. "No," she said, "we will wear galoshes and take our good shoes in a carpetbag and we'll just have to manage with umbrellas."

The couple made a humorous sight, picking their way between puddles in fine clothes, rubber wellington boots and two big black umbrellas—one of which had seen better days with its ribs sticking through the holey silk fabric like an aroused hedgehog. They couldn't have been more happy than to see Doctor Wilson pull up alongside them in his new motor car.

"Jump in," he said, "I thought you might not come with the weather, so I thought I'd run out and pick you up."

George and Amy climbed aboard, stepping carefully onto the running board, then closing their umbrellas and shaking off the raindrops so as not to get the good doctor's car wet or muddy. "Thank you, Doctor," said Amy. "We would have come if there was snow and a howling gale; we really do want to sort out this dreadful mess with our Evie."

George remained silent.

"Some people call me panglossian," said Doctor Wilson. "I always look on the bright side, but I think this time I am not so sure."

Amy and George looked at each other. A bewildered Amy said, "Is that serious doctor?"

Doctor Wilson laughed, "No of course not, it just means that I look for the good in everything. Or something like that anyway."

The shining new motor car proceeded gently down the bumpy and bepuddled lane, avoiding the overhanging weeping willow trees and brambles that reached out from the hedgerows. Doctor Wilson obviously didn't want to get his new red and black automobile scratched. Amy stroked the leather seat and thought about how much things had changed in her lifetime alone. It wasn't that long since a ride in a pony and trap had been a luxury. Then George got his bicycle, and now here they were sitting like a lord and lady in a motor car. And really, they were only sitting in all their grandeur because of Eva.

The streets in town were packed. It was market day, and the stalls lined the town centre with their gay striped awnings and colourful wares. Amy looked at the oranges displayed like a pyramid on the end stall. "Look George, when did we last have an orange?" she said.

"I will get you an orange, woman, if that's what you want, but for now, can we just concentrate on what is important?"

"But George," said Doctor Wilson, "I hope you don't mind my two penn'orth, I think if your wife mentions she'd like an orange, it is important. More important sometimes than a new pair of shoes. Am I not right Amy?"

Amy blushed. "I didn't mean it like that, Doctor. I just saw them and they made my mouth water."

"It is a marketing ploy," said Doctor Wilson. If there had just been one orange, you probably would not have even noticed. It is very clever, and it worked, didn't it?"

By the time they'd finished the discussion on oranges in which George, once more, fell silent, they'd arrived at the doctor's house. Doctor Wilson helped Amy descend from the motor car while George climbed out on the opposite side and came around to join the two of them, and together they went into the house through the front door.

They removed their coats and wellingtons and donned the shoes Amy had brought with them. Coats were hung on the hallstand beside an ornate mirror. Amy caught sight of herself as she passed and stepped back to see to her hair and her white lace collar which had become a little askew. They were then shown into the parlour expecting to see their Eva sitting there demurely waiting for a round-table discussion. But the parlour was empty. Gleaming, was Amy's first reaction. Everything was highly polished and smelled of lavender. A large potted aspidistra stood in the bay window, and opposite was a piano with the lid up and sheet music open at hymns.

It was a world she didn't know; it made her feel honoured to be there, yet in awe of this life she knew nothing about. And Eva had actually been staying there. She hoped it didn't give her daughter ideas above her station. But then again, what was Eva's station? A young woman who had had a good education, who had a strong and open mind and had already shown that she could hold her own in company of which Amy and George had no experience.

At that moment, the parlour door opened. Amy expected to see Eva, but it was Mrs. Aggie Wilson carrying a tray with a silver teapot and cream and sugar. "Eva is on her way with the scones and jam," she said.

'As if,' thought Amy, 'that is the most important thing.' She immediately wanted to retract those thoughts, because Aggie was probably right on the nail.

Aggie had left the door open and in walked Eva, carrying a tray. Amy and George looked in her direction, but Eva didn't look back at them. She placed the tea things on the rosewood table in the centre of the room. She adjusted the chenille tablecloth where it had rucked up from placing the tray, made sure everything was just so and then took a seat beside her mother on the chaise.

Amy reached for her daughter. Eva took her mother's hand and gave it a slight squeeze. Both hands were cold as ice in spite of the room being fairly warm, with a nice fire burning in the grate.

Doctor Wilson stood in front of the fire with his back to the flames, then turned and warmed his hands. When he turned back, he smiled at everyone, "Well, here we are." he said. Amy thought that was stating the obvious, but just smiled sweetly back. "Eva, can you stand up," he said.

Eva stood, with a little awkwardness, and walked across to the doctor. He took her face and pointed it towards George. "George Matson, do you see what you have done?" he said.

George grunted then said, "I know what I have done Doc."

"Look George," said the doctor. "Just look at your daughter."

Their eyes met and George looked at his daughter's bruised face and her eyes red and swollen from crying.

"I'm sorry," he said.

"Oh Dadda, so am I," said Eva.

Amy looked at the two of them and stopped herself from speaking just in time.

"Will you come back?" said George.

There was a silence in the room. All apart from the ticking of the mantel clock. The clock then began to strike 4 o'clock. And Eva spoke as soon as the striking had ended.

"Oh Da," she said, "I think it is time for me to make my own way in life. You cannot take care of me as if I was a small girl any more. I love you Da, but I think this is for the best. I will come home for visits, as I will miss you both," she looked at Amy "And I'll miss Grandma too."

George opened his mouth to speak. He was beginning to get red in the face. Doctor Wilson held up his hand. "Let her finish George."

"Ma, I will come up to the house later in the week to sort out a few belongings, once I have made my arrangements."

"Arrangements, what arrangements, our Evie?" she said.

"I'm going to London, Ma. I have landed work in a hospital there. I will live in the nurses' home. You won't have to worry about my safety. The matron is like a general in the army."

25. Eva

Nigel waited in the kitchen until Eva's parents were gone. He knew they'd be distraught at the thought of their daughter going to London, a city so far away from home.

"She's still in the front parlour," said Aggie Wilson. "Will you take another cup of tea with her now? If so I'll bring an extra cup."

Nigel nodded. He entered the parlour to find Eva sitting serenely, looking into the fire, its flames licking up the chimney and giving her once pale face quite aglow. She also had a look of satisfaction, as if she'd made a major decision without prompting from others.

"Nigel," she said, "I'm so glad you stayed. Have you seen my father?"

"You mean, I should see your father first," said Nigel.

"Oh Lord no," said Eva, "you've taken that the wrong way indeed. No, I just wondered if you'd seen him leave. If you could tell how he was."

"Why," said Nigel, "what has happened? Has he said sorry for what he did?"

"He has," said Eva. "He is sorry, and so am I. It was thoughtless of me to have him worry so about me, so I've made a big decision."

Nigel looked crestfallen, as if the wind had been taken out of his sails.

"Ah," said Eva, "here's Mrs. Wilson with more tea. I will be awash with tea if I drink too much more."

As they drank their tea and nibbled on chocolate biscuits, Eva told Nigel about her plans. How she was heading for London to work at the children's hospital and that she would be leaving in just one week.

"Amazing," said Nigel. "I came to tell you I've been sought out by The Times. I start with them on their celebrity news desk next month. I'll be in Fleet Street and I have to find myself lodgings so I am off to the big city next week, too. I've told Ed Durrell, 'Thank-you for everything, but I must move on'."

"My word, Nigel, what a coincidence. We couldn't have arranged it much better if we'd tried, could we?" said Eva. "It means we can still see each other from time to time."

"Indeed," said Nigel, "maybe we can travel on the train together, too, it may—or may not—put your father's mind at rest about your safety."

"Oh golly," said Eva, "I'm travelling with Doctor Wilson in his motor car, he has made all the arrangements and I have to go and meet Matron. Doctor Wilson is my reference."

Nigel looked down at his boots. Then up at Eva, "Ho hum," he said. "That's good, it may have put the cat among the pigeons if we'd broadcast that we were going together, mightn't it?"

Eva looked uncomfortable. "But we are not together in that way, are we, Nigel? We are friends and colleagues with much in common, and we should just leave it like that, shouldn't we? Still, it will be good to know there is one other person in London who I will know. We must exchange addresses as soon as we have them. But you can always write care of the hospital."

26. EVA

Life for Eva in London was both a shock and a delight. The job was hard work. Most illnesses in children were brought about as a result of poor nutrition and living conditions. At least, in the country, Eva knew there were always foods such as fresh eggs and cream and home-grown fruits and vegetables to keep bodies healthy and fit. But here in the city the food seemed old and stale and lacking very much in all the things Eva knew to be good for you.

Unless, of course, you were at a fancy restaurant with Nigel and his newspaper friends eating chops and mashed potatoes and spotted dick with custard for afters. Nigel looked to be in his element to Eva, very much the spiv in his derby hat and corduroy jacket. Neither was he a slugabed; up with the lark in search of new human stories that would sell more newspapers and help him rise through the ranks. He was eagerly and enthusiastically looking for a sub editor's desk—although he still liked combing the streets for news. Being on the spot when things happened.

"Can I come to the hospital and do a story about you and the children?" he asked over a foaming pint of beer in the bar at The Thistle in The Strand.

"Me?" said Eva. "Why me? There are plenty of others."

"You are very photogenic," said Nigel, "and you tell the story really well, from the heart, it is as if you feel for these children and want, more than anything in the world, for them to be fit and healthy."

"I'll need to clear it with Matron and the administration," said Eva, "I know the hospital is short of money, there is even some talk of closing or at least laying off many of the nurses unless we agree to work some of the time for nothing. And I would if I had to," she said. "This may take some time, as letters will get written and replies awaited. You know how it is."

"I'll need to clear it with my editor too," said Nigel. "It's pretty much the same kind of thing."

That night, thinking of letters, Eva wrote home:

Dear Ma and Da,

London is a very busy place. It is dirty and noisy with smog most mornings and trams and charabancs snorting and hooting at all hours of the day and night.

My work in the hospital is very fulfilling. I have been given the job of working with little children who have illnesses and diseases rather than those who are having operations. These poor little mites are thin, just bags of bones and many of them I can bring back to health just by making sure they get a good broth and an egg every day.

It makes me realise just how lucky all the children in the Dorset countryside are. It makes me realise what a good healthy childhood I had myself, and for that I can never thank you enough.

Talking of health, how are you both, and Grandma too. I think of you each day and include you in my prayers.

I will write again next week, you can reply to me at this address. It is the nurses' home and crammed with young and jolly women all trying to do their best for the sick of London.

With my love as always,
your Evie.

Eva sealed the letter and addressed it. She was very aware she hadn't mentioned Nigel and his friends, or the night life she was also enjoying in the city—the jazz clubs and the restaurants and the friends she was making in her own right. She didn't mention Lois either.

Eva met had Lois in her first few days in London. Lois had come down to do the same kind of work. She was from Lincolnshire, out in the country among the sugar beet fields not far from the fishing port of Grimsby. "Not Grimsby really," said Lois, "closer to the Humber, near the watercress meadows. The name of the place is Barrow Haven. A tiny hamlet with only seventeen houses surrounded by fields and a wide, wide horizon."

Eva was intrigued, it sounded so different from her own open countryside with its chalk escarpments and cliffs and undulating hills. Lincolnshire was flat, with a vista of around ten or eleven miles, really as far as the eyes could possibly see. Lois got the hint of a tear in her eye as she told Eva about it over a cup of tea and a sticky bun in their break.

Eva had reached her hand forward across the blue checkered tablecloth to comfort her. She felt a tingle as their fingers touched. A feeling she had never before experienced.

Two nights later, they arranged to go for a meal together. Eva wore the green silk, the only formal dress she had taken with her to London. Lois appeared in a tweed two-piece suit, a white shirt with a man's collar and a woven tie in blues and greys. She wore lisle stockings and a pair of stout brogues. "My walking shoes," she explained to Eva. "My most comfortable attire."

Eva took this all in her stride. It was Lois's style, she told herself, and the fact that Lois had the courage to wear her own style in public made her admire the woman even more. She was six years older than Eva, but Eva was not in awe, just admiration and the beginnings of a touch of fondness.

On one of these excursions, they were spotted by Nigel and his cronies who asked if they could join them. Nigel began to whisper sweet nothings in Eva's ear, and Eva could tell that Lois was shocked by the way she announced, "Well we two are off to the Odeon cinema to see Mary Pickford in Baby Gladys, been nice to meet you." And with that, Lois gathered up their hats and coats and Eva followed her, just a little bewildered, to the door.

"The pictures?" she said, "I didn't know…"

"No," said Lois, "neither did I, but it should be fun yes? Just the two of us."

Afterwards, over tea in Lois's room, Eva said, "I danced with him you know,"

"Who?" said Lois.

"Why Douglas Fairbanks," said Eva. Lois shrieked with laughter, "Hush," said Eva, "You'll have Matron along. Yes, I danced with him in a jazz club. Nigel took me. It was the night everything went wrong and I left home."

"What was he like?" said Lois.

"Who? Nigel?" said Eva, "you've met him."

"No, you nincompoop," said Lois, "Douglas Fairbanks."

"He was all over me, whispering in my ear. His breath was quite smelly. Nigel rescued me and took me home. It was the night I had my first champagne."

"Golly gosh," said Lois. "I wonder if she knows what he is like."

"Who?" said Eva, "Mary Pickford? I wouldn't be surprised, but they were good in the film, weren't they?"

At Christmas, Eva was given leave to go home for ten days. "Oooh, take me with you," said Lois, "I'd love to see your countryside."

But Eva stood firm. "Not this time, Lo," she said, "I have things to sort out with the parents. I haven't seen them since I first left home. It could be awkward."

"I understand," said Lois, "I suppose I'll have to make do with flat-as-a-pancake Lincolnshire and nothing to do but a jigsaw in the window seat at home."

"Lucky you," said Eva, "there will be much work to do at mine, all hands to the wheel."

As she took the train from Paddington, Eva thought about what lay ahead. How would her parents receive her this time, she wondered if they would see a change. Eva had seen much suffering in the months she had been away. She had lived in a smoky, dirty city where the noise never stopped. She had met people she had no idea she would. And she was earning her own money. Had her own bank account and was planning for an independent future.

The lull of the train caused her to doze. She dreamed of Dorset, of celestial skies with clouds scudding across the rolling green hills down to the cliffs and the blue sea beyond. Of the mellow stonework of the pretty cottages lining the leafy green lanes, of the cows gently grazing in the fields. And of her parents and Grandma, in the warm kitchen smelling of fresh-baked bread and plum jam.

After many hours, when the train jolted to a halt in Weybridge, the sky was the blackest of black and all Eva could see in the window was her own reflection.

She alighted to find her father with Doctor Wilson waiting on the platform. She threw her arms around George without saying a word. "Alright my girl," said George, "I've got you, you're home now."

"Welcome home, Eva," said Doctor Wilson. "We have the car waiting and can get you home in style."

Eva was nothing short of relieved. She had dreaded the idea of a pony and trap. George laughed, "Indeed," he said, "if the good doctor here hadn't offered, you would have been going home on my cross bar."

They all laughed as they boarded the car and, with a quick crank of the motor, they were on their way. Eva peered out at the dark treeless lanes, the houses with no lights, the mud and puddles on the roads and the fact that there were no people about and no noise apart from the motor of the car.

"Quite a change for you, Eva," said Doctor Wilson. "You wait until you wake up in the morning. We are expecting snow tonight."

They pulled up at the house on The Tops well after midnight. A lamp burned in the front parlour window and at long last Eva felt like she was home.

Her mother and grandmother were at the door to greet her, give her hugs and kisses, George took her bag and the doctor said, "I'll be off now, Matson family. I'll no doubt see you on Christmas Eve, Aggie has quite a spread planned judging from all the stirring and baking that has been going on. I see my good brandy bottle has gone down a bit too."

He left them with the family's heart-warming laughter resounding in his ears. He climbed back into his motor car and trundled his way back home.

The following morning, Eva woke early. It was still dark, but she could almost feel the sun rising as the glow shining through her fine yellow curtains began to throw a beam of light on her bedroom wall. The light picked out the picture 'At Low Tide', a mermaid on the rocks just five miles down the coast where rock outcrops formed tunnels and arches reaching out into the sea. She lay back and studied the picture. It dawned on her that it wasn't a mermaid at all, but a nude young woman with red hair flowing over her shoulders and hiding her body, with the exception of her peachy pink arms and legs. She had a beautiful, sweet face, with blushed cheeks and small rosebud lips. Her eyes were the bluest possible. Eva lay back again and thought, 'why have I not seen this as it really is before?' It struck her then, and only then, that leaving Dorset and living and working in London had opened her eyes to another view of the world. Had she become more worldly then? This was something she needed time to work out. While she had been so busy working and surviving in the city, she'd had no time to really think about the world in which she was living. Maybe these few days at home would provide her with that space and time.

Eva heard the rattling of the kettle in the downstairs kitchen. She reached her toes out from under the eiderdown and found her bedroom slippers on the cold floor. She tip-toed to the window and flung open the fine yellow curtains to see the morning begin in the fields behind the house. There had indeed been a fine sprinkling of snow. The green fields she had dreamed of were dusted with white, just like icing sugar. The leafless trees stood bare and stark against the early morning sky.

She looked down and there, sitting on the handle of Da's garden fork, was a robin redbreast singing his little heart out.

Eva smiled. "Hello little fellow," she called, opening the window. She closed it immediately as she felt the icy blast against her flannel nightdress and hurriedly donned her big woollen dressing gown. It was in a beige plaid with cording around the edges and pockets. She tied it tight with the belt and crept down the stairs to see Grandma standing at the range. She crept up behind her and hugged her tight.

"There you are," said Grandma, "I thought you might be up first if I made a big pot of tea. I was going to bring you one up. I'll bet you haven't had a cup of tea in bed since you left home."

Eva smiled, "Tea in bed? Grandma, you have no idea. Life in the nurses' home is quite different. There is a kitchenette we all share. It works out quite well as long as someone remembers to order more milk from the milk float."

They sat together in a familiar silence. Grandma reached across, taking Eva's fingertips in her warm hand. "And you've been a good girl while you've been away? A good girl for your Mama and Dadda?"

"Grandma, of course. I have worked really hard, and I am always exhausted at the end of each shift. And in any case, I have been brought up to be good. Haven't I?"

They smiled together. "I just thought I would ask," she said, "because I know your parents are thinking it, but will not say."

The day got under way as George came into the kitchen scratching his belly and lighting his pipe. "George Matson, take that smelly thing over there and smoke it," said Grandma, pointing at the rocker on the far side of the range. "Young Evie doesn't want to get her beautiful curly brown hair smelling of your St. Bruno."

Eva was surprised. She hadn't thought anyone had noticed her hair in its marcel waves. She blushed. George grunted. "Marcel waves is it, where did you get that done then, some fancy beauty parlour?"

Eva approached her father. "Da," she said, "we have no time for beauty parlours. We are working in a hospital bulging with very sick children. We, the other nurses and I, help each other doing our own hair late into the night when we have finished our long twelve-hour shifts." But she put her arms around her father, "You can smell it up with your pipe smoke as much as you like, I have missed this smell of you, this smell of home. So much."

Grandma placed thick rashers of home-cured bacon in the frying pan and added freshly laid eggs from the chicken coop out the back. Amy came downstairs to join in the conversation. The eggs had rich orange-coloured yolks, mostly doubles and Eva was filled with a homesickness she didn't know she had. She began to understand just what home meant and almost regretted that in ten days she would have to go back to London.

Breakfast seemed to go on for hours as more and more fresh food appeared, bread cut into thick slices, spread with bright creamy butter. Plum jam, just as Eva had remembered and dreamed of, was in the middle of the table in a large blue bowl. Fresh pots of tea were made and the family didn't seem eager to move or get on with the day until Eva said, "What can I do to help?"

"Not much really," said Amy, "we have been busy for weeks preparing for your home-coming. We have been making mincemeat and Christmas puddings and cakes—but that still has to be iced," she added. "So there is something. Your father has to kill the goose tomorrow and let it hang. You probably won't want to help with that, will you?"

"And why not indeed," said Eva. "Whatever you need me to do, I will do."

The following day, Eva received a letter. It had a Lincolnshire postmark. "Who is it from?" asked Amy, shyly of her daughter. "Do you have a friend in Lincolnshire?"

"I do indeed Ma," said Eva. "In fact she wanted to come with me for Christmas. Here. But I said 'no, not this time,' I wanted you all to myself."

Amy nodded. "Aren't you going to open it?"

"Maybe later," said Eva, "we have plenty to do first." And with that she pushed the letter into the deep pockets of her dirndl skirt and carried on making the icing for the cake.

When George came in from the fields, Amy said, "Our Eva's got a lady friend in Lincolnshire, she's written a letter to her."

"She's a nurse with me," said Eva. "We work together. Sometimes go to the pictures or to a tea room when we are off duty. It's good to have a friend when you are in a strange place. Her name is Lois, and she started new, the same day I did. We have rooms in the same nurses' home."

On Christmas Eve the family were invited to Doctor Wilson's house. Grandma packed up a dozen mince pies and Amy wrapped home-made toffee in a cotton cloth. George had made a wreath from the holly and mistletoe in the hedgerow, and Eva had a picture frame in pewter she had bought in London for the doctor and his wife. Her way of saying thank you for all the help they had been.

They dressed in their Sunday best for the occasion. Grandma had her fox stole around her shoulders; it had little tails hanging all the way round and Eva remembered how her grandmother had allowed her to play with it when she was small. Such happy memories of her childhood kept flooding back, much more so now she was home again than when she was away.

The Wilson's front parlour was warm with a roaring fire in the grate and a table set with delicious delights. Sherry was offered to the ladies, but they declined and took a sip of plum brandy in small glasses instead. George was offered something stronger. At first he looked at his mother for approval, then at his wife, but both were busy talking with Aggie and

Eva about the latest recipes for the festive season, and so he said, "Why not indeed, kind sir," to Doctor Wilson who rejoined with, "It won't hurt you one bit George. Anyway, it's Christmas."

To the rest of the parlour Doctor Wilson announced, "We do have other guests coming, it will be quite a party, Aggie is going to play for us so we can gather around the piano later and have a good old sing-song."

For Eva, it was a Christmas never to be forgotten.

27. Amy

The day George took his stroke, Amy was away in Dorchester. She had an appointment with a specialist at the General Hospital arranged by Doctor Wilson, who took her in his car. Amy had been suffering from abdominal pain for some time and as she lost weight and grew more and more pallid, Doctor Wilson recommended her to the specialist.

After many tests and two nights in the hospital, Amy was released with a loose diagnosis of ulcers and given some peptic medicines to take morning, noon, and night.

It seemed fate that George should take his stroke while both his wife and his doctor were away and there was little Grandma could do about it other than cradle him in her arms and sing soothingly to him as if he were still her baby.

When Amy and the doctor arrived home, that is how they found them, an elderly woman and her ageing son cradled as if it was sixty years prior. George needed feeding and taking care of and there was no-one now to take care of the garden or the home. "I need to go and talk to Eva," said Amy. Doctor Wilson agreed, and made all the arrangements.

She sent a letter in advance, telling Eva that she would arrive on Tuesday at 8.05 pm at Paddington, and to please be there to meet her. Which she was. She had arranged a camp bed in her own room at the nurses' home with Matron's approval. Amy was glad to see her daughter, even in the sad circumstances.

Over cocoa, she told Eva what had happened to her father. She didn't tell her about her own health problems, just that she had left George in the care of Grandma, who was now of an age where she needed looking after herself.

"I'll come home, Ma," she said. "I'll need to speak with Matron in the morning, but I need to come home and see what we can do."

The following day after a breakfast in the little café on the corner, Eva left Amy wandering around the Army and Navy Store in Victoria and went for her meeting with Matron. "You've been such a good nurse, we'll be sad to lose you," said Matron.

"Oh," said Eva, "I hope I will be back, but I must see what I can do to help my parents, mustn't I?"

"Of course, my dear," said Matron. "Get your packing done, we will arrange for your things to be sent on, but we will keep your post and your room open until we hear from you."

Eva introduced her mother to Lois over lunch of bangers and mash. "Ma, this is my very best friend of all time. Lois. Lois, this is my dear mother."

Lois appeared distraught at Eva getting the handsome cab to the station with her bags and her mother. "What is the matter with her, our Evie?" said Amy, "does she always cry when someone goes away, doesn't she understand this is about family?"

"She's my best friend Ma, and I hers," said Eva. And left it like that.

The hospital was in trouble, and Eva knew it—but her priority was to her family. Before she left she said to Matron, "My newspaper friend Nigel has some ideas about the money side of things Matron, I will write to you once the plan is in place."

Matron had scratched her head. She had told all the nurses the week before about the penurious hospital board and the shortage of funds and cut backs. She showed that she had faith in her nurses and that as a team they might well find a short-term solution. They needed two thousand pounds. And that was a small fortune.

28. Eva

It was a shock for Eva to be away from the hospital, from London, from her friends, but mostly away from Lois. Back home with her family, a family in ill health, Eva soon understood that her nursing skills were of paramount importance.

With Doctor Wilson's help, a regime and routine of rest, medication such as there was, and good wholesome food, was what Eva needed to concentrate on.

And each day there was at least one letter in the post for her. While the family slept each afternoon between two and three o'clock, Eva read her letters. The first was from Nigel:

Dearest Girl (this always made Eva smile)

I trust you are well and that your ma and da and Grandma continue to regain better health. I know they couldn't be in better hands than yours and the good doctor's.

There is also that good healthy Dorset air and fresh food that will help. Oh, how I miss that salt sea air and the view of the far horizon over the ocean. And you dear girl too, how I miss you. (Eva smirked over this too)

Now regarding the huge problems that we are all facing back here in the big smoke. We may be getting somewhere. I have suggested to the editor-in-chief that we follow the lead of the Americans and organise an event that will swell readership and lift us out of the doldrums.

And if we do this right, it could be a big help to you—you may even be able to help your hospital, at least stop it closing for the short term.

To that effect I have enclosed a cutting from today's paper carrying the first advertisement.

I wish you were here, or I were there. It really doesn't matter. I don't see enough of you, you know that, we are each either too busy or out with other friends.

But remember this, Eva, my sweet lady, you are always in my thoughts,

Yours

Nigel.

Eva grimaced, 'sweet lady indeed' she muttered. Then she looked at the newspaper clipping.

Soon to be announced. A beauty contest. Open to any lady married or single. The forms will be available in this very newspaper next month. In the days and weeks to come, there will be details of what you need to do to enter. The prize will be substantial financially. Encourage your families and friends to buy the newspaper between now and then as you will need copies of every coupon in order to enter.

Eva could see Nigel's hand in this. She could see how it would encourage and increase sales. She wasn't sure how it involved her or how it could help the hospital, but she knew Nigel, and gathered he had it all worked out.

Her second letter was from Lois:

Eva, you are very missed around here, not least by yours truly. Matron has turned into a wildebeest, and I reckon it is all to do with threats of closure. They have turned off the heat now it is April and the poor little mites in Ward 11 are freezing as we need to keep the windows open for their lungs, especially now there is a tar boiler down the street. Matron is convinced it will help their breathing. I reckon they will die of pneumonia or something much worse.

Enough of troubles here. I hope your parents and grandmother are on the mend and that you are not wearing yourself out. Your old friend from the paper came sniffing around for you, so I told him you'd gone back to the country and that things weren't good at home. I hope that was OK.

And finally to me, I am bereft without you. With whom can I eat jam tarts at midnight? With whom can I make marcel waves?

When can I come for a visit? Matron says I can get three days off next month.

L x

Eva was touched. Sad and happy at the same time. Sorry that she was causing herself to be missed, but happy that she was. She resolved to write back to both Nigel and Lois, along with a note for Matron, that evening once the family was fed and bathed and settled again. But for now she could hear Grandma moving around in the back bedroom and hastened to put on a big kettle for a heartwarming and healing herbal tea. She pushed the letters into the pocket of her blue dotted pinafore, swept tendrils of hair behind her ears and patted where her marcel waves once were, and tried not to think too hard about the contents of the letters and her other life so far away.

As Grandma improved, she spent the late afternoon and early evening hours—what she liked to call the twilight hours—with Eva knitting. "You need to begin to get a few things made ahead of time," she said.

Eva looked at her quizzically, "Things? Time?" she said.

"Yes," said Grandma, "you know, for when you marry and when you have little ones of your own. You will need more knitted things for babes, I'll grant you. Here, let me show you a sweet little lacy stitch."

And so for reasons known only unto Grandma, and because Eva didn't want to upset her, they first made a matinee jacket for a new-born baby. The stitches seemed complex to Eva to begin with. Grandma drew them out on a piece of paper with squares and slashes and circles, indicating where the wool was wrapped over the needle and where to slip a stitch, thereby producing the little holes to make the look of lace. The complexities arose when the little holes needed to line up in the shape of a leaf or a diagonal line. Here Eva had to say, "wait a moment please, Grandma, I need to double check I have this correct."

Between them they made matinee jackets, leggings, bonnets and mitts, bootees and little coats enough to clothe twenty babies, and Eva had a good notion as to where these knitted jewels would be most useful. But she decided to go along with Grandma for the time being.

"Do you think he will ever ask?" she said.

Eva replied, knowing full well to whom Grandma was referring. "Who?"

"Why the young fellow from the paper, Nigel Thomas, do you think he will ever propose marriage to you?"

Eva laughed the loudest she had laughed in weeks. "Oh Grandma, Nigel and I are friends. And friends only."

"Oh goodness, my girl, you are blind. There is a saying that men and women cannot be 'just' friends'. You know he has affection for you."

"And I for him also, Grandma, but not like you think. We have similar minds, we enjoy similar things, but in London he has his own friends, and I have mine."

"But isn't that a letter from the same young man, peeping out of your pinafore pocket?" said Grandma.

Eva explained what was going on in the world of economics in the big cities of the world. "And London is no exception," she said. "Places are closing down for lack of money. The newspapers are in trouble and even the hospital may have to cut right down on things to save money."

"My word, our Evie, you have gone up in the world, knowing about such men stuff. But I admire you, girlie, for understanding what makes this world tick. The wars have a lot to answer for, they may well have created an industry in armaments and military clothing, but I think the place wouldn't be in the mess it is in now if there hadn't been the wars, I pray there is never another, they say the Great War was the war to end all wars, but when you have men at the helm who knows what foolish ideas they'll get. I reckon us women could teach that Mr. Stanley Baldwin a thing or two. Don't you?"

Eva nodded in acquiescence. "I think we should be able to vote along with our menfolk, then we might have a say in who gets into government—that's what I think," said Eva.

Together they folded the knitted baby clothes and added them to the trousseau. "They are beautiful," said Grandma, "you have such fine hands and do fine work Eva, it's a pity you never learned the piano."

"It's never too late Grandma," said Eva, "maybe one of these days I will learn."

29.

As spring turned to summer and George and Amy were more and more able to get out and sit in deck chairs on the lawn, so did their health improve and Eva began mentioning the possibility of returning to London.

"Maybe in June, if you keep up like this," she said.

It was early when Lois came for a visit. Eva had warned her parents and Grandma that there was to be a visitor, "It is my nursing friend from London," she said. "Actually, she is from North Lincolnshire, she has never been to countryside like ours before."

Grandma shook Lois by the hand and said, "Welcome, young lady. Any friend of our Eva's is a friend of ours. We have a fine Dorset spread ready for you, Eva will take your bag upstairs."

Amy and George seemed excited to meet their Eva's best and truest friend, they had heard so much about her over the months. It had been 'Lois says this', and 'Lois does that, and this', they recounted over tea and scones with cream and plum jam. All home-made of course.

Lois showed them her good manners. They had difficulty at first understanding her Lincolnshire accent, but Eva translated and, all in all, it was a jolly time. "I've been saving these for you," said Lois and produced a large manilla envelope with newspaper cuttings. "Nigel said I should bring them down to you."

Eva took the envelope and peeped inside. "Of course, I thank you."

"He says he will be down on Saturday. To take the photographs, and you should wear something nice."

Eva looked quizzical, as did her family. "Me? Something nice? What on earth is he referring to?" she said.

"Why the beauty contest of course, He reckons you will win the two and a half thousand pounds."

Grandma began choking on her scone at the sound of the money. George went red in the face at the sound of the beauty contest. And Amy sat there speechless and let all the commotion go on around her. Their peace had certainly been shattered with the arrival of Lois.

"I think you had better explain all this to us," George said to Eva.

"Dadda, I have no idea at all." she replied, "I know that companies and businesses are trying these things to save themselves from bankruptcy, and the hospital may close through lack of money. I know Nigel has had this notion for a while; it has worked in a small way in America. But I have no information about that kind of money whatsoever. Can we wait until Nigel gets here on Saturday to explain? Please?"

Eva has been doing a spot of reading on beauty contests—the pamphlet was tucked in the envelope from Nigel with a short note saying, 'E, read this first, it will give you the background'.

It was dawn before Eva found a moment alone, and, in the garden listening to the spring and the dawn chorus of blue tits and thrushes, she pulled the pamphlet out of her dressing gown pocket. Before opening it, she looked across the gentle, rolling slope towards the sea. The surf was breaking softly as it often did in the early morning, just as it did in the evenings when the moon was coming up. Eva breathed deeply and thanked God for all the mercies he had shown her: how to use her head, how to use her talents, how to avoid being manipulated. She wasn't sure why that one popped into her head—but she was sure it had some meaning on that morning.

She looked down at the glossy pamphlet in her hands. On the front was a drawing of a girl in a very revealing bathing suit. Eva shuddered, 'Oh Nigel, what have you got me into now?' she whispered.

Inside was packed with information. How the first beauty contest in America was in 1880 to promote a seaside resort. The original idea was that of P.T. Barnum, the chap who had the famous circus. 'Hmmm,' was Eva's reaction to that.

But she went on to read how it was all part of a cultural change, how women were beginning to care more about how they looked as a result of watching films, just like the ones she had been to with Lois, and she thought she could understand a little, as the following day she and Lois had gone out and bought lipstick and rouge.

She then read that a newspaper had held a beauty contest about twenty or so years earlier, when she was just a little girl, but they were stalled because it was difficult for the newspaper to reprint the photographs. And then it dawned on Eva—why of course— this was right up Nigel's alley. She could see now why he he'd been pushing for it. And that the intention would be for the general newspaper reading public to be able to vote on their favourite and result in a winner.

Nigel had added more notes inside, saying that the beauty contest he had persuaded the paper to run with would not be a bathing suit style contest. That was for the rags of newspapers, not a quality weekly like his. Nigel's paper was renowned for being a little on the upper crust side and read by lords and ladies and gentlemen's clubs.

And that gave Eva a touch of concern, the idea of pictures of young women circulating gentlemen's clubs. Would it make young women vulnerable? All these thoughts were flickering through her mind like the dragonflies that were skittering across the pond, to and fro as if they had forgotten something and were turning back for it, whatever it was.

Lois crossed the lawn in her stockinged feet with a tray on which she had balanced two cups of tea. "Saw you out here all alone with your thoughts," she said, "I hope you don't mind."

Eva smiled at her friend, "Why should I ever mind," she said, "when the person you think more of than anyone in the world shows up with tea at six a.m. How could I ever mind? I wouldn't mind if it were three in the morning."

They sat together in silence. Lois reached for her hand and their fingertips brushed, then they pulled away and laughed. "Watch the thrush," said Eva, "see how he takes the snail and cracks the shell on the rockery stones."

"Amazing," said Lois, "and what a beautiful song. We have thrushes in Lincolnshire, but at six in the morning I'd probably get my head blown off out at Barrow Haven. The wind seems to come in from the North Sea. Which, I might add, is as grey as steel, not this lovely inky blue like yours."

They sipped their tea and looked out to the sea. "Let's go to the beach later," said Eva. "Once I have everyone settled. Just you and I, we can take a picnic. Ma won't mind a bit. She will never forget the day Nigel took us in the car."

At Nigel's name Lois looked a tiny bit crestfallen, "Are you and he...?"

"Lord no," said Eva, "whatever gave you that idea? Nigel and I are good friends from our school days. He bounces ideas off me sometimes and I him. That kind of friend. He did take me to a jazz club once. That's what got me into trouble, the night I danced with Douglas Fairbanks."

"Eva Matson, you are quite the girl," said Lois. "One day you must write a book about your exploits and dedicate it to me. After all, I have just suggested it."

"Right," said Eva, "I will, one day before long, I will begin my book, but it will be fiction. A novel but based on my life. I will call myself Virginia. Virginia Welland. How about that? I will go into great detail of how I learned to drive an automobile when I was just fifteen years of age."

"There you are you see," said Lois. "You'll have plenty to write about, and a whole chapter about Douglas Fairbanks and his smelly tobacco breath."

The two women were roaring with laughter when Grandma called from the kitchen door, "The bacon is in the frying pan, you two hussies, laughing and cavorting on the lawn in your nightclothes and bare ankles. Whatever will the postman think?"

Lois and Eva linked arms and skipped across the dewy lawn to Grandma, their cheeks flushed with fresh air and the joy in each other's company. Their conversation still buzzing in their heads with thoughts of what their future could hold.

EPILOGUE

Where to begin? I think starting at the end is best. At least you'll know I'm still alive. Although, according to family stories, Uncle Arthur, when he was a boy, wrote in his school composition, 'and then I was dead', which begged a question—one that always had the family laughing.

I am here now, rapidly approaching 70, in our villa in Cyprus, sipping a Keo beer by the pool.

It was Lois's idea for me to write this. Poor old Lois. She's been gone a few years now, leaving me with her dog, a collie called Ben. He reminds me of Lois if I look at him in the dusk, a few whiskers sprouting from his chin, big brown sad and liquid eyes. His coat on top is roughed up and never tidy. And when he runs through the villa, the whole place shakes as in an earth tremor (and we've had a few of those.)

And it was Lois's idea to retire to Cyprus; she had a family friend who had been stationed here with the army and we came for a holiday, and noticed some lovely places being built with sea views and swimming pools and we said, 'why don't we?' and the answer was 'why not?" So we pooled our resources and when we turned 60 and got our first pension payment at the post office, we each packed a small bag, and well, that was it really. A life of sun and sand and ice cold beer.

Grandma would turn in her grave. Actually, Grandma would have turned in her grave multiple times if she'd known half of what happened to Lois and me.

We made a handsome couple. Our friends and colleagues joked that we really should have gone to the Greek island of Lesbos, much more appropriate, they said. We took it all in good part, and so did they; nurses can be like that, empathetic, understanding, and they make allowances for people being different. I was convinced that quite a few of the elegant British and American men around, and some Swedes too, had some pansies among them. I didn't like the term pansy, but it seemed to be used a lot.

It was a worrying time, to say the least, for people in those years, with Enosis and Eoka making it hard to feel very free, as much as we wanted to, and we did think that a Greek island could be what we'd have to move on to, but we hung on, as did many of the others, and eventually things sorted themselves out. It also made the villa really inexpensive as the 'trouble', as it was called, put a lot of folks off and houses were hard to sell. We learned the Greek language, which helped, and dressed in simple cotton shorts and shirts with sandals. A far cry from the silk cocktail dresses of my early years.

And it was beautiful. Away from the noise of London, and into the sunshine, with fresh oranges and lemons, fresh eggs, wonderful grilled red mullet. The grapes were delectable; small seedless Aphrodite grapes. Cyprus was known as Aphrodite's birthplace, and we could see her rock in the sea from the terrace of the villa. The rock. Where she was supposed to have emerged from the sea. Aphrodite, Goddess of Love, Cyprus, the island of love. An island for lovers.

I miss Lois in our big double bed the most. The bed where we curled around each other and held each other gently until we fell asleep. And when we woke each morning, we looked into each other's eyes and said, 'your turn to make the tea,' and laughed, because that is what love is, taking turns to make the tea.

When she knew she was dying of cancer, she told me that she wanted her remains to stay here, where we had been happiest. Mainly because we felt so free. One day, I took her ashes out in a little fishing boat with Andreas put-put-putting his motor as slowly as he could, around Aphrodite's rock, and gently let her—my Lois—float away in the gentle evening breeze into the sea where Aphrodite had once risen. I imagined that one day Lois would rise again, just like the Goddess of Love. Imagination is a wonderful comfort sometimes, isn't it?

It was almost like losing her again, letting her ashes go, but I'd hung on to them for two years, and it was time. Afterwards I walked with Ben along the shore. I wore my best embroidered Cypriot skirt and sang into the waves, 'My bonnie lies over the ocean, my bonnie lies over the sea, my bonnie lies over the ocean, so bring back my bonnie to me…' Ben howled and so I imagine he was missing her too and understood what it was all about. I threw him a stick and, like a good, well-trained collie, he brought it right back and dropped it at my feet. "Just us two now, old chap," I said. And so it is.

But Lois suggested I write about anything that popped into my head, anything to give you an idea of what a full and interesting life I had, not just with Lois, but on my own too.

We were apart for quite a few months in the early fifties, when Lois volunteered for nursing in the Korean War. I think she thought I'd go along too, but Ma was really ill and I stayed home and nursed her. Ma was alone in the world by then, and it was with much trepidation I waved Lois off on the troopship. She looked different in her Qarancs uniform. She was a Queen Alexandra's Royal Army Nursing Captain. A captain, I assumed, because of her wealth of experience—in her career she had specialised working with amputees, and it seemed (sadly) appropriate that she should be snapped up. "The pay is good," she said, "I'll have nothing to spend it on, so it is going into our special retirement fund for you and me."

Because that is what dear Lois was like. Always thinking of us both and our future together. She wrote often and told me about the miserable conditions, about her colleagues, and about the amputations she had done that day. But she also told me about the wonderful local people, and that she had bought paintings to adorn our retirement place when we eventually did really retire. The paintings are here now, hanging on our dining room wall. All reds and golds and vivid blues. Each time I look at them, I see something new. A new dimension. A different form. Ever shifting like the sky. Or the sea. I understand why she bought them, but at the time I thought it was frivolous. Paintings were not something Ma or Da went in for. Their house could be what was called, 'austere' at the time. But comfortable. Plain. Homely. Home.

Lois brought back other things too. Fabrics which we made into curtains and cushion covers. I say we; it was me, Lois couldn't thread a needle if her life depended on it. So how she stitched up her amputees, I am not sure. I suppose being a captain, she probably had an assistant to do it for her. The textiles are wondrous. Deep blues with gold threads. White, as white as pearls, with silver threads. As curtains they are drifty and when the evening breezes begin, in front of the open windows, they waft and dance as if they are alive. Mesmerising. Most evenings now, I sit with Ben at my heels and watch Lois's curtains dance until the moon comes up, and the breezes drop and they are still, once more, until the next day.

It took me a long time to move some of Lois's belongings out. But her shoes and clothes I wear myself, we were the same size if not the same taste. Lois's clothes were more like boys wear: practical, robust. She didn't go in for pretty. So I wear them now, I can see why she preferred them—you can do all kinds of things wearing trousers and shirts, that dresses and blouses would not allow for.

There are some other things I couldn't bear to part with. Her collection of postcards and letters. Mostly from me. But also from our old matron in the London hospital. If you put them all together in chronological order, they tell quite a story. Maybe one day if I need something to do and there is nothing on FBS wireless, I will do that. But for now they are stacked in shoe boxes at the top of the wardrobe.

Nigel came for a visit last month. Nigel Thomas, my lifetime good friend. As young children, we ran across the beach together, chasing the snipes. We gambolled like spring lambs over the grassy hillocks before the dunes, hiding, finding, laughing. And he was, and still is, a very good confidante. He knew about me and Lois without me saying anything. Of course Nigel is a 'man of the world', being in the newspaper business all his working life.

He went to university after the grammar school, just like I went away to nursing college. So apart from summer and Christmas holidays, we didn't see much of each other, and we made new friends from further afield. But at the end of the day, at the end of a phone line, and in air-letters from exotic places, there was always Nigel.

I was full of gratitude and delight when he sent me one of those exotic air-letters from Tripoli, I think it was, saying he was here in the Middle East and how would I like company for two weeks. 'Don't write back. If you are not home, I'll find a hotel', was what he had written. So I didn't write back, but I did get some new pillows for the guest bed, and a striped bedspread in gay colours to brighten things up a bit. The guest room had become a dumping ground, and so I rescued our record collection and got those sorted out too. All ready for playing in the evenings.

He arrived late on Friday, all duffle bags and camera cases and tripods. His hair was still thick and wavy, hanging over his eyes and halfway down his back in a ponytail. Still the newsy corduroy sports jacket and cavalry twills, I noted, without saying anything. But I knew a good little shopkeeper in Paphos who would soon kit him out in a pair or two of khaki shorts and some Aertex shirts.

"I thought you were in North Africa," was my second sentence after, "Oh my giddy aunt, it is so bloody good to see you, Nige."

He laughed and explained he had stopped in Tripoli on his way back from New Zealand, where it was winter. You see, he knew I was referring to his heavy non-summer clothing; I didn't have to tell him. That is the way it has always been with us.

After dropping his bags he scooped me off my feet and carried me through to our big comfy sofa with its cool cotton covers, plonked me down saying, "Evie, old girl, I hope you have something cold ready for me."

The Keo went down a treat along with the little dishes of peanuts and olives. "We are eating out tonight. Celebration," I said.

"Celebration?" he looked at me, raising his left eyebrow as always.

I laughed, "Yes, I've written that book," I said. "If Larry Durrell can do it, so can I."

He picked me up again and whirled me around the room. Ben crouched in the corner. He hadn't seen such activity for months. Not since the Christmas party.

We ate down at the seafront at my favourite restaurant. The tables were at the water's edge, across the road from the main restaurant. All the seafront tavernas are like that here. Waiters had to keep nipping between cars to cross the road with trays of food and drink. It was, and still is, all part of the charm.

"So how are you, Evie?' he said.

I knew what he was asking. "She has gone," I said. "But she is still here, very much here." I patted the empty chair between us. "We had a good life the pair of us, but yes, she is gone."

"Have you thought about going back?"

"To England?" I knew that was what he meant, but it seemed a good way to fill a space. A silent gap. A quiet that would say even more. I looked out at the bright blue and white-painted fishing boats tied up at the wharf. At the octopus dishes being brought across to the restaurants. At the children at the next table eating pistachio ice cream out of tiny glass bowls with miniature silver spoons. I loved the fact that children could eat at restaurants at night here, not like England where children had to be seen but not heard and made to stay home with babysitters.

"Not yet," I said. "Maybe not ever. Lois is here." I pointed out to sea.

He understood. He said nothing but reached his hand across to mine and our fingertips just touched.

"I'll have to come more often," he said.

It was a beautiful evening, and as the sun went down and we drank local white wine, and ate those tiny pearl grapes, I said, "Come as often as you would like. Stay as long as you like, I would most certainly love that."

"I'll hold you to that," he said.

Coffee arrived in too-small cups with a glass of water on one side and two squares of Greek Delight on the other. We took our time. We watched the moon over the water, not noticing the activity behind us; the waiters were clearing tables more rapidly than when they brought the dishes—dashing across the road with plates piled high, no doubt so they could swing their legs across their bicycles and get home to their families. They worked so hard.

We sauntered back up the hill along the dusty lane. It was nothing like Dorset with its lush greenery. Paphos is dry, dusty and hard baked. Tomorrow I would take Nigel to The Tombs of the Kings.

We talked, Nigel and I, in the two weeks he stayed with me last month.

We talked about Ma and Da. And Grandma. "You know she became a widow the year I was born," I said.

"That doesn't make sense," he said. "What on earth do you mean?"

"Grandpa was executed for desertion. It was the Boer War. He had got lost by all accounts, according to his mates. He tried to rejoin them, but when he found his regiment, they reckoned he'd run off as a coward. Grandma told me that Grandpa was never a coward. Why, he was one of the first from the village to go off and fight. Anyway, it all happened round about the time I was born."

"That must have made it hard for Grandma to celebrate your birthdays," he said.

"Not a bit of it," I said. "Grandma said she wouldn't let the army or the war destroy that, too. They had already robbed her of her husband."

'I had no idea," said Nigel. "Do you still have his squeeze-box?"

"No," I said, "it disintegrated in the end. I don't think it would have survived this hot weather anyway. Lois bought me a new one before we left England." I showed him the case in the corner of the room, but didn't open it. I will one of these sunny days. When I am alone. I will.

"I'm glad you came to the funeral," I said. "In fact, you came to all of them. Lois, Ma, Da, and Grandma. You are the best friend a girl like me could wish for Nigel Thomas."

He laughed then. "And we were both there for Doc Wilson's, do you remember?"

"How could I forget," I said. "We all went to the pub afterwards and raised a glass to the good doctor. Look how he helped us though. When I ran away from home, where did I go? Why Doc Wilson's, of course. I'd say that was a major turning point for me. I would never have gone up to London. Never met Lois. And look at you, too."

"Yes," said Nigel. "He supported my desire to get into a bigger national daily. 'Follow your dream, young man,' he said to me." Nigel smiled then. "Funny how we went to the big city at the same time. I reckon people thought we were a couple, you know, courting, even then."

"But even before that, tongues wagged, didn't they? Do remember Douglas Fairbanks? How you saved me?"

"I do indeed. He was quite the ladies' man, you know."

"Oh, I know now what his reputation was," I said. "I don't know how Mary Pickford put up with it. Anyway, his breath stank of stale tobacco, goodness knows how actresses got on, kissing him in the films."

And this was how we reminisced over those two weeks during Nigel's visit, one thought trickling through to another like a tiny babbling stream. Filled with pleasant thoughts and memories, just babbling on with glasses of wine, good fresh salads, and lots of locally grown fresh fruit.

Nigel relaxed during those two weeks, too. The frown went from his forehead and the pink went from the rims of his eyes. He told me how he'd been many nights without sleep, how the story he'd been sent to cover had gone haywire and it was a fruitless journey. And he told me how he longed to stop.

"Stop? You?" I couldn't believe what he was saying. "I never thought I'd hear the words, I thought you would want to go on until you dropped."

"Being here with you has made me realise there is probably much more to life than work and making money. I could still write, but mostly take photographs. This island fills me with inspiration."

"You are the best photographer I ever knew," I said. "Do you remember the beauty contest?"

"Remember? The beauty contest? How the hell could I ever forget," he spluttered.

Nigel had come up with this idea that if his newspaper ran a beauty contest, it would serve two purposes: it would boost sales, as the readers would be the ones voting for their best beauty. And the prize, if I won, could help me save my hospital.

He'd bowled up in his latest automobile one sunny morning, announcing that he had come for the shoot.

"Shoot?" I'd shouted, "we've had enough of shooting around here." And then laughed because I knew that he was talking about a photographic shoot.

Lois was with us. Ma made me put on my new embroidered blouse she'd made for me, after Nigel informed her it just needed to be head and shoulders for the first level of entry. And he sat me with sheets draped all at the back of me, covering over the bookcase and the dresser in the front parlour. 'Plain background,' Nigel said.

He rolled off three full films of portraits. Took a few of Da and Ma and Grandma, and Lois too, 'just for fun,' he'd said. Those are the photographs I have here with me now in silver frames, in pride of place.

"Yes, you were always a good photographer," I said. "You always said a picture speaks a thousand words."

He laughed. "Never a truer word. I'm thinking of a book of images. Just regular people going about their business, in the fields, at work, at play, and not just people—look at the blindfold donkey going around the well, this could almost be biblical times. You gave me the idea last week when we were at the tombs. You said you'd never seen any postcards or photographs of the tombs. I dare bet there are wonderful places like that all over the island."

"Food for thought, eh Nigel old chap," I said.

"Indeed Evie," he replied. "In fact, if I wire my editor on Monday, I might be able to pick up an assignment here, and that will kick the entire thing into life. The Times publishes those kinds of books too. This may well be the solution."

"I had no idea you had a problem," I said.

Having Nigel stay made me think about the years gone by; of the splendiferous times we had in the early days of the automobile. Of picnics and jaunts. Of course, more recently there was the time Lois and I bought the Morris Minor. It was green and didn't go particularly fast. But we trundled around England for three glorious weeks.

She took me to Lincolnshire, a county I had never visited. I had come close with Leicestershire and Nottinghamshire, but Lincoln cathedral stood out like a distant monument from about ten miles away as we moved along the A46. You just couldn't not see it. It was like a guiding finger, pointing into the sky, but also telling us, 'Come on ladies, cross that border and experience this beautiful city.' And it was beautiful. We found a hotel close to the cathedral. It was a shock of course when the bells struck midnight, but we'd had that when we were in Bath, and Durham, and all the other cathedral-close hotels we had stayed in on our bi-annual holidays. In those days no-one questioned two women sharing a room. There were no raised eyebrows or, what is that saying? 'nudge nudge, wink wink!'

And it was fun to snuggle together in big four-poster beds, whose springs squeaked and timbers groaned, but we made a point of hunting places like that, and it was always Lois, my clever Lois, who wrote ahead and made the booking.

The George and Pilgrim Hotel in Glastonbury was a fabulous place to stay for a week. With its ancient hallways and secret passages. It was built in the 1400s, The George and Pilgrim is the oldest purpose-built pub in the South West of England. Situated in Glastonbury, it is steeped in history and old tales.

The building has a panelled stone frontage, mullion windows, and old oak beams. Unusually, for those days, the rooms had en suite bathrooms and televisions. Plus, the luxury of being able to make tea and coffee in the room meant we didn't rely on room service. In the evenings, we would bathe together, neither of us were too heavy to both fit into the George and Pilgrim's generous tubs, using Badedas bath foam—'things happen after a Badedas bath'—remember the old slogan? Well it really does work, so after the bath we would sit, Lois and I in the comfy velvet chairs sipping wine, and telling each other tales of our pasts, the pasts when we were not together. Then we tumbled into the very impressively draped four-poster bed.

The bar was always inviting, with its little nooks and crannies, and often stayed open late for residents. There was also a superb restaurant with an à la carte menu, offering succulent homemade food.

Our many trips were memorable. Over the space of ten years we drove that little Morris Minor not just around England, but also to Scotland. We took a ferry to the Isle of Skye, and I remember Lois softly singing The Skye Boat Song. Speed bonnie boat like a bird on the wing/Over the sea to Skye. The words, 'Though the waves heave/soft will ye sleep/Ocean's a royal bed/Rocked in the deep…' stay with me to this day, and I hope Aphrodite's Rock also makes a royal bed, so soft will she sleep.

It was the first time I had heard her sing. She knew every word. I was entranced. Others on the boat stopped chatting and listened too. At the end, she received a small ovation. I was so proud of her.

After the Isle of Skye, we went on to Lochmaddy on the Outer Hebridean Island of North Uist. Approaching the island we could see the tiny white croft houses with their walls made of thick stone and the roofs of wood and thatch made from straw or rushes. When these houses were built, people had to use whatever materials could be found locally, and often wood from old boats was used. They had just one door through which both people and animals went into the house. I understood that people from the mainland thought it strange that islanders lived with their animals, but it was, apparently, the way of life.

We stayed for three days. Unforgettable days. We couldn't understand the language most of the time, but we got into the swing of it. And we found that the roads were very narrow and on the rare occasion when we met another vehicle there was quite a palaver to pass, but it happened with much nodding. Mostly we talked, it seemed that Lois and I never ran out of things to talk about. We were both in our mid-fifties by then, yes, it was 1955 and we began to talk about early retirement and where we would like to be. We did look at one or two crofts for sale, as we did like the solace offered by the Outer Hebrides, but at the end of the day, it wasn't very warm, even if it was September, and in spite of the really fair prices, we were not tempted.

"We'll find somewhere," said Lois with confidence. "The right thing will show up, just you see."

By the end of the three days, I understood what she meant. North Uist was simply lovely for a visit, but not for us year round. We saw where they had made the film Whisky Galore, with Gordon Jackson, just a few years earlier. It was one of the Ealing Comedies we'd seen when it first came out. We went to the pictures a lot—it was always our staple night out when we were working dayshifts. Tea at a Lyons Corner House followed by the 7 pm showing at The Odeon. Anyway, North Uist and Benbecula hadn't changed at all, and you could just imagine the antics and goings-on. Lochmaddy featured in the film quite a lot—well, it would—it was where the boats came in. Benbecula was a little different. It had been a landing strip in World War II and held its own secrets behind barbed wire.

The journey back south was tiring. We shared the driving, but I suspected Lois was having trouble with her eyesight because we were just about half an hour before Loughborough in Leicestershire when the accident happened. We had taken our time on the return journey, stopping a night in Glasgow, and a night in Carlisle and again in a little village in Yorkshire not far from Hebden Bridge. We'd stayed up late that night, drinking in the after-hours-for-residents' bar in the White Horse. So maybe we were just tired and even slightly hung over.

By 2 o'clock the next day we were passing through the Midlands and I have no idea where the tractor came from. It must have just pulled out of a field. I was dozing off as Lois was singing The Skye Boat Song again to me. Jolt is the wrong word for what happened. There was an almighty bang, and I opened my eyes to see Lois slumped over the wheel of the Morris.

It was no good screaming; sound wouldn't come out. I could see the blood on her forehead and I thought then, that I had lost her forever.

The interminable waits at the hospital. The weeks of recovery. I made arrangements for Lois to be transferred to our own hospital in London, and then to a convalescent home for her recovery, but as soon as she made sense, it appeared my lovely, stubborn, confident Lois was still in there somewhere. "Take me down to Dorset," is what she said.

I was surprised; I thought she might want to be in Lincolnshire, but no, she loved my home village. She loved the sea air and the coolness of the dewy dawn grass. We sat out there many mornings on the old bench in front of the old empty house that was now mine.

It took six months for Lois to return to her normal convivial self. "Where do we go from here," I asked her as we sat on the old bench as we had always done.

"I think," she said, 'I think I'd like to go in search of sun and sand and sea."

"Isn't that what we have?" I said.

"It's getting cooler," she said, "especially in the early mornings and evenings. I remember a place…" She drifted off, her eyes closed, and I was worried she might have a relapse—the damage to her brain was, apparently, all healed and she could pursue a normal life, they'd said.

"A place?"

"I was there with the Qarancs," she said. "Another Island, you know how we love our islands, Evie."

I smiled then and thought about our island adventures, and how the last one had resulted in disaster. The accident.

There are hints of wisdom from the penetralia of the mind. And Lois's mind was a mine of little secrets; I'd always known that. It was one of the things I loved about her.

Three weeks later, an airmail letter with exotic stamps arrived for her.

"We'll open this together," she said, "I will let you in on my little surprise."

The following month, we took the Cyprus Airways flight to Nicosia from Blackbushe, just outside London. The night before we stayed in London at The Regent, and went to the pictures, to the Odeon one last time. We saw The Seven Year Itch with Marilyn Monroe. And afterwards we went out for dinner. It was a special night, so we chose a Cypriot restaurant in Charlotte Street. Lois wanted us to get into the spirit of our destination.

The waiter was smashing. He was attentive and when we told him where we were going he said, "You must say hello to my parents. They are in Famagusta." We took down the details and smiled and nodded. Only to discover that nodding meant 'no'. It was a night to remember, and later back in the hotel, Lois said, "We will remember this holiday. I hope you will write about it in your book."

"Book?" said I. What book?"

"The book you will write very soon," she said.

So this is what happened. We landed in Nicosia, after a flight lasting ten hours. It was about 120 degrees in the shade. I probably exaggerate, but everything sizzled. And was so dry and brown.

Lois's nursing friends were there to meet us in a battered old Land Rover and we drove for what seemed like hours to Larnaca. These girls were nurses at the British Military Hospital (BMH) in Dhekelia. They lived at the nurses' home there, but had found us a nice little seafront hotel to stay in for our two weeks.

They were grand lasses, but soon got the message that Lois had been through a bit of a bad experience, and eventually left us to a peaceful time, occasionally dropping by to take us on excursions.

Fig Tree Bay and Aya Nappa still resound with me. We donned our homemade cotton bathing suits and swam in the Mediterranean with the tiny fishes. The water was crystal clear and calm and, each day, I saw more colour return to Lois's face. Then back came her smile. Soon she spent almost all her waking hours beaming.

"Should we talk about money?" I said one evening as we sipped our brandy sours under a vine-draped pergola.

"I was waiting for you to bring that up," she said. "And tonight is as good a time as any."

There was a silence, not unusual for us, we often had pauses for thought during conversations that were of importance. "You like it here, don't you?" she said.

"I love it, Lo," I said. "I especially loved our road trip to Paphos, and it was so good to spend two nights there and really get to know the locals, too. Kantara was nice, in the mountains, but I always love being able to see the sea, don't I?"

"I know," she said. "It is important to you. Look here."

And out came a bundle of papers. With details of small villas for sale. All in Paphos, all with views of the sea. The prices were unbelievable. "Do you mean what I think you mean?" I said.

And so the following day we went back to Paphos. We stayed three nights. We changed our return tickets back to Blackbushe to make it all possible.

We looked at eleven houses. They were very similar in as much as they had marble floors for coolness in the hot summers. They had two bedrooms, one bathroom and everything else was pretty much open plan.

The one I loved the most had a walled courtyard at the back. It caught the early morning sun, and the evening shade. Bougainvillea rippled over the walls. There was a lemon tree in the front garden and from the sitting room, through the picture window, was the most expansive view of the sea. The Mediterranean glittered in the afternoon sun and reflected rays of light across the entire room. The house was approached down a narrow dusty lane. All the other houses were occupied by local people. In one back garden was a donkey. I was sold.

"Can we?" I said.

"I reckon so," Lois said. And I could see that this was her favourite, too.

We had to return to England to sort out the finances. We found ourselves a good Cypriot solicitor to sort out the legal side of things in Cyprus, but we also wanted our own solicitor in Dorchester to have a good connection with him too.

The house, now referred to as a villa, is in Spyrou Kypriano Avenue. Not on the beach, but with that wonderful view. We didn't really want the beach, we could walk, it was only about five minutes. And we got ourselves a couple of tricycles with boots on the back for our swimming stuff. It worked well. People probably thought we were crazy.

Back in England, it meant I had to put my house up for sale. It felt like a huge leap of faith. Huge. I was letting go of everything that my family had worked for, for generations, selling it to buy a house in a foreign land. It was frightening. Scary. Lois didn't quite get that, she had never owned property. Like the majority of the population in the 1950s, it was more common to rent. But I was parting with Grandma's house. Her's and Da's. Side by side. The agents thought selling both together would get a much better price—but I was having second thoughts— maybe, just maybe—I should retain a foothold back in the old country.

In the end, I didn't let go of Da's house. I wanted to come back from time to time—and I wanted that safety net. It left the finances lean, but Lois had a good pension from when she served with the military and we both had our nursing pensions. It was tight, but we managed to buy the house in Cyprus without applying for financing.

But I'm getting ahead of myself.

***

I nursed them all in the end. First Grandma, then Da, Ma not long after, and finally, back here to nurse Lois. She didn't want to return to Lincolnshire, but to stay here in Paphos.

Grandma was determined, as with all of her life, to be in control. She moved back into her own place after living with Ma and Da for years, while just popping in to her own for a bit of dusting.

But it was old age for Grandma; a woman who had seen more than most. A woman who had held her own counsel. But a woman who was not afraid to speak her mind. "You've done so much with your life, young Evie," she said to me. I reminded her that I was not so young. "You'll always be young to me," she said.

"And you've done so much to help people, especially the poorly children in London. Remember all the knitting? I thought one day you would have babies of your own. Instead, you had hundreds of other people's babies. And all the layettes you and I knitted together. All those little bootees and bonnets for the prematures. It was something we did. Do you think it helped?"

"Of course it did," I said. "Some of those tiny babies would have perished without them. They are now grown-up people, out in the world. Some of them write to me even after all this time."

And they do. I receive a postcard or a letter now and again. One young man is a teacher in a school for deaf children. Another is a small star on the stage, but going places, from the reviews. It does make you realise that you might have made a tiny difference.

I nursed Grandma until, one afternoon, she just fell asleep and didn't wake up. She looked peaceful in the hand-knitted shawl with the intricate stitching we had once worked on together. She still had a blush in her cheeks and a slight smile on her face. I hope she died remembering good times, of Grandpa playing his squeeze box, and Da coming through the door with the Christmas tree, his eyes shining with excitement. And no memories of the wars she had lived through.

I went back to London to work at the hospital once the funeral was over. Then the letter came from Ma. 'Can you come home for a week or two - it's your Dadda, I think he is getting sicker.'

'Getting sicker?' I wondered why she hadn't told me he was sick at all, but I said nothing when I arrived. It sounded like his lungs had flared up again. I don't think he ever really recovered from the TB during WWI. It left him with a weak spot and somehow in the past few weeks he had picked up a cold. Doctor Wilson was no longer with us. He had passed on a couple of years before and it was a new young doctor with new ideas. I was always open to new ideas, and she came up with these things called antibiotics.

They seemed to help to begin with; the coughing subsided after a week, but it left him with no strength. He slowly got weaker until he said to me, with difficulty, "I can't go on, our Evie. You take care of your Ma."

By dawn the next day my father had died. The death certificate said, 'lung disease' and it was about right. But I know my Da, and he just couldn't fight things anymore. And so I was committed to staying with Ma until things settled.

My hospital was good about things. 'Leave of absence for family reasons' was granted, and I stayed with Ma. Grandma had left me her house and so I got it ready for Lois's visits and visit she did. Almost every weekend.

Once we had Ma settled in an evening, we sat in Grandma's house—to which I had moved many of my possessions, paintings and books and records. It was starting to look like a place of our own. Grandma had taken good care of it, but it was cold in the evenings with just the fireplace. Lois stumped up the cash to have central heating put in and that caused quite a furore in the village. 'La-de-da' they called us, but they were just joking. Everyone in the village was always so kind and thoughtful.

We took Ma off on holiday. She had never seen mountains, and so we took her for a week to the Lake District. It was a trip of a lifetime for Ma. Of course Lois had stopped driving after her accident and so we used the train. It was a good service and we could sit back and enjoy the passing countryside. We had to change in Bristol, but on Lois's suggestion we stayed overnight at the station hotel and took some time to explore that pretty city. With the boats moored and the grand esplanade. I think Ma was mesmerised. She said, "I am beginning to understand why you two travelled around the country so much."

It was nice for her to say that. In the Lake District we had a hotel right on the edge of the water, looking across to the hills. We sat out on the verandah and drank tea, and ate cream cakes, and marvelled at the scenery. It was good to see Ma get some colour back in her face. "You know you have to go back to work," she said one evening, the night before our return to Dorset.

"I suppose I do," was my reply. "When you're ready."

"I'm quite ready," she said, but there was a look of uncertainty on her now rosy face. Ma had never lived alone, and this was going to take some getting used to.

The solution lay in Grandma's house. As much as I loved having it for my own little get-away with Lois, I thought it would make a good holiday let. On our return, Lois and I packed up our personal possessions and advertised the house, leaving Ma with the job of greeting the holidaymakers on a Saturday afternoon, cleaning after them when they left, and generally taking care of the place.

Ma thrived on the job. She took to it like a duck to water. She discovered new friends and made a cake each Saturday morning to put in the pantry next door for the holidaymakers' arrival. She made sure there was fresh milk and butter and eggs, along with tea and coffee. And soon the property got a reputation for being most desirable. Ma had a purpose.

Lois and I popped down every few weeks. On our last visit we noticed Ma getting frail. It was Lois who saw it first. "Do you see how thin she is getting?" she said.

And I must admit I hadn't. So I called a halt to the holiday let. I didn't advertise anymore and, while we still got enquiry letters, they slowly dropped off. I stayed with Ma but whatever was wrong was something she couldn't stay home with; she was admitted to Dorchester General with a form of dementia and slowly declined until she didn't know who I was. I still sat by her side each day, going home to the houses at night. Lois came whenever she could and then stayed to see things through with me. We knew, from our nursing experience, that Ma wouldn't come home.

We stood in the cemetery four months later and looked at the stones all in a row. Ma and Da side by side and then Grandma. No-one really knew what Grandma's name was. The stone said, 'Grandma Matson - she saw it all'. And so she had. She had lived through wars and suffered their effects, first losing her beloved husband and then, World I—to end all wars, made her son so ill.

Lois and I placed our flowers and walked slowly back up to The Tops. We sat out on the old wooden seat, took off our stockings and shoes and let our bare feet feel the damp evening grass. We held each other's hands and looked far out to the horizon. To the whitecaps. To the cliffs across the bay.

I suppose that was my most major turning point. It was just a few days later that Lois suggested we take the holiday to Cyprus.

It had been a long time since anyone had mentioned the beauty contest. But the following day there was a piece in the paper. And there was my picture from 1925. Lois brought the paper in with the milk and put it on the breakfast table. "You're in the news," she said. "It's been an age since you made the papers."

I'm not sure who wrote the article. It was fairly accurate though. It recounted the financial state of the country at the time and how companies needed to come up with a ruse to increase sales etc. It quoted Nigel as the bright young man who had come up with ideas, and yes, there was his picture, a little grainy, but certainly a young Nigel Thomas. "I wonder where he is now," Lois said.

"Nigel? Oh, he is in the Far East I think. He keeps in touch. Always has. He does more photographic journalism now. Makes good money."

Lois cut out the article. It went into detail how I had won the national contest and how the prize money was huge. Enough to buy a row of houses but stated how, instead, the children's hospital was saved with the money. It added that Nigel's newspaper was also saved from ruin as many more people rushed to buy the paper each week, to see who had been put through to the next round and to vote for their favourite.

A whole page devoted to people in the area who had made a difference.

***

Nigel's here. He arrived about a month ago. He decided Cyprus suited him, and it was time to step back from all the travelling and follow his heart. He is taking wonderful photographs.

We have had one room converted into a dark room. Yes, of course he has moved in with me. What did you expect? We are lifelong friends.

It wasn't a big decision. We talked one night, drank quite a lot of wine I must admit, and then it was all settled. He needed to go back to England to sort out his affairs there and put many of his belongings into storage. "You don't need to do that," I said. "I've still got the house."

It is all about sharing now. We each do our own thing. I am writing, as Lois always wanted me to, not under silly pseudonyms though, and Nigel is out on shoots and then in the darkroom. Yes, he has his publisher and is pretty certain they will publish my next novel too. He produced the newspaper clipping, like a rabbit out of a hat, at the presentation he did. You know the clipping from the local paper that I told you about, where both Nigel and I were purported to have made a difference. That.

We've framed the clipping. It hangs on the wall beside the portrait Nigel took of me for the beauty contest, and the photos he took of Ma and Da and Grandma, especially the day we went out in the automobile to the beach. There's a beautiful photo of Lois looking strangely demure. And a whole series of Lois and me on the wooden seat, rippling our bare feet through the dewy grass. Excellent black and white photographs with the driplets of dew spraying. Our mouths open with unabashed joy. Our eyes sparkling just like the dew on the grass in the evening sun. We are wearing bathing suits with great abandon. It is a picture of pure happiness.

There are few photographs of Nigel himself. But there is one of him and me when I won the beauty contest. Me clutching the giant cheque and Nigel a glass globe for his achievements in bringing the newspaper back to life. He has his arm around my shoulder. I am wearing the green dress. The one I wore at the jazz club.

And it reminds me of the points in my life that caused it to run the way it has. If I hadn't learned to drive the ambulance, and then the automobile, Nigel wouldn't have connected. If he hadn't taken me to the jazz club, I would never have had that foolish skirmish with Da and stalked off, leaving home. But I did. I went to be a nurse and then met Lois. It all changed from there on.

I still drive around Paphos and beyond. And yes, I have a little green Morris Minor. Nigel has bought himself a secondhand Riley with a running board and a walnut fascia, very debonair. He has taken to wearing a white panama and a linen jacket atop his baggy shorts. I have had him teach me how to use one of his cameras, so there will be more portraits of him to add to our wall.

Nigel also has Reverend Jones's cedar box. Left to him in the good vicar's will. The box with all the messages left at the village stone, written by villagers with hope. One day we might look through them and then lock them up for good.

We have also become very uxorious with each other. A geniality that has only come about because we have known each other for over sixty years. A true and honest friendship.

***

I have supper made; it is my turn tonight. Oh yes we have divided the chores equally. Quite novel for this day and age, I think. He should be home soon. Parking his Riley beside my Morris. He will pat the cats as he comes in. Two tabbies also called Riley and Morris. Well, why not?

We lost Ben, the collie, some time ago. I miss old Ben. But he was Lois's dog really, and he grieved when she died. He lost weight and one night, without a murmur—because he was never any trouble at all—he just never woke up. His ashes are with Lois's in the waters around Aphrodite's rock. I see the rock now as I look up away from my typewriter. Aphrodite stands proud in the turquoise sea; a pillar of hope. A sign of perpetual love.

I put a record on the turntable, the soundtrack from the musical The Pyjama Game. It is just one of our collections of the most wonderful musicals. We catch a couple each year when we make our annual trip to England. When we always spend our first two nights in London. We've seen almost all of them: The Flower Drum Song, At the Drop of a Hat, West Side Story, Candide, and My Fair Lady. But The Pyjama Game has remained one of our favourites.

While in London Nigel visits his publisher, and I visit the National Portrait Gallery and think again how a portrait can tell such stories. I look into the eyes of the sitter. I see sadness. I see anticipation. I see joy. And I see a life that has been lived. All captured so well by the painter or photographer. It makes me understand why the portrait Nigel took of me won the competition. It didn't show a cocksure beauty. It showed I had lived through many things by the time I was only twenty-five. I have Nigel to thank for capturing me at that time of my life, a time when I had no idea what was to come. He continues to add to the collection he calls his 'Eva Works'.

If I've timed things right, as Nigel comes through the door the track, Hey There, You with the Stars in Your Eyes, should be playing. And he will take me in his arms and swing me around the dining room floor, and I will remember Douglas Fairbanks, and the night at the jazz club, all over again.

I have chopped a tasty salad of our own homegrown tomatoes and cucumbers which we will have with some grilled red mullet caught just this morning. The Keo beer is in the fridge and the nuts are already in the bowl on the coffee table. I will ask him all about his day.

And he will ask me about mine.

- end –

Photo courtesy of Stuart Bailey

ACKNOWLEDGMENTS

My thanks to the late John Marshall for sending brown paper parcels over many years. And for the specific package from which dropped Eva's wonderful, mysterious photograph. For all the additional kind generosity, eternal thanks.

To National Novel Writing Month 2015. That was when Eva was first drafted. This story, and others, wouldn't exist at all without the motivation of NaNo every year since 2006.

Thank you to Sally and Sally's Mum for shedding a little light on Eva and the Dorset connection, and for the thumbs up for me to write Eva a fictional life story. My thanks, too, to organisations that find homes for retiring racing greyhounds. Without our Nelly (RIP) who lived out her retirement with us, and the connection with Sally (who also homes retired greyhounds in the UK), there wouldn't be this quite extraordinary coincidence.

I write, for the most part, without conscious thought and thank Canadian author, playwright and poet, Susan Musgrave whose workshop all those years ago left its mark.

To the literary journals and magazines around the world that gave, and continue to give, my work homes over the years, that's the best validation a writer could ask. Thank you.

A giant thank you goes to my writer family: the members of the international online writing group, Pens Around the World.

Thank you to my loyal and oh-so-honest alpha and beta readers: Kat, Elke, Vicki, Marg, Pam (RR), Pam (S), Kimberly, J.P. Vincent, Bruce, Joan, Sally, and Catherine. Your eagle eyes, especially with the new reading glasses, are remarkable. And invaluable. Forever grateful.

In an odd way, I feel the need to thank the person(s) who documented the memorial stones in the churchyard at Chickerell. Tripping over the document on the internet, late in the re-writing of this story, renewed my determination to complete Eva.

To my flag-waver-in-chief, Vicki, for the hours, nay—days, weeks, and months when you've been there for me, extinguishing my doubts, cheering me on, and making me laugh. Non-stop showerings of love for you.

None of my books would exist without Arne. My loving thanks for your support, encouragement, astuteness and love. And for dragging me off down the coast for fish and chips when you knew I just needed a break.

To Summer for saying 'yes' to my novella proposal, based merely on Eva's photograph and my enthusiasm, thank you. And thanks always to all the team at Unsolicited Press for turning my manuscripts into books. For making them hand-holding real. And for making the entire book creation process an absolute joy.

And finally, thank you always to this peaceful corner of the world, where thinking, observing, dreaming and creating can happen.

Fishermen's Fingers

a novella

For Elke and Kat
my sounding boards

Author's Note

National Novel Writing Month (now known fondly, around the world, as NaNo) is an event where writers of all ages and genres write their hearts out in the thirty days of November. There is no time to plot, write character studies, consider settings, research, edit, rewrite — all of those good disciplines normal to a writer.

No, the idea is to bravely bash out around 2,000 words a day, and to enjoy the liberating feel of writing mostly without conscious thought. Letting the story have its head.

I have done this every November since 2006. Fishermen's Fingers is one of three novellas I wrote during NaNo 2018. It was indeed written without conscious thought, this story bears no resemblance to characters or places — it's all fiction.

*

ACKNOWLEDGEMENTS

To all the good folk at National Novel Writing Month, without your continued commitment to the project, this story would not have been written. To the international writing group, Writers Abroad, your support keeps me motivated and inspired. To the eagle eyes: Kat, Barbara, Chris, Laura, Elke, Kimberly and Pam. I do thank you for your spotting of all my blunders. To wonderful small fishing communities along this coast and to all fisherfolk, who put to sea before dawn in all weathers to put food on tables, you and your families deserve medals for bravery.

To Summer Stewart and all at Unsolicited Press, you have turned me from a writer into author. Thank you.

And to Arne. You keep our home ticking over through those November writing indulgences, and the rest of the year during my writing hours. Thank you for making all things possible. And for the stories about the pig in the liquor store and the drunk ducks.

Red sky by morning, sailor take warning.
An ancient rhyme often repeated by mariners.

Miss Watson stood before her class of ten-year-olds and moistened her lips. She needed to warn them. It was her job. She looked at their faces of innocence, at their lack of street-wisdom, at their trust and acceptance in every member of the fishing community. She looked at the empty chair on the back row. She began to tell them about Betty. And why she wasn't in school today.

CHAPTER 1

BETTY SITS ON the bank contemplating her parents' discussion around the table last night. She kicks at the skeleton. She knows it was a porcupine from the shower of quills along the gravel edge. She toes the curved spine, perfect in its formation and wonders what kind of brain was once in that small skull.

Alongside the spread of bones is an unmoving chickadee. "Must've been hit by something," the ten-year-old murmurs, reaching down to stroke its minute head of still-silky but dead feathers. She touches its beak, smaller than a grain of corn.

Betty remembers last night's heated talk then. About the poor crop. How there'll be no money for anything. How Ma said she'll go back out West and take Betty with her.

How Pa said, "Over my dead body."

There's peanut butter sandwiches for supper, "Ain't no money for more," says Ma, but gives Betty a sideways grin, "Lift the corner of the tablecloth," she whispers, "when Pa goes out to the tavern."

Betty's not stupid, she knows the correlation between not enough money for food and Pa going to the tavern but keeps her own counsel. She's learned well from the best; her ma, who learned from her own mother. That was before Nanny went to jail for shooting Kenny who wouldn't let her play the spoons in Hank's band—but that's a whole 'nother story.

It is past six o'clock before Pa leaves and Betty is getting real anxious to lift the corner of the oil cloth with its faded blue flowers among the rubbed-off green. But as Pa swings his rough brown coat from the peg by the back kitchen door, she is ready with her mouth watering.

Ma has left her the latest copy of the story book magazine Betty collects. This week there is a free notebook inside the packet too and a small red ready-sharpened pencil. 'Write Your Own Story,' it says on the cover of the magazine. On the front of the notebook it says, 'My Story by dot-dot-dot.' That is the place for Betty to write her own name.

She wonders if she should use a pseudonym—she knows what that is — just in case people recognise themselves in her book and come after her. 'Nom-de-Plume' is what her teacher, Miss Watson, called it. 'French' she'd said. 'Pen Name.' Betty liked that idea and carefully printed on the cover of the notebook. 'Elizabeth James.' She'd heard that sometimes lady authors take their husband's first names as their nom-de-plume last name. And as Betty's full name is Elizabeth and as she dreams her one-day husband will be James, then Elizabeth James had the most perfect ring to it. That's what Betty thinks anyway.

CHAPTER 2

THE NELLY-MAY PULLS away at dawn. The bay is flat-ass calm and 'I'll be at the traps before the rest of 'em,' thinks Lenny as he lets the Nelly-May have her head. She's an aging lobster boat and belonged to an old man, that was Murray, the only person to ever really believe in Lenny. To give him a chance. The licence and boat got willed to Lenny when Murray died. That's how they did it then.

He sees the sun come up — well part of the sun. There's an eclipse today and for Lenny that could mean trouble. He knows he has problems working stuff out, but this eclipse is something else and he understands it. The sun rises above the horizon like a red scimitar, blade pointing off at 2 o'clock. The absolute stillness gives him a chill, he's felt it before, years before when he's done things he later knew he shouldn't.

Like taking young Florrie Henderson into the woods and making her take off her knickers while he watched. Drooling, playing with himself. Watching her shiver and sob like a small defenceless animal. He didn't touch her. Not once, just himself until oh joy, he came onto the soft carpet of moss, over and over, while she shut her eyes and held tight to her pigtails as if they would pull her out of her nightmare.

When he was done he told her, "Sort yerself out you wicked child," and dropped her back on the hauling road so she could walk home, "say anything and I'll tell about your wickedness," he said.

He heard no more, Florrie's mother came to the wharf often when the boats were coming in and bought lobster from him. Never said a word. So it must've been OK. Florrie was sent away soon after, he heard, to a special hospital for the nervous. Well, she were a bit edgy, again he tells himself, if only she'd just stood still and let him see without him having to be so bossy, she needn't have cried like that. He didn't much like the look of her dirty knickers either. Dirty child.

There'd not been an eclipse since then — not here anyway — 1993 was it? he can't remember. That dirty little Florrie must be all growed up now. At least twenty anyway. He doesn't know what happened to the rest of the family. Moved away, they said. Lenny felt nothing when he heard that. It was nothing.

There have been times when he'd needed dirty little Florrie and was pissed off that she'd been sent away. He wouldn't have given her a two-dollar bill if he'd known she wouldn't be around for long. Money wasted.

There is a stillness over the water that is uncanny. No sign of life at all. No other boat as the water turns from peach to purple to aquamarine. No dolphins breaking the water, no sharks, no whales. He sits back in the wheelhouse with his first beer and unzips his pants.

Chapter 3

IT'S 'SHOW AND TELL' at school today. Chrissy has brought in the teddy bear her nanny has made for her. It is knitted in yellow itchy wool with a black stitched nose and purple buttons for eyes. They've been stitched on with green wool that make crosses. The kids laugh and Chrissy is about to cry when Miss Watson produces balls of yarn and knitting needles for everyone.

She puts one ball and two needles before each child. "Now how do you make an animal out of those?" she says.

Everyone looks at her with open mouths and even wider eyes. Todd Matthews holds up his hands. "We could take them to Chrissy's nanny for her to show us," he says.

"Good suggestion Todd, but no," says Miss Watson, "we will begin to learn ourselves. Together."

She shows the children how to make the first stitch by putting a loop over the needle and tying it in a loose knot. They all copy her. She walks around the classroom, checking that they've done it before continuing with 'binding on' as she calls it. This is where they need to add 9 more stitches to the needle to make ten in total, by using their thumbs, they loop the yarn over the needle, pull it not too tight, then continue on.

She has to put a few back on track. Ronny has let his ball of yarn fall and roll across the classroom floor picking up dust and grit as it makes its way between the table legs, but Betty picks it up under hers and begins to wind it, hands it back down the line until it's back with Ronny. He grins and waves his needles in the air.

"You must always respect your knitting needles," says Miss Watson. "Rule numero uno."

The children all laugh. Miss Watson often uses interesting ways of reminding them of things. Numero uno means it is important and they all remember that.

As they sit with ten stitches on their left-hand needle, she continues to show them how to knit a row. One stitch at a time, "Just like life," she says, "one step at a time, a good life lesson."

The children count out loud as they knit their first row. Ronny finishes last. But at least he finishes after getting mixed up around 7 and 8. He finishes with a, "Whoop - TEN."

The class applaud him. Miss Watson gives him a button for his achievement. "When you've finished making your animal," she says, "this will be his first eye. The animal will be what?"

She looks up at the class. They look at the ten stitches on their knitting needle. "Not a teddy bear then?" says Ronny.

Miss Watson opens her desk and brings out a scarlet sausage dog. It has black as coal button eyes and little dumpy legs. The class all gasp in unison, like when the school bus slows down with that unique noise.

"The piece we've started with is a leg, we have to make four of them before we do a body and a head."

"And a tail," calls out Betty from the back row.

The class cheer because Betty doesn't always say too much.

Miss Watson hands Ronny a bright blue button. She tells him that it will go perfectly for his sausage dog in his pale green yarn. "He will be a blue-eyed puppy dog," she says, "you'll need to give him a name."

The rest of the class then go forward to Miss Watson's desk to pick out their own first button. Betty picks black for her pink sausage dog which will be a girl puppy.

"Now keep your eye buttons very safe," says Miss Watson. "And put your needles and yarn in your backpacks, safely at the bottom. Take them home but bring them back on Monday. Now we'll have our Friday afternoon story."

Chapter 4

LENNY LEANS AGAINST the bar. The tavern smells of old fish, wet woollen clothing, tobacco of many kinds, and talk that would make their grandfathers blush.

But for Lenny it's where he feels most at home. There's a comfort in the smells. It is dark and woody. The bottles don't shine too bright. Everything has an amber glow to it when he's had a few pulls on his weed. And all is right with his world.

He guesses people know that he has weaknesses. He's only been arrested a few times and only because of people's complaints, he has never been charged. Kept in the jail overnight a few times which has never bothered him. He gets a free meal and to watch TV which he can't normally do as he doesn't have one himself.

There is one in the tavern but it's usually set to the sports channel, sometimes the news. Lenny isn't interested in sports unless it is darts. And he doesn't give a shit for the news — he says the media folks are manipulative. A word he has picked up recently when listening to some of the women shopping in the grocery store. They'd been talking about the president of America.

Lenny doesn't give a chickadee's dick for America. Or for politics either. But he keeps his own council until he's had a few more beers and rum chasers. Then he lets it all out and look out anyone who's around then. Sparks will fly and Lenny's language is off the wall.

But for now he leans against the bar and thinks about his day. How he watched all the little kids come out of school with their book bags. How they clambered up the high steps onto the school buses. How he wishes he could have helped lift them up, especially the little girls. With their pink tee shirts and tight leggings around their tight little bums. He thinks about what they have for bum cracks. And how he'd like to wiggle his fingers there and then taste them.

"Another one Lenny?"

"Wha…?"

"Beer?"

"Yup," he says with no manners. They know he doesn't use manners at all and accept him for what he his — or what they think he is.

He wants to knock this beer back and head out to the other side of the bridge. Where the school bus turns. Where the last of the little kids get off and saunter back to their nice warm kitchens with their wood stoves and their moms having milk and cookies all ready for them. Where they'll turn out their homework onto the kitchen table and their loving moms will lean over and point out what they should write.

Lenny never had a mom like that. And he never rode a school bus. In his day you walked from the orphans' home to school in all weathers rain or shine. You got there and had to bring wood in for the stove, empty the slop bucket before you even learned to write your own name. He hated school. Hated the teacher who used a cane to whack them for the slightest thing. That man struck Lenny every day. Every day he promised that one day he would get him.

He was thirteen when he cut the brake cables of the teacher's car. When the guy disappeared into the lake that was the water supply, drowning in the ice and algae, "Good for 'im," Lenny told himself.

No-one was ever held responsible. 'Came off in the ice on the bend, accidental death,' they'd said.

"Good riddance," said Lenny.

But the damage was done. Lenny was broken as a child and from then on was a broken man filled with badness that no-one could repair even if they'd known. Some said a good woman would sort him out. But what good woman would want anything to do with the snarly man who didn't take care of himself? Never bathed or shaved. Never washed his clothes and got all of his nutrition at the tavern, or his weed supplier or at the still he'd set up himself in the middle of the wooded land that he'd won years before in a bet.

It was a lucky bet really. Lenny came in right at the end and the other guys had turned to him and said, "What card do you think it is Lenny?" Lenny had picked out the Jack of Spades. The result: 28 acres of dense woodland with a single-track laneway leading in. He'd let the laneway get overgrown so no-one would ever find it. Never find him, if he ever wanted to take himself off for a bit.

And never find out what he really got up to when he wasn't out fishing.

Chapter 5

BETTY IS FILLED with excitement about her knitting project and rushes off the bus and through the gate at the entrance to their farm lane. She's wearing her pink rain boots, which is just as well as the farm lane is muddy most of the time.

Her mother is baking molasses cookies, if there is one thing Betty likes more than ice cream, it is molasses cookies. She smells the ginger and the brown sugar as her mother adds to the eggs and flour. She watches, her mouth watering, as her mother spoons the batter onto the cookie sheet.

"Ten minutes," says Ma, "they'll be hot, but if you start your homework you can have two, one for each hand."

Betty thinks this is a perfect day all around and empties her backpack onto the kitchen table. Out rolls the ball of yarn and the knitting needles.

"Ooooh," says Ma. "You're learning to knit, good for Miss Watson, it is a good thing to learn you know, I knitted for years until my arthritis took over. You'll let me do a little, won't you?"

Betty nods. Slowly as if she's not sure she should let Ma do her homework. But she's excited to make her sausage dog and counts slowly as she knits her first row at home. "One... two... three..."

"What will it be?" says Ma.

"It's a sausage dog," says Betty, "Ma, what really is a sausage dog, is it like a hot dog?"

"In a ways," says Ma, "I think that's why the hot dogs are called Weiners. A Weiner is a German dog that has a long body like a sausage, and four little legs. We had one once when I was little. His name was

Solly, I don't know why. My ma named him I think when Pa brought him home. Pa won him in a raffle or something. maybe something to do with a card party he was at."

"Can I call mine Solly too?" says Betty. "Can it be a girl's name? My sausage dog will be a girl."

"I don't see why not," says Ma. "People use all kinds of names now, just look at pop singers."

Betty hums along with her knitting, "four...five...six... what a pretty Solly you will be."

CHAPTER 6

LENNY IS AT the tavern talking to Chrissy at the tavern's side-line pizza counter. "My poppy had a pig once," he said. Chrissy takes little notice of Lenny. She's well aware Lenny has no family whatsoever. That he makes things up to entertain, to get free pizzas and beer.

"He was at the liquor store with his brother Mel. They'd just bought the pig. A baby pig it was."

"That's a piglet," says Chrissy who finished her grade 12 before working at the pizza counter.

"Right," says Lenny, "a piglet then. Cute little thing it was, I was maybe seven or eight years old myself."

"Piglet," says Chrissy, under her breath.

"Anyhow," says Lenny, they took the little pig into the liquor store with them, they didn't want to leave it in the back of the truck, case someone stole it."

"Right," says Chrissy, aware that the rest of the clientele were listening in to Lenny's story now.

"Pops, and his brother, my Uncle Mel were drunk as always."

"Ya don't say," says Chrissy, rolling her eyes, but aware that the story was holding the interests of the entire pizza place.

"Well, by the Jesus didn't the little pig get loose in the liquor store," says Lenny, cracking a grin, showing his brown teeth. Eyes shining as the folks began clapping.

"You should have seen them," he cackled, "Pops and Uncle Mel chasing around the aisles of rum, the little pig running faster than either of them, squealing at them."

The folks round the pizza counter were laughing out loud now, cheering and clapping. "Buy the man a beer," says someone.

"Right," says Chrissy, "s'pose it's worth it for a laugh." she pours a tall glass of cold Coors Lite. Lenny's eyes light up even brighter.

"I have more stories about the old days," he says. "Shall I save them for another time?"

"You do that Lenny," says Chrissy, rolling her eyes, as she pushes the glass towards him, wondering if she'll need to disinfect it when he's gone.

Chapter 7

"CAN I GO outside and play?" says Betty. "I've done one whole row Mom, that's ten whole stitches."

CHAPTER 8

LENNY IS IN the coffee shop. He orders a Boston Cream doughnut and a double-cream, double-sugar, coffee. He removes the lid immediately and takes it to a seat in the far corner, away from the gaggle of giggling white curly-headed shoppers. He's no time for these gossipy women and he knows full well how they don't like him, with his raggedy beard and his long greasy hair. His dirty fishy clothes and black fingernails.

He slurps his coffee and his old friend Billy joins him. Billy in his dirty donated jeans. 'Birds-of-a-feather,' whisper the gaggle of grey-haired grannies in the opposite corner before getting back to their knitting and their current victim of gossip.

"You told 'em the story of the pig, I hear," says Billy. "You haven't told that one for some time."

Lenny grunts. "I don't know what kicked me off," he says, "but you know what folks are like, everyone sinking into their beer, no-one talking, thought it might liven things up a bit."

"You should tell the one about the choke cherry wine and the ducks next time," says Billy, "They'd like that, especially in the tavern."

"You remember that?" says Lenny.

"Sure do," says Billy, "I could've bin there miself, seen the ducks all laying on their backs with their webby feet in the air, happy as pigs in muck."

"It did for them though, din it?" says Lenny. "All those poor ducks went into someone's supper that week. Apparently they tasted good, very moist and not one bit fatty."

Billy nods. He remembers now. It was his story really, he'd told it to Lenny, how his ma was angry at the boys. How they'd filtered off the wine and were told to take the remnants, all the bits left over and put them in the burn barrel. How they'd done no such thing. How they'd tipped all the old berry skins out onto the lawn in back of the house, laughed and run into the barn to watch through the tiny broken window as the ducks waddled out. Cackling with excitement at a new treat.

"You wus just kids though," says Lenny. "You didn't know them ducks 'd git drunk, did ya?"

Billy nods. Then shakes his head. It's a Billy thing. Generous with giving Lenny his stories. But he's a fence sitter. He'll answer yes and no to most all things. He did get into trouble that day. Got a good beating from his father. Those ducks were to be the family's income for Christmas. They had orders for ducks that year and it would be another month before they were ready to be killed and sold. Now there would be nothing.

Lenny remembers Billy first telling him about that Christmas. How here wasn't much. Potatoes and turnip for dinner. That's about all. He'd hoped for a trumpet. Wanted to play like Louis Armstrong. He'd practiced his voice over and over, got the growl just about right.

But Billy never did get a trumpet. Never learned to play an instrument. He'd only ever told Lenny about his time as a boy. The only time Lenny ever saw him with a tear in his crusty eyes.

Lenny saunters out of the coffee shop, kicking at stones like a ten-year-old would. He is sixty and never been loved, not really loved. And never had anyone to love in return.

He sees young Betty playing in her front yard in her pink boots. He leans over the fence. "Hi Sweetie," he calls.

"Go 'way," she says, "Ma says I mustn't talk to strange men."

"I'm no stranger Sweetie, am I? I'm a good friend to your old uncle Billy."

"Oh," says Betty, "s'pose that's OK then. I'm learning to knit," she says, being polite as her mother always told her. "I'm knitting a sausage dog at school. That's a dacksoond or something," she says.

"Do you want to see some real puppies?" says Lenny. "I can take you and show you."

Betty hesitates. Then she hears her mother calling her in for supper. She leaves Lenny at the fence, "See ya," she says, to be friendly. She waves and Lenny sees her little pink boots plip-plop across the muddy lawn and into the back kitchen of the house he has never been allowed into.

Billy pulls over in his beat up old Dodge. "Ya wanna come?" he says.

"Where ya goin'," says Lenny.

"Liquor store," say Billy. "They are opening today for cannabis."

"Right with ya," says Lenny, "Mebbe I'll git me some."

It is the first day of the Cannabis Act. It has caused somewhat of a stir with users, dealers, non users and the medical profession.

Lenny and Billy park the truck what seems like miles from the normal parking lot. The line-up at the liquor store is right around the block. Some folks are still in their pyjamas. Some are in shorts with bare chests. It is October. That's still summer for some folk. There are people in business suits. There are women in stiletto heels. It is a complete cross-section of humanity.

By the time Lenny and Billy get to the counter which is in a separate section with a toll gate inside the liquor store, there is not much left. "We have the oils," says the clerk. "What do you need the cannabis for?"

"This ain't a question we've ever bin axed," says Billy in his best voice, trying to stop two of his teeth falling out of his rotten mouth. "We just like it."

Lenny says, quite out of the blue, "For pain, for relaxation when we're stressed."

"The oil is best," says the clerk, "you can order it online."

Billy looks at Lenny. "On Line. Dja know what that is?"

"Here, says the clerk. I'll show you." She walks around to the client side of the counter and opens up her screen.

"Ahh like TV," says Billy.

"I'll give you a card with a number," says the clerk, as it dawns on her that she's fighting a losing battle with these two. "If you go to the library, or even a school computer lab, they can show you how. Well, maybe not a school, you have to be over nineteen, so there'll be no computer access there." she adds.

Billy and Lenny return to the truck each with a little plastic card with a scratch panel on the back. Apparently, they've been told that is their unique number with which they can order online.

"Well, that weren't much good, were it?" says Billy.

Lenny nods as Billy shakes his head. "Let's go to the tavern," says Lenny, "we don't need to go to a computer for that."

Chapter 9

BETTY AND RONNY got married last year, both twenty-two and both so sure of what they each wanted. Needed.

Ronny brings Betty breakfast in bed. Toast with her favourite marmalade made by his mother each winter. They have to make six bottles last a year — "that's yer quota," Ronny's Ma told them, so go easy. "If you want to make marmalade cakes, you'll have to get it from the grocery store."

It's not been easy for Ronny. He helped Betty through her trauma from when she was ten years old.

She still doesn't say much about it. But she hangs on to her little pink sausage dog that she was making at the time. He is pink with brown eyes. The black buttons were lost in the mud. Miss Watson had the rest of the class share in the finishing of Betty's sausage dog after Betty was found back in the woods by the big rocks. When all they'd found to start with was the ball of yarn. It was the ball of yarn that led the search party to her. Crouched beneath a rock. Unable to speak. Unable to cry out. Unable to move.

Beside her was Lenny. Blood congealed across his face. One of Betty's knitting needles sticking from his eye. The other from his throat. Billy sitting beside him, crying like a baby.

The search crew had never seen anything like it. They all had counselling afterwards that went on for weeks. Betty's counsellor tried in vain to get Betty to talk.

But she never has.

Ronny spreads the marmalade for her. The toast is just how she likes it, with real butter, not Becel. Her doctor has monitored her progress and Betty has responded well, but twelve years. Twelve years of nightmares. Twelve years of learning to trust. Twelve years of Uncle Billy still coming to visit Ma and Pa.

Betty immersed herself in learning very soon after it all happened. Home schooling was not an option so Miss Watson visited three times a week and set Betty assignments. Guiding her through a curriculum that would set her up for university.

The community held fund raisers. What happened was on the conscience of many townsfolk. 'We should have seen the signs,' they said. 'We could have done something…'

And so, funds were raised. Betty sailed through all the academic grounding for college. The funds were there to see her through for at least three years.

But in the end, she hadn't the confidence to leave her home, her family, and the love that had grown with Ronny.

Miss Watson retired round about the same time, and so together they pursued a correspondence degree course, using the computer and once a semester travelling to the city for tutorials.

CHAPTER 10

THE MORNING OF Lenny's funeral is dank and dark. A storm's been brewing through the night and hurricane force winds are in the forecast. Folks have been warned of power cuts and told to fill their kettles and bathtubs with water, and charge anything that can be recharged.

The funeral is not at the church. But in the back room of the tavern. "Seems right, somehow," says Billy.

Others agreed, although no-one really knew Lenny like Billy. But Billy's footing the bill for this, "Least I can do," he mutters as other folks in the town glower at him. "The guy was not all bad."

No-one nods. Billy nods and shakes his head, as only Billy can, and appears on the stroke of 11 o'clock in a rumpled grey suit he's picked up at the thrift store. He wears an off-white shirt with a collar. And a tie. Albeit a polyester tie with a picture of a naked woman down the front. "The only one left at the thrift store," he says, when one of the guys says, "Well Lenny would certainly approve of that."

There is no official music, but Danny behind the bar switches on 100.7 which is playing Willy Nelson's Blue Eyes Crying in the Rain. Turns out the entire morning is given over to Willie Nelson. Billy reckons he couldn't have organized it any better if he'd tried.

Lenny is in a purple plastic container on the bar. His ashes anyway. Danny places a ring of rum shot glasses around the ashes. As Willie begins By the Rivers of Babylon the assembled company lift their tot of rum and say, "To Lenny, RIP."

The morning turns into the afternoon and the rains come down like someone hosing the town from a thousand fire trucks. The power flickers.

The guys are ready with their counting. It flickers the second time. They know that a third means the power will go out. And could do for days.

They sit in darkness and in silence. Danny reaches for the 40-ouncer of rum and refills the glasses. Billy has had lobster rolls made up and they are still in a large Amazon box in the stock room. He takes Danny's flashlight and brings them out. "Fill yer boots," he says. "The lobster's on Lenny. This was his final haul."

By six o'clock as the waters rose the funeral party was in full swing in spite of no power. Out came the cards and the dollars were flying fast and furiously. Nobody mentioned Lenny after a while, and Billy nodded to himself, then shook his head, not deciding on whether this was a good thing, or a bad. He supposed that what they'd done was given Lenny a good send off. Better than a pyre on the Nelly-May in the middle of the bay, which is how Lenny had once described the way he wanted to go.

CHAPTER 11

LENNY WATCHES FROM his rusting brown Dodge Dakota truck at the end of the laneway. He sees the little pink boots tottering around in the mud, he looks up to see Betty's sweet face. She is ten but looks more like seven or eight everyone says.

She's still in her own yard, splashing up and down the once gravelled pathway. She smiles, her ponytail bobs up and down just like a pony's would trotting around a green field on a sunny day.

Only today looks like more rain. The dark clouds on the horizon are so familiar to Lenny. He always knows when, and when not, to take out the Nelly-May. When it comes to his boat Lenny takes no chances. Unlike now. He pulls on his smoke, the last of his weed, and the last of his money to get more. It makes him antsy when he's got neither one nor the other.

He fidgets in the truck. The cracked plastic seats irritate him. The smeary windshield irritates him and he gets that uncontrollable urge in his groin.

He watches Betty more closely. She hasn't got breasts yet, 'probably a late developer,' he tells himself. 'Not like those other brazen girls in her same grade at middle school, they bounce up and down like young maidens on a mountain side.' He has no idea where that turn of phrase has come from other than he once saw The Sound of Music on a TV in a store window. Saw the pictures, but with no sound. All he saw were maidens' breasts jigging up and down with the mountains behind.

The drizzle eases off and he climbs out of the truck. At the same time Betty opens the garden gate, she sees Lenny and politely says, "Hi, how are you?" Not waiting for his reply.

He calls back, "Fine and dandy, young lady, I'm off to see how my puppies are making out. Wanna come along?"

Betty hesitates, thinks about what her mother has told her about strangers. But Lenny is not a stranger is he? He's a friend of Uncle Billy and she has spoken with him before a few times now, so he is no stranger.

"OK," she says, "I'll just tell my ma in case she worries."

Betty runs into the house, her little pink boots plopping up and down along the muddy garden path.

Lenny gets a lump in his throat, not just in his nether regions and returns to the truck, climbs in and hopes Betty's mother says, 'no.'

But here she comes, little Betty with her little pink boots, and shining pink face filled with expectation and anticipation. His heart leaps and then sinks. She climbs into the truck with difficulty. "You OK?" he says.

"Yup," she says, "I can do it."

"What ya ma say?"

"Can't find her, she must've gone to the store for more butter, she's making a cake for my birthday tomorrow."

"Your birthday tomorrow?" asks Lenny, "How old?"

"I'll be ten," she says, puffed up with pride, her ponytail swinging. Lenny notices the little pink plastic butterfly that holds her ponytail in place. He swallows hard.

"Puppies?"

"Yes, please," she says, remembering her manners. "How old are they?"

Lenny is caught out by the question. Has to think very hard. "Six weeks," he says, off the cuff.

"They must be so tiny then, what kind?"

Again, Lenny is stumped. He doesn't know dog breeds that well other than Duck Tollers. So that's what he says, "Tollers, Nova Scotia Duck Tollers, the colour of taffy"

Betty settles down on the bench seat of the truck beside Lenny. The old crocheted afghan thrown over the back stinks of tobacco and weed, she knows the smell. There's also the smell of booze and that she doesn't like. It was booze that caused her pa to leave home. To leave her and her ma to struggle without him.

"Actually," she says, "can we just stop at the store, I want to get some candy first."

Lenny's heart lifts at the thought of candy and has no problem pulling in at the curb by the FoodMart.

Betty doesn't come out for the longest time. He wonders why. Through his smeary windshield he sees Betty talking to her mother. And he knows he is probably in the shit.

He moves on without switching on his motor. He rolls the truck out into the road on neutral as he has done on many occasions and then starts her up. He heads for the tavern, something, anything, to take away the longing. Surely someone there will buy him a beer.

"Whatcha doin' Lenny," Billy calls to him down the length of the bar, "Wanna beer?"

Lenny is glad that his panic is over. He never gives a thought to the fact that things happen in his head and with his crotch over which he has no control. But knows beer with Billy will go a long way to quenching everything. He puts the frothing bottle back on the bar after a swig and says, "Back in a bit."

In the gents washroom he wanks off to feel better. Doesn't feel one bit better, in fact feels fucking miserable, but puts on a brave face and goes back to Billy at the bar. The other guys have gathered around, "I told them you'd have more stories," says Billy.

"Not today guys, sorry," says Lenny. "Maybe tomorrow. Unless of course each story is worth a beer."

That works, they perch on bar stools and lean against the bar as Lenny begins, "My ole pa 'ad a still, ya know," the guys all nod, as if they really do know, but no-one had a clue that Lenny had no idea if he had a father, or who he might be.

Lenny's ma was just a young girl around fifteen when she had Lenny. He was born in the back of old Gordie Levi's barn. Behind a bale of hay with the goats chewing at one end of the bale. Lenny's ma (no-one knew her name then) was not a fragile little thing, no, a robust girl with legs like tree trunks and a bosom like the rocky mountains, so legend had it. She shelled out the baby, a boy, stuck him to her breast where he latched right on and guzzled.

Once she'd given him a good feed, she'd wrapped him in a towel she'd plucked from some old washing line and left him in the barn with the goats.

Old Gordie Levi found him that night and took him into the kitchen where his wife, Ada, was just serving up the turnip stew for their supper.

"What in the hell have you there, Gordie?" she squarked.

"It's a goddamm babby, can't you see woman, can't you hear?"

Lenny was screaming his little lungs out at this point and Ada said, "Gimme here," she dipped her finger in a bowl of milk warming on the Enterprise stove all ready for making Gordie's nightly coffee, and the baby suckled.

"We canna keep him ya know," said Gordie.

Ada, knew this, she'd never had children. Never had anything but Gordie and all his animals to take care of. A baby had eluded her and here she was over sixty years old. Childless, and no-one to look after them in their old age.

"We'll hand him in in the morning," said Gordie.

The couple sat up with the baby all night, Ada dipping her little finger into the warm milk every so often. They wrapped him in a shawl that Ada's mother had knitted years before, when Ada and Gordie got married, thinking there was sure to be a baby on the way soon after. It didn't happen, but Ada had kept the shawl in the cedar trunk all these forty years or more.

"What will we say?" she said to Gordie.

"Well, the truth of course," said Gordie, "how we found him in the barn."

Constable Brown at the station took one look at the screwed up little newborn at 7.30 the next morning and slowly wrote out their statement. "We'll get it to the hospital in the city," he said.

"Him," said Ada, "it is a baby boy…"

"Right," said Constable Brown. "A boy. What should we call him?"

"We called him Leonard last night," said Gordiie. "If we'd ever had a son, we'd have called him Leonard."

"Do you want that back?" Constable Brown held up the fine lace shawl.

"Ada?"

"Well," said Ada, "I guess not, we've no use for it now, the wee mite needs something to wrap around him."

As they walk down the wet grey steps of the police station, Gordie takes Ada's arm, "We couldn't keep him you know," he says.

"'I know," she says, "if only we'd been 20 years younger, then…"

"Even then," said Gordie. "Even then, it wouldn't be right."

They never saw the child again. Often they wondered as they sat by the stove, keeping their toes warm in the winter. But they hoped he'd get a good home and be loved, as they might well have loved him.

CHAPTER 12

LENNY FINGERS THE piece of rag in his pocket. It is grey with age. And fragile too. His rough hands catch in the fine wool. There have been times when he could have thrown it out. But something always stopped him.

Maybe Billy calling up the track, "Hurry up Lenny, I've been waiting for you," when they've been going to snare rabbits. Or when his truck broke down, as it often did and he'd looked for a rag to wipe his oily greasy hands, the piece of lace would find its way into his clutches and then he'd say, "Nah," and push it back in his pocket — right to the bottom of his pocket as if to say, "stop popping up, stop haunting me, stop reminding me."

Because without knowing it, the piece of rag was the only thing Lenny had from his past. He sometimes held it to his nose. He imagined he could smell hay. Or goats. One thing he could not smell was a mother.

He tries to forget the home for outcast children. The cold. The hard work in the fields from dawn until dark. The leather strap if you didn't yield enough blueberries, or cranberries, or whatever it was they'd been sent out to gather and pick and collect for the higher-ups to make money.

He was fourteen when he cut his way through the fence with a pair of stolen wire cutters. He still has those somewhere in his truck. They are another reminder of where he came from. He has no recollection of anyone kind. No smiling face. No gentle touch. The harshness seems unfair to him now somehow when he sees how other people treat their children. Even those kids with only a mother. Or only a father.

Lenny just longs for a gentle touch. Someone to stroke his forehead when the headaches come on. The blinding headaches that send him into a rage. Just a tender touch from a tender hand.

He has never had a girlfriend, or woman friend for that matter, much as he has tried. There was a girl, Alexa, who said, "Clean your act up Lenny, and I might be interested."

But he didn't understand. He thought she meant something totally different, that he had to act a part or some such thing. He did try cleaning his teeth with spruce gum once, like the first nations people used to do, he was told, but that just left horrible black stickiness in his mouth and so he needed a joint to take all of that away. And one joint would follow another and he never saw Alexa after that.

Billy got a girlfriend. Lenny was totally pissed off that he went off with a woman called Ginny or something, short for Virginia, Billy told him.

"Is she?" said Lenny.

"Is she what?" said Billy.

"You know," said Lenny. "A virgin. Never been fucked."

Billy kicked him in the balls at that comment before replying. "I don't know and I'll not tell you when I find out either."

CHAPTER 13

"STILL NO REPLY?" says Ada.

"Nothing," says Gordie, "nothing in the mailbox. We'll probably never hear what really happened to the little fellow.

"They did give you the right address?"

"Yes. I'm pretty sure it's the one Constable Brown gave us. We'll try again next month."

"OK," she says, "I have his birthday card to mail, he'll be four."

CHAPTER 14

BILLY STANDS AT the small memorial in the town centre. It is November the 11th and everywhere is closed, 'as it should be,' Billy thought.

It is a while since Lenny passed over. Billy still misses his funny friend. The guy he'd known pretty much all his life. Billy places his poppy on the cement that the memorial stands on. There is only one other. That's besides the wreath placed by the mayor on behalf of the town. 'A pretty raggedy thing,' thinks Billy, 'probably made in China.'

He wonders who has placed the other poppy. It is there before the right time and no one normally places anything before 11 am. Billy has stood on the opposite side of the road beside the closed farmers market for at least half an hour waiting, needing a pee really, but waiting regardless.

And he hasn't seen anyone. Other than the person in a green car, a Pontiac, he thinks, slow down, and pause, as if in respect and reflection. Billy had thought nothing of it, it was all quite normal really, but then, maybe that is where the other poppy had come from.

He picks it up. There is a little sticker on the back. In memory of my baby, it says, I should never have let you go.

That's a mystery for Billy. Does it mean Lenny, his friend Lenny? Or is it someone who went away to war and didn't come back. 'That must be it,' thinks Billy, 'it cannot be for Lenny.'

Chapter 15

HER NAME IS Frannie. She lives in the city with her granddaughter now. In a big house with a grand back yard with lawns and rhododendrons and arbours with climbing roses in the summer. A pool for koi and water plants and a gentle trickling waterfall. Frannie often sits beside the pool, even in cooler weather, looking at her own reflection, seeing the young fifteen-year-old that she was.

She sees the barn where he was born. She hears his cries still now after all these years. It wrenched her heart out then and still does.

Her granddaughter, Eleanor, had helped her trace what happened. Using the internet. It took months of careful crosschecking. Eleanor kept copious and detailed notes.

There was one hand written slip of paper from a police station, with a scant report by a constable, stating that an elderly couple had brought in the baby that had been left as a newborn in their barn. Eleanor and Frannie have their names and the name of the community. She imagines if they were elderly then, they would be long gone from this earth. But still, the name of the community is there. In black and white.

She is horrified to find that her little boy had been placed in care right from day one really, as soon as he was well enough to leave the hospital.

She'd visited the hospital a few weeks ago, walked the halls. Imagined the care her boy had received.

But she hadn't visited the homes he'd been put into. Institutionalised right from a few days old. She cannot forgive herself.

Eleanor discovered that, as an adult, the boy, as a young man, had moved back to the original community and become a fisherman. With a boat, the Nelly-May. Frannie took comfort in that thought and with her granddaughter planned to visit, to seek him out. To say sorry.

The death notice in the archived paper caught them both with a jolt. It happened months before their planned visit. "Too late," weeps Frannie, "just too little too late."

"Grannie, do not cry," says Eleanor. "We can still go. One day we will go anyway."

"I often wondered if he would try and find me," she said. "Obviously not. Maybe he just hated me."

"So many if-onlies in this world," says Eleanor.

Frannie pulls her close and kisses her forehead. "Indeed," she says, "if only we knew what the future held. I just hope he was loved. But it doesn't really look like it."

"Grannie, I've never asked you before, but what about his father?"

Frannie swallows so hard she feels like she might choke. "He was a bad man," she says. "A very very bad man. I just hope my boy took after me. And not him."

CHAPTER 16

LENNY RAN AWAY from the home at fourteen. A lean and hungry looking boy just beginning to get fuzz over his top lip and on his chin. He'd picked up a cocky swagger with his walk and always had his hands in his pockets.

He wore his scars like a secret though. The welts across his back from the repeated beatings at all the homes he'd been in. All, mostly, for standing up for himself and others. For asking for clean sheets for another boy who repeatedly wet the bed and was repeatedly beaten for it. Lenny got the beatings, too. Lashings across his back, leaving scars that would only be seen if he ever showed them to someone. Or if he was in an accident of some kind.

And he did think as he got older that he was heading for an accident. The way the masters and matrons at the home told him, "You're a bad 'un alright young Lenny, you'll get your come-uppance."

'Well, now they can get their come-uppance,' he told himself as he stole out through the dark midnight corridors, pockets filled with thieved coins and paper money too from the office. The place he'd come to know. The place with the padded doors so no-one would hear the screams and cries of beatings.

He'd taken it all in each time he'd been bent over the sawhorse to get eight or ten lashings, depending on just what he'd done. Or what was said he'd done.

Between gasps he'd noticed where drawers and cupboards were, where keys hung on hooks, and he even manufactured misdemeanours in order to glean as much information as he could.

He stuffed a pillowcase with as many clothes as would fit: socks and shirts. No underwear. The boys in this home didn't wear underwear, all the easier for the masters to beat their bare flesh he supposed. It might have saved on washing too, but washing was not uppermost in his mind as he wove his way down hallways and stepped through the big barred heavy wooden doors with their iron bolts.

Once clear he ran for all his worth to the far woods and then through the fields beyond. He'd seen the envelopes in the office addressed to him. Letters that he'd never been given. Letters he'd asked for and been beaten for asking. He knew someone was trying to find him.

And he noted the town on the postmark. And that was where he was heading.

Chapter 17

BETTY SINGS AS she skips the garden path. Her mother watches through the kitchen window. She knows the song that Betty is singing, she taught her years ago before Betty could even walk. It goes, Mary, Mary, quite contrary, how does your garden grow, with silver bells and cockle shells and pretty maids all in a row.

She watches Betty place shells along the edges of the flower bed. Large scallop shells. "Now where did that child get those shells?" she says.

Betty has a supplier. It is Lenny. Once Lenny has moored the Nelly-May and sold his catch to the buyers he loads his latest haul of shells into a plastic FoodMart bag for the pretty little girl with the pink boots.

He usually leaves them by her garden gate, but this time she is in the lane to meet him. He stops the truck, smiles at her through his very whiskered chin and hands her the bag.

"Thank you mister," she says.

"You are welcome pretty lady," he says. "I'll try and get more for you in a few days, just look out for me."

CHAPTER 18

WHEN LENNY HITS the town he's just about on his last legs. He's managed to hitch a ride most of the way, but the last fifteen miles he walked. A truck driver had bought him a big mac yesterday. And a fisherman had bought him fish and chips the day before. "Are you looking for work young fella?" he'd asked Lenny.

"Yessir," Lenny had replied. "I may not look it, but I am strong."

The fisherman knew this without asking. He could see that the young man, or boy, had strength and stamina. "Be at the wharf next Tuesday by four in the morning and we'll give you a try," he'd said.

Lenny spent all Monday night on the wharf so as not to be late, plus he had nowhere to stay anyway. The fisherman, whose name Lenny learned, was Murray, handed him a floater jacket and special gloves and showed him what needed doing this first trip.

Lenny was a quick and eager learner, and before he knew it he was going out every day of the season catching lobster for the international market. The Nelly-May became his home. Unbeknown to Murray, Lenny sneaked back on when all had gone home each evening and slept in the wheelhouse. Clearing away all evidence before 4 am the next day.

For his hard work and dedication, Murray took him under his wing to a certain extent, and when he had to give up fishing for his rheumatism, he handed the boat over to Lenny. He also made sure Lenny was named in his will. The Nelly-May would be Lenny's.

Lenny did quite well for a few years, kept his nose clean, kept off the rum. He smoked to calm his nerves and one night he ran into Billy who quickly became his friend and confidant.

It was Billy who got Lenny started on the weed.

And it was the weed that began Lenny's inevitable fall. He began missing days out fishing. Days and days at a time. Sometimes weeks. He didn't know where the time went. He had lost it. He still had nowhere really to live until Billy offered him a place to stay. And that caused Lenny to stop going to the boat day in day out as he'd been so keen to do in the early days.

CHAPTER 19

"HERE YOU ARE again pretty lady," he says to Betty. She is standing on the wharf near his mooring as he brings in the Nelly-May. He throws her the mooring rope and she tries to heave it over to the rusting cleat. He laughs and hops out of the boat. "Like this," he shows her how to loop the rope and secure the boat. "What can I do for you pretty lady?" he says.

"Have you forgotten about the puppies?" she says.

He hasn't forgotten his promise to take her to see fictitious puppies. How he wishes he hadn't used that line. How he wishes he could just be normal with this sweet little girl. How he wishes things were different...

"Let me get my truck," he says. "Wait for me by the highway up there." Lenny doesn't want anyone to see him let Betty into his truck. He has a good idea what people might think. And he knows that in some respects they are probably so very right.

She knows how to climb into a truck. She knows where to find the hand holds and the foot holds. She pushes aside the old newspapers that cover the bench seat. She opens her bag.

"What have you got there," he says.

"It's my knitting for school," she says, "I'm knitting a pink sausage dog. I told you before, that's when you told me about the puppies."

"Shit, you're right," he says, then covers his mouth and grins. "Sorry," he says, "naughty word!"

"S'alright," she says, "Ma says it all the time."

Chapter 20

FRANNIE SITS IN a corner of the small restaurant on the side of the harbour. She sees the fishing boats coming in about midafternoon. She is bewildered by the hive of activity and doesn't remember it being at all like this from when she was here sixty years ago.

Then it was run down. Miserable. Nobody had a thing. Times were hard. The day she was raped called a halt to all her dreams. She told no-one. She didn't know the man who pulled her under the wharf and ravaged her until she passed out. Who held her down with one hand over her face while he ripped her body apart.

And then left after calling her a little slut who didn't even deserve that.

She told no-one. She knew nothing about life, about pregnancy, about her body. As she grew larger she just thought she was growing up quickly, getting fat like all the other women in the village. When her time came she hugged herself with what she thought was a bad belly ache, lay down in that old barn and gave birth.

It was like a nightmare from which she dearly needed to wake up. She ran, covered with blood from the birth of the baby. Frightened as a rabbit. She ran all day and all night until she hit the Salvation Army in a big town where no-one knew her. They took her in. Cleaned her up, fed her and made sure she was OK. She didn't tell them her name was Annie. "Frannie," she said. "Frannie Bennet."

They were good to her and helped her find work and somewhere to live.

Frannie looks down at the steaming cup of cappuccino that has been set before her in a dark green French coffee cup with a gold rim. Just like something she saw in an English movie recently. Then the little tiered cake stand, with assorted fancy cakes. Miniature iced sponge cakes, chocolate éclairs, cream horns, and blackberry tartlets. A little pot of clotted cream on the side with a silver soon.

As she looks up from this array of mouthwatering treats, she sees a tiny union jack flag in the corner of the restaurant's window. "Of course," she says, "it just has to be British, how on earth did the British find this forgotten corner of the planet?"

"By accident," came the reply. It turns out the owner is sitting at the next table having tea with a friend. "We saw the need, gave up the rat-race in Europe, and just, as they say, did it."

"Successful, yes?" says Frannie.

"More than we could have hoped," is the reply.

Frannie looks around, she sees every table is taken. It is around 4 o'clock when in England everything used to 'stop for tea'. She notices that the women are doing the ordering for the men. And it is the women who take their bank cards to the till on the way out and pay. The men are told to leave a tip.

"How things change," again she says aloud.

"Been here before?"

"I was born here," she says.

"We are doing a project on local history, would you like to stay a while and talk with us? Many folks have drifted away, we are trying to find out why."

"I'm not sure," says Frannie. She doesn't want to turn them down flat, she wonders if they may be able to help her find her boy. "I'm staying in town at The Best Western, just ask for Mrs. Lambert, that'll be enough to put you through. I do have a cell phone too, here's the number. But right now I am doing some personal research."

She leaves the restaurant with mixed feelings. She'd hoped to bump into a familiar name, or at least a descendent with a familiar name. She stands on the wharf and watches the boats tie up. One boat seems that it hasn't left the wharf in years, rusty and uncared for, the Nelly-May.

"Do you know whose boat this is?" she asks a small boy.

"That's old Lenny's boat, he's gone now."

Frannie doesn't reply, she knows what the small boy means.

"Ask Billy. He's always in the tavern. He'll tell you all about Lenny."

The tavern is in the centre of the community. Bicycles lean against the peeling painted wall. She can hear the guffaws of beery men within. Beery guffawing men don't bother Frannie. She can deal with them.

She's wearing a smart black worsted skirt suit with a faux mink stole around her shoulders. She has on black velvet ballet style shoes and a matching handbag with a gold link chain handle.

Her hair is coifed into a French twist and a gold clasp holds it in place. Slightly made up, she is still quite the beauty at 75.

The clamouring talk stops as Frannie enters the tavern.

Red nosed faces turn to see who has just entered. Men push back the beaks of their ball caps to see her a little better through the tavern's gloom.

A wolf whistle comes from the far corner. It is Billy.

"A gin and tonic," she says, "please."

"Ice and lemon?"

"No thank you."

"I'll bring it over if you'd like to take a seat."

Frannie looks for the cleanest table, the one with the least amount of stains, and the bench with the fewest crumbs.

Billy is the one with the curiosity. He picks up his beer bottle, wipes the froth from his top lip and saunters, in a way that a chubby sixty-year-old can saunter, over to the table. 'May I?" he says, all polite like.

"Please do," she says, "I'm Frannie."

"Howdy, fine lady," he says, remembering how Lenny called all females 'pretty lady' and making him swallow hard with the memory of his dear friend.

"I'm here to find out about someone," she says.

"Oh yeah," says Billy, not as a question, more as a concern. Wondering what he might have done, and if this was someone from the council. Although she looked old, surely not still working for the government. But you could never tell, could you?

"Yes," she says. "I'm looking for a guy called Billy."

Billy turns to stone. Has he been found out? But found out for what? His conscience obviously was playing snooker-balls in his pockets at this very moment.

"Are you Billy?" she says.

"I s'pose I'd better come clean," he says, "I sure am Billy as everyone here will tell ya."

"Oh good," says Frannie, "I thought you were. I understand you knew my son."

The tavern goes deathly quiet. You could hear the birds sing outside, a rare moment indeed in this tavern.

"If you mean Lenny, yes," says Billy, lowering his voice, solemnly looking at his friends at the bar, trying not to let the tear that he knew would come, roll down his cheek. He can feel his nose prickle like it did if he cried, when his nose would run down over his top lip and into his mouth.

"What can you tell me?" she says.

"I'm so, so sorry," says Billy. "Lenny died."

As Billy reaches for his drink, ash drops from his cigarette on to Frannie's black skirt. Frannie doesn't notice. She was still coming to terms with the bombshell. It seems more real now she is in the company of someone who knew her son.

"I'll take you to the grave if you like," he says.

"My son has a grave? Should I take flowers?"

"He'd like that," says Billy.

"Give me one of those," she says. "Please."

Frannie pulls hard on the cigarette. Breathes deeply and closes her eyes. "I should have come here sooner," she says, dropping her ash too, on her black skirt.

"He'd have liked that," says Billy.

"What else can I take?" she says.

"A beer," says Billy. "He always liked a beer."

They stand over her son's grave. "I should have loved you more," she says, gently pouring the beer over the earth.

"He'd have liked that," says Billy.

"Who's this?" She looks closer at the headstone next to Lenny. She recognises the names from the only clue, the slip of paper, she had a while back.

"Oh, that's ole Gordie and Ada, died a long time back. Fifty years or more. That's their old farm over there."

Frannie shields her eyes and looks over the fields at the crumbling farmhouse, "Nobody living there?"

"No," says Billy, "they had no family, it's bin for sale forever."

CHAPTER 21

LENNY FOLLOWS THE little girl. He likes her and he reckons she likes him more now, especially now she knows he likes puppy dogs too.

He sees her pink rubber boots bounce up and down, up and down along the muddy ruts in the lane. Her mother had waved her off at the garden gate, given her a small basket and a five-dollar bill and told her to come straight home with the bread.

Lenny knows it's Betty and that she is ten years old, small for her age, but sharp as a thumb tack Lenny hears. 'She must be clever if she can go shopping for bread,' he tells himself.

She stops at the end of the land, looks left and right. Then sees the daisies growing along the edge, she begins to pick the flowers, their little white petals surrounding the golden centres. 'Picking them for her ma, I guess,' says Lenny to himself, 'oh how I would have loved to pick flowers for my ma, if only I knew where she went, where she is, I could give her a flower and she would kiss my forehead and make the bad bad headaches go away.'

Betty sees Lenny then, "Hi," she says.

"Hi back atcha," says Lenny trying to be cool.

"Did you get the puppies?" she says.

"Not yet," he says, "but I know where they are, I c'n take ya."

"I'm not allowed to go far today," she tells him, "Ma sent me for the bread, then I must go straight home."

"Huh," says Lenny, "maybe some other time then."

Betty's mouth turns down at the corners, he thinks she is going to cry.

"Don't cry pretty lady," he says, "you'll spoil your pretty little face."

Betty perks up then, "'Nother day then?"

"Sure," he says, come find me at the wharf tomorrow after school."

"I will if it doesn't rain," she says. "'bout four o'clock? But I must be home for supper and to do my homework."

CHAPTER 22

FRANNIE SITS DOWN in the muddy grass beside Lenny's grave. "There is supposed to be a headstone," says Billy, "but it isn't made yet."

"You?" says Frannie.

"Yes, of course," says Billy. "Lenny was my bestest friend in the whole world."

"I'm glad he had you for a friend," she says. "That gives me some comfort. What kind of a life did he have?"

Billy does his best to disguise the fact that Lenny actually had a pretty miserable life. "He changed when he got the boat," he says. Billy closes his eyes. He shivers.

"Come on, let's go and get warm," says Frannie, "and let's get you some better clothes and a good meal in your belly. It's the least I can do after what you've done for my boy."

Billy is embarrassed but lets himself be drawn in by this old but elegant woman, with her fine gold rings and her rich woollen coat. With her earrings that sparkle like early morning frost on the grass behind his welfare apartment.

She smiles at him, "Don't be scared, I won't eat you."

Billy laughs then, "Lenny always said that," he says. "Quite a lot actually."

"It's no use us being miserable over what might have been," she says, "so let's look to the future. I'd like for you to come home with me, I have a big home. If that's what you'd like."

Chapter 23

BETTY PULLS LENNY by the hand. They climb up the lane to the top of the knoll. He follows like a dutiful child, letting Betty take over, as if she has suddenly become a mother to him. He wishes Billy were there too, so that they could see the view all together. Like a family. Like a Mother a Father and a little boy Lenny.

There is a large granite rock at the top. It is shaped like a scoop of ice cream that's had a bite taken out of it leaving an overhang, a sheltered place.

Betty has arranged a dolly's tea set in pink with flowers around the rims of all the cups and the saucers too. She has them laid out on an old raggy tea towel for a tablecloth.

"Sit down," she says.

Lenny is surprised at her bossy little squeaky voice. She had been so meek and docile down on the wharf, wheedling at him to take her to see the puppies. Now the little minx was squinting her eyes at him as if hypnotising him.

He watches carefully as she pulls her knitting out of her bag. He wonders what else she might have.

"Ya got a biscuit in there too?" he says.

"Only if you're good," she says. Smiling in a sneery way, showing a row of tiny white teeth.

"Oh, I'm always good," he says.

"Show me then."

He is unsure what she means. Does she want him to tidy the little she-cave she's made? Or does she want him to tell her a story or something? He decides the story is the best way forward and begins:

"There was once a little puppy called Elsa."

"That's a funny name for a puppy," she says.

"There was once a lion called Elsa," he says, "that's not in the story, that's true."

"OK."

He begins again, "There was once a little golden puppy called Elsa, her mistress called her Elsa after a lion, a real lion also called Elsa who lived in Africa, in the jungle."

"That's more like it," says Betty. "You are getting close to being good."

Lenny feels that age old quiver between his legs, low in his belly and he really is hoping it will go away soon. It seems the bossier and stricter the little pretty girl gets, the more it arouses him. He doesn't want to spoil anything. He just wants a biscuit really.

'She's such a pretty little thing,' he thinks, 'to look at anyway, but she seems to have turned nasty on me.' "So Elsa goes to live with a little girl with pink boots. The little girl is good at knitting and decides she will make a coat for Elsa. She gets her friend Lenny to take her to town to the yarn store in his truck. Together they choose the colours of the rainbow for the doggy coat: red, orange, yellow, green, blue, indigo and violet..."

"What's indigo?" she says.

"Indigo. It's a greyish blue colour, the colour of the clouds over there. You know we should probably head back now, it looks like rain on its way."

"You are going nowhere yet," she says.

Lenny is struck dumb and begins to stand, first on his hands and knees. Before he can get himself upright she is onto him. Stabbing at him with her knitting needles. In his face. In his eyes. In his throat.

"I know you," she says. "People like you. Dirty old men like to mess with kids like me. I've seen stuff on TV. You're supposed to know better. You're supposed to help us kids."

Her stabbing is frenzied. Over and over until she is out of strength and out of breath. Until she collapses on the side wall of the granite shelter. Her dolly's tea set strewn across the ground, some pieces have tumbled part way down the hill.

She looks down at what is left of the man she has been talking to. In disbelief she tries to pull out her knitting needles.

"Now I won't be able to finish my sausage dog," she says before fainting back, hitting her head on the rocks.

CHAPTER 24

322

WHEN THE SEARCH party finds Betty, she is comatose against the rock. If Billy hadn't spotted the dolly's tea cup in the dark they may not have found her before morning. By then hypothermia would be set in.

It was too late for Lenny, he had bled out from his jugular, probably only took minutes for him to die. What he could see through the one eye still functioning was anyone's guess.

But he would have seen little Betty revert to her normal sweetness having no idea of what she'd done.

It was too far off the road for an ambulance to bring back either of them. Betty's mother carried her in her arms to the bottom of the lane where the ambulance waited. Forensics soon arrived and after an initial examination, Lenny's body was carried out on a stretcher. Yellow police tape was run around the entire area as far as one of the dolly's teaspoons had rolled.

CHAPTER 25

BILLY DOESN'T TELL Frannie all of this, he really doesn't fancy reliving the entire trauma. He found them both. The little girl in the pink boots and his oldest and best friend together. He'd scratched his head later completely confused as to what they might have been doing there.

Lenny's pants were halfway down his legs. His flaccid dead penis shrivelled like a walnut, no, an almond more like. Billy zipped up Lenny's pants, he thought it inappropriate that anyone else should see. And he smoothed down the little girl's clothes too. If that was tampering with a crime scene he couldn't help that. It was the right thing for Billy to do. For both of them.

In the end, 'misadventure' was the conclusion. No-one could talk to Betty. She just wouldn't open her little red rosebud mouth for any authority. When she did it was to ask for her knitting.

"I'll get you some new knitting started," said her mother.

But Betty declined that, she wanted the knitting needles Miss Watson had given to her, and the pink wool. Miss Watson visited every afternoon after school was out. She talked to Betty, or just sat with her. She went over the lessons the class had had that day.

Betty looked through her, to the wall and window beyond, to the view of the hill where it had all happened. Then, "Where is Elsa?" she said.

"Who is Elsa?" says Miss Watson.

"Elsa is a puppy dog, a golden-haired puppy dog. The man. The man Lenny was taking me to see puppy dogs. Elsa was to be mine."

Miss Watson repeated this to Betty's mother as they sat round the kitchen table drinking coffee later. Betty's mother just shook her head.

"She's delirious," she said. "It doesn't make any sense. Lenny, you say? Not that Lenny?"

"He is, sorry was, the man she was with. The man who died," says Miss Watson.

Betty's mother is beside herself, "I told her not to go off anywhere, I told her not to talk to strangers. Do you think she will ever be OK?"

"I hope so," says Miss Watson, "but I think it will take some time, we will just have to be patient."

"I never really knew him," says Betty's mother. "Do you know any more?"

"Not a lot. He was a buddy of Billy Mac. He had a boat, the Nelly-May, so a fisherman I guess. Some say he was born here in a barn and was taken and put into care by social services, but it is only gossip.

CHAPTER 26

FRANNIE PUTS A notice in the newspaper. It is Lenny's obituary:

Leonard Francis. Died September 14th of unnatural causes aged sixty years.

Son of Frances Catherine Lambert originally of Hellings Cove.

Best friend to Billy also of Hellings Cove.

'Unloved in life, now loved in death, no time for regrets'

CHAPTER 27

EVERYONE IN THE coffee shop has the paper open to the obits pages. "Who is this Frances Catherine Lambert?" they ask each other.

Of course the moment Billy waltzes in through the doors, letting in an icy blast, they are on him. "Who is she?"

"That's his ma," he says. "She'd come looking for 'im. Didn't know he was dead or nuffin'. I don't think. Just too bad. Just too late. Poor Lenny."

Billy doesn't tell them that she's offered to take him back with her. He doesn't know what to do, whether to just leave quietly without a fuss. What? Without Lenny there is nothing for him now in Hellings Cove. "She is going to sell the boat though, or maybe just give it away."

They want to know how to get in touch with her. Billy says, "I'll give her your messages if that's OK."

He has suddenly become quite an entity in the community, almost celebrity status. People clamouring around him like he's a superstar or something. A cup of coffee, double double and a Boston Cream doughnut is put in his hand without him ordering.

"This is just plain embarrassing," he says, "but thanks a lot, much appreciated." With that he swings out of the coffee shop and heads off down the road towards the hotel.

"That's where she must be staying," the cry goes out and at least a dozen people pour out onto the freezing cold street and head to the Best Western.

The staff at the hotel are non-committal about who is staying where. The guys are too late to see Billy disappearing into the elevator and pressing 4 for the fourth floor. For a while they sit around in the hotel foyer in the hopes that at least Billy or the woman will appear. But no luck. Eventually they drift off, "It's my supper time," they say to each other.

As the last of them slip out through the main revolving glass doors, the hotel receptionist calls Frannie in her room. "They've all gone," she says. "But I'd give it half an hour, if you like I'll ask your car to be brought to the side exit."

Billy sits stiffly in a new pair of jeans with a plaid shirt and a leather jacket. Frannie says, "We'll get you a decent haircut and some more stuff when we get home." Billy shivers.

Frannie has noticed his discomfort about everything in the hotel, how he wasn't sure about which spoon to use for his soup, how she knew he really needed to pass gas and went red in the face to stop himself. How he sits on the edge of his chair as if about to bolt. She wonders if taking him with her will work.

"You don't have to come," she says. "There's always Lenny's boat, we could get it fixed up."

Frannie sees Billy's eyes light up. How he takes a deep breath and sits back n the chair. She's also thinking about the visit to the Real Estate office earlier in the day, and her offer on Gordie and Ada's ruined farmhouse.

- end -

About the Author

Once described in the writing world as a 'third space inhabitant', S.B. Borgersen, originally from England, writes, makes art, and loves gardening on the glorious shores of Nova Scotia, Canada.

Sue's favoured genres are poetry, flash, and micro fiction. In addition to solo works, she is published internationally in anthologies, arts, and literary magazines. An extensive list of publications covering work of the past two decades can be found at www.sueborgersen.com.

S.B. Borgersen is a member of Genre Writers of Atlantic Canada, The Society of Authors UK, and a volunteer reader for the Scottish Arts Trust writing awards.

Collected Novellas is her 7th book to be published by Unsolicited Press, bringing together, within one cover, three of Sue's highly acclaimed novellas: *Passport to Perdita, Eva Matson,* and *Fishermen's Fingers.*